The Limits of Intervention

(an inside account of how the Johnson policy
of escalation in Vietnam was reversed)

Townsend Hoopes

DAVID McKAY COMPANY, INC.

NEW YORK

In Memory of

JOHN T. McNAUGHTON

THE LIMITS OF INTERVENTION

Revised and Updated, September 1973

International Standard Book Number: 0-679-30241-7

Library of Congress Catalog Card Number: 78–94505

MANUFACTURED IN THE UNITED STATES OF AMERICA

Preface

THIS BOOK is first a memoir and then, perhaps, a history. It deals primarily with a finite chronological slice of the Vietnam agony—the six-month period culminating in President Johnson's decisions of March 31, 1968 to reject the military request for 206,000 additional troops, to initiate a partial bombing halt, to ask the North Vietnamese for negotiations, and to take himself out of the 1968 presidential race. The events in question are still too recent and their ultimate consequences still too largely unknown to form a basis for anything resembling definitive history. Moreover, the book is necessarily written from a particular vantage point in the civilian hierarchy at the Pentagon—a position not at the center of policy, but on the near periphery. Also, one must cheerfully acknowledge that no participant in controversial, unfinished enterprises can pretend to unblemished objectivity; while I have made every effort to be faithful to the facts as I know them, either at first hand or as acquired through diligent search, no claim is made that the discussion here is confined to the facts or that the facts as presented are argued with scientific detachment.

The Vietnam War has nearly drowned us in facts—infiltration rates, weapons-loss ratios, aircraft sortie rates, expended ammunition tonnages, allied troop contributions, enemy body counts, and friendly casualties. Individually these have provided only modest enlightenment; collectively they may have served primarily to dull the national sense of awareness, softening the harsh flesh-and-blood realities of the war for policymakers and general public alike, through a form of presentation that has tended to equate this intractable tragedy with a range of domestic enterprises whose progress or regression we also measure by a set of statistical indicators.

Though few perceived it in the beginning, the Vietnam War is now recognized as the probable high watermark of America's tidal impulse to political-military intervention in the period following the Second World War. What course U.S. foreign policy now takes is far less clear than the fact that its failure in Vietnam has arrested the growth of an implicit American universalism, born of our extraordinary effort and exhilarating triumph in the great struggle that began in Europe before Pearl Harbor and ended when the second atomic bomb was dropped on Nagasaki. That development became self-conscious in 1945–46 when we first grasped the somber reality that we were facing, in a world of shattered allies, friends, and enemies, the iron challenge of Stalinism, a system whose philosophy and apparatus were well suited to the exploitation of disorder and to the scavenging of genuine new social and national movements. It was nurtured through the next two decades by attitudes that were themselves the product of our involvement in the world struggle—a doctrinaire anti-Communism, a social evangelism forming around the idea of American-financed economic development in the Third World, and an unquestioning faith in the ultimate efficacy of military alliances and of U.S. military power. How Vietnam came to represent the outer limits of feasible American intervention, how the working of the democratic process finally forced the President to abandon a policy of escalation, and why the particular events of March 1968 signaled the end of an era constitute the subject matter of this book.

My exposure to foreign-military affairs began in 1947 with a privileged apprenticeship as Assistant to the Chairman of the Committee on Armed Services, in the House of Repre-

Contents

"... The men who create power make an indispensable contribution to the nation's greatness, but the men who question power make a contribution just as indispensable ... for they determine whether we use power or power uses us."

JOHN F. KENNEDY

CHAPTER 1

Roots of Intervention

MY FIRST impression, on returning to government in January 1965, was that it was difficult to find out what was going on in foreign policy—even from the vantage point of the office of International Security Affairs, that strong and influential "Foreign Office" under the Secretary of Defense which, though not well known to the general public, stands in fact at the crossroads of foreign-military affairs in the U.S. government. I felt the absence of an explicit framework of policy for both global and inter-regional issues. With respect to particular regions and countries, small interdepartmental groups of flexible membership conducted day-to-day operations with ability and zeal. But the bridging mechanisms needed to relate policy in one region to policy in another, and to link them to general problems of global implication— like the proliferation of nuclear weapons, or the progressive withdrawal of British military forces from East of Suez— seemed weak. Moreover, there appeared to be a serious lack of the kind of comprehensive assessment and long-range planning that was a remembered feature of those days during the Truman years when George Kennan and later Paul Nitze headed an elite Policy Planning Staff at the State Department.

Closer examination confirmed the impression of no central guiding philosophy in foreign policy, as well as of slackness

1

in coordinating the disparate elements. An important cause lay in the fact that President Johnson, a man of little background and much uncertainty in foreign affairs, had inherited an organization for their conduct that had been made deliberately loose and flexible by President Kennedy, a man of broad knowledge, intuitive grasp, and determined initiative in that field. This inheritance, which adversely affected both the scope of deliberations on Vietnam policy and the quality of President Johnson's decisions from the fall of 1964 onwards, showed itself in the structural weakness of the National Security Council and in inadequate attention to longer-range policy planning. The principal results were fragmented debate, loose coordination, and an excessive concentration on problems of the moment.

EVOLUTION OF THE NSC

The establishment of the National Security Council in 1947 had reflected a determined effort, born of painful experience, to bridge the gulf between considerations of foreign policy and considerations of military force which had historically characterized, and plagued, the U.S. government's conduct of external relations. As the nation drifted toward the supreme ordeal of World War II, our governmental structure provided absolutely no organizational linkages between the State Department and the Military Services; there was no joint planning, not even provision for a systematic exchange of views. And indeed the situation was almost as bad between the War and Navy Departments. Between Pearl Harbor and V-J Day such coordination of foreign-military considerations as existed was entirely *ad hoc;* and though much of the improvisation was brilliant, the absence of established structure and channels led frequently to major decisions that suffered from a failure to consider highly relevant implications. A few were grave blunders, like the missteps that permitted the Russians to occupy Berlin. In the sobering afterlight of victory, a nation painfully aware that it now stood at the pinnacle of world power and responsibility concluded that the continuance of such organizational disorder had become intolerable.

There were two overriding, interrelated needs: to bring the separate organizations and traditions of the Military Services under sufficiently central authority to ensure an end to multiple and conflicting strategies for defending the nation and its interests; and to bring the Military Establishment as a whole into close and continuous relations with the State Department, the intelligence agencies, and the economic counselors—for the purpose of planning foreign policy, weighing its military risks, judging the demands on national resources, and coordinating day-to-day operations. The National Security Council, which owed its inspiration to James Forrestal and Ferdinand Eberstadt, was conceived as a cabinet committee composed essentially of those officials who form the nation's high policy triumvirate for matters of war and peace—the President, the Secretary of State, the Secretary of Defense. Supported by designated military, intelligence, economic, and public affairs advisers, the NSC was designed to ensure detailed coordination of all the major factors that bear upon U.S. foreign policy decisions. It was written into law in 1947 as part of the "Unification Act," which placed the three Military Services under a single Secretary of Defense.

President Truman benefited in his first term from a group of wartime advisers (Marshall, Acheson, Forrestal, Lovett, McCloy, Patterson, Eisenhower, Spaatz, Bradley, Clay) who could be compared in distinction and ability to the original Virginia Dynasty, and he got the NSC off to a solid and orderly start by making it the central forum both for developing major national security policies and for considering how the U.S. would respond to particular crisis situations. Below the Council itself, Truman established a committee of Assistant Secretaries (later called the Planning Board), which addressed the substantive questions in depth, endeavored to ensure a full hearing for each interested department or agency, and made recommendations to the Council. Below the Planning Board were several drafting groups whose flexible composition reflected the shifting needs for particular expertise. Certainly the initial system had shortcomings: it was slow moving and it lacked an adequate mechanism to coordinate the *execution* of policy actions, once they had been approved by the President. But judged against the chaotic past, it represented a revolutionary advance in responsible U.S. decision-making, an almost miraculous victory for organizational principle, reason, and coherence.

In the Eisenhower period, the NSC became a more formal and more detailed structure. Under a new Assistant to the President for NSC Affairs, Robert Cutler, a Boston banker whose fussy attention to minutiae brought to mind an elegant Old World dowager, it adopted stricter procedures and developed a formal statement of U.S. policy in relation to nearly every country in the world and for nearly every conceivable political, economic, or military contingency. These changes, which were in tune with President Eisenhower's penchant for elaborate staff work, resulted in prodigious labor; unfortunately, they also produced procedural rigidities and tended to ensure that a large percentage of NSC papers were soon lifeless, like wills in a safe deposit box that have been rendered irrelevant by altered circumstance in a fluid world.

President Kennedy, acting on the advice of McGeorge Bundy and Walt Rostow, scrapped the entire structure of the NSC and chose to rely on small groups of flexible composition that were given responsibility for both *policy formulation* and *execution* with respect to particular countries, regions, or functional problems. Bundy, as the Assistant for NSC Affairs, provided the nexus, and the President was often personally involved in the early stages of discussion. This loosely woven mosaic was capped by irregular meetings at the White House attended by the President, Rusk, McNamara, and Bundy, augmented from time to time by the Chairman of the Joint Chiefs of Staff, the Director of Central Intelligence, and others—notably the Attorney General, Robert Kennedy.

This was a more comfortable mechanism for a President with a broad knowledge of foreign affairs and a strong distaste for being hemmed in by too much organization, yet one feels the irony here. For Kennedy could surely have operated a formal NSC structure with more deftness than his predecessors. He might thereby have avoided an excessively bureaucratic process, while at the same time ensuring against the risk of having important considerations slip between stools. His own highly informal system carried with it serious dangers of insufficient coordination—as the sad travesty at the Bay of Pigs soon showed.

It was, then, this somewhat amorphous set of arrangements for foreign policy formulation, coordination, and control that President Johnson inherited. While it is speculative, to say the least, whether a man of his galvanic temperament, irregular administrative habits, and passion for secretiveness could or would have used a more formal structure to good advantage, the fact is that he was bequeathed a rather fragile apparatus tailored to John F. Kennedy's specifications and heavily dependent upon the kind of affinity for foreign affairs that Kennedy possessed and Johnson did not. This seemed another of those incongruous inheritances, with which our recent history is liberally sprinkled, that produce an unfortunate, even a tragic effect, but are traceable to no villain.

DECLINE OF THE LONG-RANGE VIEW

More serious than the structural weaknesses of the NSC was the erosion of comprehensive, integrated, longer-term policy planning. A radical decline in the influence of the Policy Planning Staff at the State Department had occurred during the Eisenhower and Kennedy years, and it fell to even lower estate under Johnson. In the Republican period, its work had been largely assumed by Secretary Dulles himself, and in the following period by a small White House staff

5

under the direction of McGeorge Bundy and later of Walt Rostow. Dulles, it was said, carried State Department policy and planning in his hat, spent much of his time in travel, and implicitly discouraged his staff from either initiatives or penetrating reflections in his absence. The White House proved, at least in the Kennedy-Johnson years, to be a post primarily of action and reaction, and not an ideal place for reflective thought on difficult, longer-term problems. The result, as I perceived it in early 1965, was a notable absence of the kind of comprehensive policy analysis (and its lucid documentation) that had constituted our national policy guidance in the Truman-Acheson period. I had, for example, played a part in preparing NSC 68, a prescient blueprint of U.S. military and foreign policy requirements for the 1950s, written during the winter of 1949–50 in the shadow of the first Soviet nuclear explosion. That task had been accomplished by a small State-Defense group under Nitze's able leadership. In 1965, there appeared to exist in the U.S. government no current planning documents of comparable scope, authority and quality.

As head of the Policy Planning Staff from December 1961 to March 1966, Walt Rostow had tried to fill the vacuum, first by the issuance of an "Overall National Policy Paper" and later through a series of "National Policy Papers." The first effort died quietly because the principal department heads—Rusk and McNamara—were unwilling to spend the personal time required to reach agreement. The second effort became a continuing exercise, but of marginal value, for the second and third levels of government, taking their cue from Rusk and McNamara, treated the National Policy Papers with indifference. Prepared by earnest and diligent young men, these papers set down the relevant facts and considerations in admirable fashion, and proposed reasonable lines of policy for the U.S. government to follow. But no one topside would take the time to read or endorse them. It could be argued with some cogency that the pattern of world power

6

relationships was measurably more complex in 1965 than in 1949, and that to define U.S. interests in the context of the more intricate tapestry of the later period required something more than a resort to general principles. The fact remained that a foreign-military establishment as large and as far-flung as ours requires that policy be something more tangible than a thesis carried in the minds of an Assistant Secretary and a few opposite numbers. Granted its fluid and perishable nature, policy must be generalized, written down, and each major part coherently related to the other. There must be an agreed and stated vision of the whole. Otherwise the many parts of the establishment will function and comprehend in the manner of the blind men examining the elephant.

I believe the decisions and actions that marked our large-scale military entry into the Vietnam War in early 1965 reflected the piecemeal consideration of interrelated issues, and that this was the natural consequence of a fragmented NSC and a general inattention to long-range policy planning. Consultation, even knowledge of the basic facts, was confined to a tight circle of presidential advisers, and there appears to have been little systematic debate outside that group. Still, it would be incorrect to place undue emphasis on the organizational and procedural shortcomings of the U.S. decision-making process in 1965. They were important, but they were not decisive.

THE COLD WAR LEGACY

What seemed in retrospect to have made large-scale military intervention all but inevitable in 1965 was a fateful combination of the President's uncertainty and sense of insecurity in handling foreign policy, and a prevailing set of assumptions among his close advisers that reinforced his own tendency to think about the external world in the simplistic terms of appeasement versus military resolve. The President seemed, from the beginning to the end, uncomfortable and

7

out of his depth in dealing with foreign policy. His exposure to the subject as a member of relevant House and Senate Committees had been long, but superficial. For reasons which seemed to have their roots deep in his personal history, he lacked the kind of confidence in his own judgments that permitted Truman, Eisenhower, and Kennedy to overrule their principal foreign policy and military advisers on major issues. In matters of war and peace he seemed too much the sentimental patriot, lacking Truman's practical horse sense, Eisenhower's experienced caution, Kennedy's cool grasp of reality. The most exhaustive search of the Johnson record reveals no solid core of philosophical principle or considered approach to foreign policy—indeed no indication that he gave the subject much serious attention before 1964. There is only an erratic rhythm of reaction to those foreign crises that impacted upon the particular elements of domestic politics that had engaged his interest or his ambition. Philip Geyelin, in his perceptive book of mid-1966,[1] said of President Johnson that "by political background, by temperament, by personal preference he was the riverboat man ... a swashbuckling master of the political midstream—but only in the crowded, well-travelled familiar inland waterways of domestic politics. He had no taste and scant preparation for the deep waters of foreign policy, for the sudden storms and unpredictable winds that can becalm or batter or blow off course the ocean-going man. He was king of the river and a stranger to the open sea."

The prevailing assumptions among his close advisers were firmly grounded in the Cold War order of things, in the frame of existing pacts and alliances and alignments—above all, in the notion that the "Communist Bloc" remained an essentially cohesive international conspiracy manifesting itself primarily in military and paramilitary assaults against that other comprehensible entity, the "Free World." An important corollary was the belief that an accretion of "communist" influence *anywhere* must redound to the direct benefit of the main power centers in Moscow and Peking, for from

8

this flowed the logic that counterthrusts in kind were everywhere and almost automatically necessary; otherwise a progressive, irreversible, unacceptable erosion of the world power balance could not be averted.

Like everyone else in the United States over forty, the President's advisers were children of the Cold War in the sense that their thinking about world strategy and world politics had been decisively shaped by that phenomenon. Still relatively young and impressionable when they emerged from the wholesale fighting of World War II, they had found that the fruit of victory was a bitter bipolar enmity stretching around the globe, and apparently restrained from the plunge into final holocaust only by a delicate balance of terror. They had lived in this political-military frame of iron for the better part of twenty years, urgently preoccupied with mortal struggle against a formidable Communist structure.

But by 1965 many of the major elements of the Cold War mosaic had undergone drastic transformation or had ceased to exist. There was an effective military balance in the center of Europe—the product of NATO counterpower sustained over twenty years—and it was a stable balance in the sense of being relatively insensitive to changes in the level and composition of forces on either side, within a fairly wide spectrum. The likelihood of deliberate Soviet attack seemed very low because it was understood on both sides that *any* dramatic attempt to alter the military balance could lead rapidly to a probably uncontrollable nuclear war. Moreover, Western Europe behind the NATO shield was no longer the weak and dispirited war refugee of 1946, but strong, prosperous, and almost confident. And on the other side of the line, time was demonstrating that not even the doctrines of Marx and Lenin could render Communism immune to the inherent traps and pitfalls of the historical process—from schism, territorial dispute, the aging process, and the effects of affluence. In combination, these factors were seriously undermining the Soviet position as the ideological fountainhead of doctrine, making

9

a shambles of party discipline in the world movement, and sharply reducing Soviet revolutionary fervor in relation to the underdeveloped world.

The Sino-Soviet rupture was a developing fact of the greatest strategic consequence. From limited beginnings it had progressed, even by 1965, to an apparently irreparable conflict over the fundamentals of ideology and power. It was a split that not only destroyed the vaunted unity of Communist doctrine, but also saved the United States and its allies from having to face the combined and coordinated resources of Russia and China. The leaders in Peking had become the most vehement radical revolutionaries in the world, but their ideological ferocity seemed to strike no profoundly responsive chord in the hearts of other backward nations. Their continuing attempt to project China as the natural ally of the world's impoverished was indeed marked by surprising ineptitude and failure, attributable, I thought, to their ingrained imperialist attitude toward all non-Chinese which alienated Africans and Asians alike. There was also the bald fact that Maoist rule had been such an economic disaster that China could offer neither meaningful economic aid nor convincing advice on how to achieve economic growth.

The loosening of Soviet control in Eastern Europe was a visible reality, reflecting the radiated consequences of de-Stalinization in the USSR, broader economic and cultural relations with the West, and the gradual recovery and reassertion of separate national identities. These developments were not moving Eastern Europe toward democracy or even a repudiation of close ties with the Soviets; and out of a deep concern for their security and a fading commitment to the revolutionary mystique, it was apparent that the Soviets would hang on in Eastern Europe for a long time. Yet their efforts to build a stable, integrated empire had failed. Nationalism had proved stronger than imposed ideology. What Stalin with total power could not do was no longer a serious possibility for his successors. In Professor Brzezinski's striking phrase: "East Europe is where the dream of Communist internationalism lies buried." [2] (This was a judgment not basically affected, but in major respects confirmed, by the 1968 invasion of Czechoslovakia.)

In Western Europe and indeed in all the areas of the world beyond the direct reach of Soviet military power, the loss of Soviet control and influence over local Communist parties was an operative political fact. The coming to nationhood of some sixty small and fragile ex-colonies whose vital concerns were economic development, political independence, and racial equality, and who were essentially indifferent to ideological crusades, was creating new centers of political initiative. These developments were diluting the ability of both the Soviet Union and the United States to manage old coalitions and control events.

The Soviet Union itself presented a curious anomaly. Presumably its leaders possessed inherited impulses to serve as a revolutionary vanguard for the world's downtrodden. But they were also masters of a powerful industrial nation, a fact which was reviving pre-Bolshevik imperial aspirations that had long been in hibernation. Just as Stalin pursued a strictly continental foreign policy because he lacked the resources to do otherwise, so Khrushchev began to give Soviet policy a wider orientation as the necessary resources and technology became available. By 1965, the Brezhnev-Kosygin leadership was giving further shape to a political strategy that seemed to commit the Soviet Union to full global competition with the United States. Russia showed evidence of a new determination to become, and perhaps even more to be accepted as, a genuine world power. There was an evident increase of military influence within the Soviet power structure, a fact which led to the disquieting possibility that the next stage of development in an industrialized Communist state might be right-wing military dictatorship—i.e., Fascism. These new developments did not materially reduce the dangers of U.S.-Soviet confrontation, but they did begin to shift the context from that of an emotionally charged ideological struggle to a more classic Great Power rivalry.

Seen in the large, these shifts indicated the gradual breakdown of the Cold War boundary lines, which had been as clear and hard as ice, and promised a proliferation of large and small power centers characterized by rather transient relationships. The world was no longer neatly divided between Free World and Communist Bloc and while these new realities did not greatly diminish the dangers of an inherently precarious century, they did alter the shape and character of problems in ways that strongly suggested the need for new analysis and new responses.

It is of the greatest significance that these new perspectives did not materially alter the judgments of the men closest to President Johnson. The tenets of the Cold War were bred in the bone. In fairness, it must be said that nothing is more difficult to confront than the need to outgrow conceptions that have had undeniable validity—have been in truth basic reference points for thought and action involving the life of the nation. It is a difficulty that persists even when one is intellectually aware that the familiar conceptions no longer fully square with the facts. As the President's advisers appraised the world situation in 1965, the Russians and the Chinese still seemed to them in full pursuit of bellicose, expansionist policies across the globe, and still quite ready and able to join in the support and manipulation of proxies for purposes inimical to our own.

Five years earlier, the new Kennedy Administration had of course inherited a still untempered Cold War and, on the basis of evidence available in 1960, had little choice but to accept the bequest. In the circumstances, President Kennedy's eloquent Inaugural Address, taken as a whole, was a remarkable effort to break free of the inherited strictures, to lift the vision of his own countrymen and of his adversaries above the ideological trenches. He asked for a new civility, called for detailed proposals to control the nuclear arms race, and pointed valiantly toward "a new world of law, where the strong are just and the weak secure and the peace preserved." The Address was to prove a harbinger of his steady efforts to dilute the moralistic tone of U.S. foreign policy set by Dulles, so that the problems of a world in seething ferment could be seen in truer perspective, through lenses less tinged with ideology, and could thus be approached with greater reasonableness by both sides. But this lofty perspective notwithstanding, the Address was not unnaturally permeated with the sense of bipolar struggle and confrontation across the globe. And it contained that famous unlimited commitment: "Let every nation know, whether it wishes us well or ill, that we shall pay any price, bear any burden, meet any hardship, support any friend, oppose any foe, in order to assure the survival and success of liberty. This much we pledge—and more."

Arthur Schlesinger might subsequently cavil at the inertia of a bureaucracy that still used terms like "Sino-Soviet Bloc" and "International Communism" in studies and staff papers, but the Kennedy Administration's considerable efforts to broaden the spectrum of practical U.S. military response strongly attested to its *own* conviction that the United States did indeed face a hostile, coordinated power bloc bent on world conquest; moreover, that the U.S. must be ready to fight at nearly every level of armed conflict to defend interests that had no apparent geographical limit.

NATIONAL-LIBERATION WAR

Indeed the Kennedy-McNamara plans to strengthen the U.S. ability to wage limited conventional and counterguerrilla war had been given new urgency by the Khrushchev speech of January 1961, the first month of Kennedy's incumbency. In the course of an eight-hour exposition, which rang with the confidence born of new economic and technical achievement, the Soviet leader described three kinds of conflict: nuclear wars, conventional wars, and national-liberation wars. Nuclear wars, he said, could have no victor because they would end in mutual destruction; and even conventional wars were unacceptably dangerous because, if they came to involve nuclear powers, they might escalate into nuclear wars. National-liberation wars, on the other hand, were a suitable means of advancing the Communist cause, and he announced that such "just wars" would have the unreserved and whole-hearted support of the Soviet Union.

President Kennedy, reportedly alarmed by the prospect that Communist expansionist efforts would now move to a concentration on stimulating protracted subversion and guerrilla warfare throughout the politically fragile and explosive underdeveloped world, appeared to believe that Khrushchev was posing a threat of global dimension. In his first State of the Union message just a few days later, he said: "We must never be lulled into believing that either power [Russia or China] has yielded its ambitions for world domination—ambitions which they forcefully restated only a short time ago. On the contrary, our task is to convince them that aggression and subversion will not be profitable routes to pursue these ends."

He quickly followed this up with a broad effort to impress the meaning of Khrushchev's new challenge upon the whole foreign affairs-military bureaucracy, and to reorient and reorganize it under the stirring, if ambiguous, banner of counterinsurgency. Robert Kennedy, Maxwell Taylor, Walt Rostow, Richard Bissell, and Roger Hilsman were in the vanguard of this effort. The works of Mao Tse-tung and Che Guevera were avidly studied and became established reference points for a new American counterdoctrine; soldiers, diplomats, and economic aid administrators of all ranks were required to take a "counterinsurgency course" before being posted to underdeveloped countries; special warfare centers were established in several parts of the world, and a high level Counter-Insurgency Committee under General Taylor (and later under Averell Harriman) was created to keep close watch on situations of incipient subversion in every corner of the globe. By early 1962, Hilsman and Rostow had developed a cogent and comprehensive "strategic concept for counterinsurgency" that emphasized the need for central control of all antiguerrilla activities within the country under attack, subordination of military actions to political purposes, and reliance on small-scale counterguerrilla units, as opposed to conventional military formations. Predictably, this concept met with determined resistance from the upper echelons of the U.S. military hierarchy—particularly in the Army—and was ironically and most unfortunately never applied in Vietnam.

As Schlesinger admitted, "there was, to be sure, a faddish aspect to this enthusiasm" for the development and application of a counterinsurgency doctrine. In terms of its effect on official attitudes within the U.S. government, a far more serious deficiency was the implicit assumption that henceforth Washington would be predisposed to view an effort to overthrow the existing order *anywhere* as a national-liberation war fomented by and for the benefit of Russia or China. In a revolutionary era characterized by profound discontent throughout the underdeveloped world (and not only there), by an epidemic frustration born of the conflict between intractable conditions and inflated expectations, such an assumption could only lead the United States toward interventions based on quite misperceived assessments. It was perfectly true, for example, that frustrated men professing radical doctrines, including Communism, were behind the revolutionary turmoil in Latin America; and that aided to some extent and in varying degrees by Maoist guerrilla doctrine, Soviet money and Cuban training, Latin American Communists and other radicals were engaged in a wide range of violent, dangerous, and subversive activities. It was far from clear, however, that such activity was controlled, or even seriously influenced, by an outside power; most evidence suggested that the motivation and initiative were largely indigenous. It was equally unclear whether, in the absence of Great Power meddling, such activity presented a situation that the U.S. could reasonably expect to ameliorate by military intervention.

THE ADVISERS

The point is that the Cold War syndrome prevailing in Washington in 1965 represented no break with the Kennedy period. Indeed all of President Johnson's principal foreign policy advisers were Kennedy men. All carried in their veins the implicitly unlimited commitment to global struggle against Revolutionary Communism which had grown out of our total immersion in World War II, and which had been specifically enunciated in the Truman Doctrine of March 1947. None as yet perceived the necessity—or the possibility—of redefining U.S. interests or the U.S. role in the world in ways that would permit the drawing of more careful distinctions between those commitments and interventions that are in fact *vital* to our national security, and those that spring more or less from our deeply held view of what the world "ought" to be and of how it "ought" to be organized—that is, from our reforming zeal and our desire for wish fulfillment. To the President's men in early 1965, there seemed no logical stopping point between isolationism and globalism.

Of the close advisers on Vietnam, Dean Rusk seemed the very embodiment of the embattled Cold Warrior with convictions rooted in the Stalinist period. An intelligent man, he could not have been unaware of the trends that were fragmenting the "Communist Bloc" and creating new problems of orientation within each Communist country. But he was careful not to allow these developments to affect his basic judgments. He was, moreover, possessed of a special mania about China and of a knack for arguing by dubious analogy. Not only in public, but in private conversations with colleagues and with President Johnson, Rusk expounded his thesis that Communist China was actively promoting and supporting aggression in Vietnam, that aggression in Vietnam was not different from Hitler's aggression in Europe, that appeasement in Vietnam could have the same consequences as appeasement at Munich. In his always articulate, sometimes eloquent, formulations, Asia seemed to be Europe, China was either Stalinist Russia or Hitler Germany, and SEATO was either NATO or the Grand Alliance of World War II. This insistent drawing on the past as a basis for meeting problems that were radically different, that presented themselves in unlike circumstances, and that involved a quite dissimilar degree of U.S. national interest could hardly fail to make a major contribution to the enormous national confusion regarding the character and meaning of U.S. involvement in the Vietnam War. Rusk thus contributed to the Administration's credibility problem—directly, because his formulations could not withstand the test of even cursory historical analysis; indirectly, because they were apt to be replayed on the President's Texas amplifier. As Philip Geyelin reported it, "The backstage Johnson . . . was quite capable of telling one of the Senate's more serious students of foreign affairs that 'if we don't stop the Reds in South Vietnam, tomorrow they will be in Hawaii, and next week they will be in San Francisco.' " [3]

Robert McNamara had blown into Washington in 1961 like a brisk and exhilarating wind. Possessed of a swift and powerful mind, training in the analytical techniques of modern management, experience in managing a large-scale industrial enterprise, and a natural affinity for the reasoned exercise of power, he quickly excited the awe and admiration of all concerned by establishing genuine civilian control over the sprawling military bureaucracies, a feat that had proved beyond the reach of all seven predecessor Secretaries of Defense. President Kennedy spoke glowingly of "that executive operation at the Pentagon," and prized McNamara as the ablest and most versatile member of the Cabinet.

By 1965, McNamara's prodigious labors to strengthen and broaden the U.S. military posture were about completed.

The land-based nuclear missile force had been expanded to one thousand modern Minutemen, and the submarine-based Polaris force was a growing reality. More relevant for Vietnam, U.S. "general purpose" forces were now organized to intervene swiftly and with modern equipment in conflicts of limited scope, well below the nuclear threshold. To this end, combat-ready Army divisions had been increased from 11 to 16; the Special Forces had been expanded from 3 to 7 groups; the Army helicopter inventory had been increased from 5500 to 8000; a fourth Marine division and a fourth Marine air wing had been raised; modern tactical airlift for troops and supplies had been expanded from 16 to 38 squadrons, providing nearly a three-fold increase in carrying capacity; and STRIKECOM, a major new command group reporting directly to the Joint Chiefs of Staff, had been established to "provide the President with tailored responses for any level of warfare" and to develop the necessary new tactical doctrines, equipment, and training for limited war.

This significant new military capability had been designed precisely to arrest or restore those deteriorating situations in the world where important or vital U.S. interests were judged to be engaged, to deal with ambiguous subversion-aggressions characterized by little warning and a low silhouette, to blunt national-liberation wars. It was now ready. To a rational activist like McNamara, with a very thin background in foreign affairs, it seemed entirely logical to employ a portion of this immense U.S. power if that could arrest the spreading erosion in South Vietnam. And such a result seemed hardly more than a self-evident proposition. For there was North Vietnam, a tiny primitive country of 19 million people, and there was the United States. Surely Hanoi could not withstand the graduated pressures of a nation of 200 million who possessed the strongest economy in the world and the most powerful military forces. Surely the use of limited U.S. power, applied with care and precision, but with the threat of more to come, would bring a realistic Ho Chi Minh to early negotiations. Nearly a year before the decision to apply direct U.S. power, McNamara had publicly expressed his fundamental confidence that in the end all would be well. While acknowledging the difficulties and frustrations that lay ahead in Vietnam, as well as the heavy demand for courage, imagination, and above all, patience, he said in a speech delivered in late March of 1964: "When the day comes that we can safely withdraw, we expect to leave an independent and stable South Vietnam, rich with resources and bright with prospects for contributing to the peace and prosperity of Southeast Asia and of the world."

McGeorge Bundy was a brilliant and self-assured pragmatist of the highest ability. Less a scholar than an activist thinker and problem solver, he brought to the analysis of world problems a solid grounding in foreign affairs and an interesting mix of ethical imperative, *real politik,* and a feel for the innate operational complexity and limited controlability of large undertakings in war and peace. In a fundamental sense, he was a "process man" who, aware of the unforeseeable ways in which events not yet born will impinge upon and alter preselected courses of action, believes that what is important is to get started in the right direction and then play it by ear. Oriented principally to European affairs and the complex issues of strategic nuclear defense, he came to focus on the Vietnam crisis only in late 1964. He concluded that the United States must be willing to stand and fight in Vietnam, or else lose not only Southeast Asia but also the world's faith in the U.S. will and capacity to cope with the Communist threat to the Asian area. Failure to respond in Vietnam, he judged, would lead to further bold insurgencies in Malaysia, Indonesia, Burma, and the Philippines. He strongly urged the intervention of U.S. combat forces in 1965. Skeptical, however, of claims that air interdiction could really halt the infiltration, he advocated bombing North Vietnam primarily as a means of forcing Hanoi to pay a price for its cruelties in the South, and to bolster the morale of the government of South Vietnam.

Writing on the "uses of responsibility" in July 1965, in response to a statement by Archibald MacLeish which had questioned the moral implications of our actions in Vietnam and had seen in the world's falling opinion of the United States the reinforcement of MacLeish's own concern, Bundy argued that from the fall of France "in that terrible spring of 1940," the continuing American attitude toward world affairs had been composed of three primary elements: first and foremost "acceptance . . . of the responsibility of holding and using power"; second, "a passionate commitment to the ideal of peace"; and third, "an assertion that the dreams of others must have room to come true and that American power must be responsive to that end." Direct U.S. military intervention in Vietnam was "fairly and correctly understood, I deeply believe, only in the context of the general, sustained commitment to a goal of less war, less struggle . . . and a readiness to judge ourselves and to be judged in terms of the effect of our behavior on others." Such advocacy and defense of U.S. intervention in Vietnam reflected, with eloquence and precision, the broader sense of a beneficent, unavoidable American universalism. This had come—through, as it seemed, the inexorable workings of history for twenty-five years—to pervade and dominate official thinking in Washington at the crucial pivot point of late 1964 and early 1965.

It was not without irony that Walt Rostow, whose views on Vietnam so closely paralleled those of the Secretary of State, had been in 1961 turned down as the man to head Policy Planning in that department because Rusk regarded him as a rather too liberal economist. It was ironic because this deceptively mild-mannered man, who showed a natural deference to authority, proved to be the closest thing we had near the top of the U.S. government to a genuine, all-wool, anti-Communist ideologue and true believer. An inductive thinker, he constructed theories—often with perception and ingenuity—but once the pattern of his belief was established, some automatic mental filter thereafter accepted only reinforcing data, while systematically and totally rejecting all contrary evidence no matter how compelling. In debate he showed a rare capacity for "instant rationalization" (as one colleague put it), which amounted to a compulsion for buttressing his views by a rapid culling of the evidence immediately at hand; it did not matter whether the support that such evidence could provide was frail or nonexistent. His insensitivity to the opinions of others was legendary.

As a result of Rusk's rejection, Rostow became Bundy's deputy at the White House, but was moved to the planning job at State at the end of 1961, on direct instructions from President Kennedy. As the President explained it to Michael Forrestal, "Walt is a fountain of ideas; perhaps one in ten of them is absolutely brilliant. Unfortunately, six or seven are not merely unsound, but dangerously so. I admire his creativity, but it will be more comfortable to have him creating at some remove from the White House." After four years at the State Department where Rusk studiedly ignored him most of the time, Rostow returned to the White House in early 1966, upon Bundy's departure from government, as President Johnson's principal foreign policy assistant and coordinator.

He saw the problem in Vietnam as a centrally directed and coordinated Communist challenge, a deliberate testing of the national-liberation war theory with global implications. Success for Ho Chi Minh would set off a string of revolutionary explosions in vulnerable areas all across the world from which only Communism would benefit. But if the challenge in Vietnam were met and mastered by a determined Free World countereffort, similar Communist insurgencies in other miserable and restless areas—in Asia, Africa, and Latin America—would be deterred or discouraged. He was an early and unremitting advocate of bombing North Vietnam,

21

although this seemed inconsistent with his own "strategic concept for counterinsurgency" which stressed small units, stealth, and knives as opposed to sizable conventional formations and weapons of large-scale destruction. But he had concluded that, because the infiltration could not be totally choked off, it was necessary to strike at "the source of the aggression." A participant in the Strategic Bombing Survey after World War II, he drew analogies from American experience over Germany and Japan that led him to the conviction that tactical airpower could make the war unbearable for Hanoi. He believed, erroneously, that there were in North Vietnam important industrial targets whose destruction would cripple the operation of that economy.

General Maxwell Taylor, a distinguished soldier-scholar, played several different roles in the Vietnam affair—as consultant to President Kennedy and co-author of the Taylor-Rostow report of November 1961; as Chairman of the Joint Chiefs of Staff until June 1964; as U.S. Ambassador to South Vietnam for the next twelve months; and thereafter as consultant to President Johnson and head of the Institute for Defense Analyses in Washington. In each of these positions he was a consistent, entirely predictable advocate of unrelenting military pressure in Vietnam as the only effective means of dealing with "the communist offensive in the Asian area."

His 1961 report found that the crisis of confidence in South Vietnam was caused in large part by uncertainty as to the seriousness with which the U.S. regarded its commitment to defend Vietnam. Evidence of Saigon's doubts, as cited by him, included the U.S. willingness to negotiate a compromise in Laos, involving a coalition government headed by a neutralist and including the Communist Pathet Lao faction (the Laos negotiations were concluded in 1962). With Rostow, Taylor felt the situation in Vietnam required a shift in the character of the American effort from advice to limited partnership, and he expressed the conviction that Vietnamese performance across the whole political-military-economic-

22

social spectrum could be substantially improved if more Americans were prepared to work side by side with them on key problems. He was confident that a larger American effort in Southeast Asia could be publicly presented as something quite different from an attempt to reestablish the colonial system. He also believed the Viet Cong had significant weaknesses, including the necessity to rely on terror and intimidation and "a declining military effectiveness against the growing strength of the ARVN," (*sic*). Moreover, he felt that Hanoi was inhibited from engaging North Vietnamese regular divisions out of a fear that this would produce a direct U.S. counteraction.

The Taylor-Rostow report recommended a very substantial increase in both civilian technicians and military trainers at every level; it called for more U.S. Special Forces teams. But what gave the report as a whole its central character, revealing the authors' essentially military conception of the problem and its solution, were the recommendations that edged the United States several steps closer to direct responsibility for conventional military operations in Vietnam. These called for American-manned helicopters to improve ARVN's mobility, American-manned Air Force units (code-named Farmgate and equipped with propeller-driven A-1s and B-26s) to provide close air support for ARVN, and the dispatch of 10,000 U.S. combat ground forces to Vietnam and acceptance of the possible need for more. To these Rostow added a special annex that recommended contingency planning for U.S. air strikes against North Vietnam. It is important to note that these recommendations, made in 1961 when the conflict was still at a low level of violence, moved directly away from counterguerrilla and counterinsurgency warfare and toward large-scale conventional operations featuring artillery, bomber aircraft, and other weapons of great destructive power. Ingrained preferences as to military means were thus already beginning to subordinate political purpose and dictate strategy. In that report of November 1961, the future was foreshadowed.

In the absence of ready alternative proposals, President Kennedy approved all but the introduction of U.S. combat ground troops and the Rostow annex on air strikes. By the time of his death in late 1963, the U.S. military presence in Vietnam had increased from a few hundred to about 16,000. By the end of 1964, it had grown to 21,000.

THE SLIPPERY SLOPE

But these impressions became definitive only through post-mortem analysis. Vietnam policy in 1964–65 was formulated by a small group, and deliberations were closely held. At the time, many officials ostensibly near the center of U.S. national security affairs knew very little. Like newspaper readers everywhere, they could only note that through a series of small, almost imperceptible, steps, the United States had become involved in large and rapidly expanding combat operations. What happened between August 1964 and March 1965 confirmed the prevailing Cold War syndrome among the close advisers; it also revealed President Johnson's passion for consensus, his instinctive feeling that foreign policy is an integral and subordinate element of domestic politics, his compulsive secrecy, and his tendency to gloss over inconvenient truth—all of the qualities that were progressivly to impair his credibility and effectiveness over the next three years, and finally to bring him down.

There had been in August the quixotic (and later much disputed) attacks by North Vietnamese torpedo boats on U.S. destroyers in the Tonkin Gulf. The second attack provoked a one-shot retaliatory air strike by U.S. carrier forces. Though it was difficult, both at the time and later, to discern any clear North Vietnamese purpose in provoking the U.S. giant, President Johnson in mid-campaign had found it prudent to respond militarily, on the grounds that he could not afford to play the total dove to Goldwater's hawk. He had found it prudent also to obtain from Congress a quick resolution that authorized him "to take all necessary measures to repel any armed attack against the forces of the United States and to prevent further aggression."

That resolution became the principal constitutional instrument by which he radically altered the character of U.S. involvement in Vietnam six months later. Its language, if read literally, supported the action and thus served to paralyze his critics in the Congress and the press for some months afterwards. Yet many believed he had brazenly distorted the Congressional intent. The Senate debate was in fact not without its ambiguities. At one point Senator Gaylord Nelson of Wisconsin seemed about to propose an amendment that would limit Congressional endorsement to those Presidential measures required to protect U.S. forces from attack. The phrase that authorized the President to take all necessary measures "to prevent further aggression" worried him. There occurred the following exchange with the floor manager, Senator Fulbright:

Senator Nelson: But I am concerned about the Congress appearing to tell the Executive Branch and the public that we would endorse a complete change in our mission. That would concern me.

Senator Fulbright: I do not interpret the Joint Resolution in that way at all. It strikes me, as I understand it, that the Joint Resolution is quite consistent with our existing mission and our understanding of what we have been doing in South Vietnam for the last 10 years.

There was an ambivalent exchange with Senator Daniel Brewster of Maryland:

Senator Brewster: I would look with great dismay on a situation involving the landing of large land armies on the continent of Asia. So my question is whether there is anything in the resolution which would authorize or recommend or approve the landing of large American armies in Vietnam or China. . . .

Senator Fulbright: There is nothing in the resolution, as I read it, that contemplates it. I agree with the Senator that it is the last thing we would want to do. However, the language of the resolution would not prevent it . . .

Later in the debate, Senator John Sherman Cooper of Kentucky returned to the question of a distinction between the President's inherent powers to defend U.S. forces and his authority to go to the defense of another country under the SEATO Treaty. Noting that Article IV of the treaty provided, in the event of an armed attack upon a member of SEATO or a protocol state, that the parties would resort to their "constitutional processes," he put the following question:

Senator Cooper: I assume that would mean, in the case of the United States, that Congress would be asked to grant the authority to act. Does the Senator consider that in enacting this resolution we are satisfying the requirement of Article IV [of the SEATO Treaty]. . .? In other words, are we giving the President advance authority to take whatever action he may deem necessary respecting South Vietnam and its defense, or with respect to the defense of any other country included in the Treaty?

Senator Fulbright: I think that is correct.

Senator Morse of Oregon called the resolution "a predated declaration of war." But the Senate was not really listening. In the midst of an electoral campaign, it felt obliged to trust and support the President. Senator Fulbright, who was later to disavow the resolution and regard his own support of it as a grave mistake, made a final pledge to his colleagues: "I have no doubt that the President will consult with Congress in case a major change in present policy becomes necessary." There was in fact no further consultation.

26

Shortly after the Tonkin episode, there occurred another of those consequential inadvertencies that seem an unavoidable element of the U.S. governmental process—in which so much is asked of a few overworked men. It came to the attention of the White House staff that the Air Force was planning, within a few days, to move a squadron of B-57 bombers from the Philippines to Bien Hoa in South Vietnam. These were obsolescent aircraft being used to provide jet training for the South Vietnamese. The training was being conducted at Clark Field in the Philippines, but no decision had been taken to turn the aircraft over to South Vietnam (among other difficulties, the introduction of jet equipment would involve a violation of the 1954 Geneva Accords). The Air Force now wished however to shift the training to Vietnam.

Both Michael Forrestal, the White House assistant on Vietnam, and William Bundy, the Assistant Secretary of State for Far Eastern Affairs, thought the proposed move was a bad idea, for they feared that U.S. aircraft sitting in Vietnam would become an irresistible target for Viet Cong attack. Hastily they took the issue to Rusk in an effort to head off the move, getting an appointment with him late on a September afternoon. Rusk was not particularly impressed by their argument, but agreed to pick up the phone and call McNamara. While Forrestal and Bundy stood by the edge of his desk, he talked to McNamara for perhaps five minutes. Then, putting down the phone, he said "Bob has so many issues with the JCS that he would rather finesse this one unless we are prepared to take a very strong position. I don't think we are. It seems to me a rather small matter."

The B-57s were duly moved to Bien Hoa. After sitting on that air base for about two months, six of the aircraft were demolished by Viet Cong mortars on November 3, just two days before the U.S. election; five Americans were killed and seventy-six wounded. From Ambassador Maxwell Taylor in Saigon came an urgent recommendation for reprisal air attacks against the North. The purely military logic of the proposal was hard to refute: failure to respond would deprive the post-Tonkin strikes of any meaning and would cast doubt on U.S. resolve. But the President's advisers presented the issue to him in low key on the grounds that it was imperative, first, to sink Goldwaterism and unify the country. Thereafter a considered national response could be made.

There seems little doubt, however, that the Bien Hoa attack crystallized official U.S. determination for intervention. The doctrine of deterrence, which had been applied with success against Russians in Europe, had proved no inhibition to the primitive North Vietnamese who were determined to finish a civil war by unifying the country on their own harsh terms. The situation in Saigon seemed to be crumbling fast, and some feared an imminent collapse of the government. Any hope for a negotiated settlement with the Communists seemed to depend on the restoration of a strong bargaining position, and that meant changing the military balance in South Vietnam. The American choices, as Under Secretary of State George Ball explained them to de Gaulle in December, were to do everything possible to strengthen the Saigon government politically and militarily, or to throw the weight of U.S. power onto the scale. De Gaulle suggested a third, which was to avoid further U.S. involvement and accept the French offer to organize international negotiations. He expressed his conviction that the United States could not win in Vietnam, and that deeper U.S. involvement would only increase the hostility and alienation of world opinion. He also thought China was backward and weak, and would not for some years pose a serious threat of military aggression. Officially at least, Ball could not agree.

It is significant that, during most of the 1964 political campaign, the President had been by his own deliberate choice insulated from day-to-day developments in Vietnam. The word was to keep tough decisions away from the White House, and to avoid new actions or policy initiatives that would complicate the President's campaigning. During September and October, therefore, the erosion went on in South Vietnam without being brought forcefully to his attention; mounting anxieties at the intermediate levels. in Washington and throughout the U.S. establishment in Saigon were muted. When the President finally focused on the problem, sometime around mid-November, it had swollen to apparent crisis proportions, confronting him with what his advisers believed was a basic choice between major intervention and a considered liquidation of the whole commitment. His advisers appeared to agree that the first alternative that Ball had put to de Gaulle—a purely South Vietnamese counter to the Viet Cong challenge—was fast becoming academic. There wasn't enough time.

It is my impression that two things then happened: the President's close advisers (excepting Ball) unanimously urged direct U.S. military intervention in Vietnam, in order to avoid further deterioration of "our credibility vis-à-vis the Communists." The President reluctantly accepted the recommendation, because it was nearly unanimous, because it reinforced his own instincts about Communism and the needs of U.S. prestige, because he lacked the experience and self-confidence in foreign affairs to devise a valid alternative through (or by overriding) his constitutional advisers, and because he was quickly resolved not to become "the first American President to lose a war." But operating always on the instinctive premise that foreign policy is merely a subordinate element of domestic politics, he perceived political safety in continuity. He thus imposed the condition that intervention had to be made to look as though nothing was changing, as though it all flowed inexorably from commitments made by Eisenhower in 1954 and Kennedy in 1961, as though Lyndon Johnson were essentially a victim of history, doing no more than his bounden duty. "I didn't get you into Vietnam," he had said in a campaign speech, "You have been in Vietnam ten years. President Eisenhower wrote President Diem a letter in 1954 when the French pulled out . . ."

To a President convinced he must take new actions, yet obsessed by a need to preserve the posture of continuity, no major and overt actions were possible. He could not ask Congress for a declaration of war without shattering the posture (and without providing a rather specific explanation as to why "vital" U.S. interests were, after ten years of involvement, suddenly at stake). Inhibited by a formula of his own devising, he could only exploit the actions of the other side, seize available pretexts and provocations, and thus start a process that would lead in a series of acceptable steps to the required enlargement of the U.S. military effort.

The Administration positioned itself for such a development. On February 7, 1965, when the Viet Cong attacked American installations at Pleiku, destroying additional U.S. aircraft, killing seven and wounding 109, a retaliatory air strike was immediately ordered. Three days later, an American billet in the coastal city of Qui Nhon was similarly assaulted. Another air strike was carried out. McGeorge Bundy, who was in Vietnam at the time, later told a newsman, "Pleikus are streetcars," i.e., if one waits watchfully, they come along. Thereafter, the air strikes were almost imperceptibly transformed into a systematic program of bombing the North, but without formal acknowledgment of the shift until long after it was established fact. On March 6, two reinforced U.S. Marine battalions were sent ashore at Da Nang on what was described as "limited duty" related to the perimeter defense of airfields. Both Rusk and McNamara assured the nation that the role of these units, the first to be organized for combat, would be strictly confined to "defensive operations." McNamara added that because of their narrow patrolling mission they "should not tangle with the Viet Cong." But as the spring wore on, there were broad contacts between U.S. and enemy forces, significant U.S. casualties, and the arrival of additional U.S. combat forces.

By June, with 50,000 American troops in Vietnam, the White House conceded that U.S. forces were "authorized" to engage in combat under carefully defined and limited conditions—but it insisted that this was nothing new. It was merely another small step, and wholly consistent with the Eisenhower letter to Diem of 1954. As one highly placed official said much later, "The President's posture during this period was to pretend the war was not happening."

Immediately following the February attack on Pleiku, but before retaliatory action had been ordered, Vice-President Humphrey returned urgently to Washington from a trip to Georgia, to make a last-ditch attempt to prevent escalation. He gave the President his view that bombing the North could not resolve the issue in the South, but that it would generate an inexorable requirement for U.S. ground forces in the South to protect airfields and aircraft. He thought the attempt to gain a military solution in Vietnam would take years—far beyond the end of 1967 when the President would have to position himself for reelection. His views were received at the White House with particular coldness, and he was banished from the inner councils for some months thereafter, until he decided to "get back on the team."

By moving with secret purpose behind a screen of bland assurances designed to minimize or mislead, by admitting nothing until pressed by the facts and then no more than was absolutely necessary, by stretching to the limit (and perhaps beyond) the intent of the Tonkin Gulf Resolution, the President carried a bemused and half-aware nation far beyond the Eisenhower and Kennedy positions to a radically different involvement in the intractable Vietnam conflict. It would have to be conceded that the performance was a piece of artful, even masterful, political craftsmanship. Unfortunately for Lyndon Johnson and the American people, it could be vindicated only by a quick and decisive military victory. But when the mists of summer confusion lifted, there were 170,000 U.S. troops in Vietnam, U.S. air forces were bombing the North with mounting intensity, and the enemy showed no sign of surrender or defeat. There was the President and there was the country—waist-deep in the Big Muddy. And the integrity, the trust, the credibility without which the leadership of great democratic nations cannot govern were all gravely strained by a pattern of actions that seemed an inextricable blend of high-mindedness, inadvertence, and either massive self-delusion or calculated deceit.

CHAPTER 2

Concurrent Events

FOREIGN POLICY ADVICE
TO THE SECRETARY OF DEFENSE

THE OFFICE of International Security Affairs (ISA) is the Defense Secretary's principal staff support in the discharge of his manifold responsibilities in the field of foreign-military affairs—that large area of problems within the general conduct of our external relations where considerations of diplomacy and military interest are interdependent, or nearly so. Numbering some three hundred people, about equally divided between civilian specialists and professional military officers, ISA exists to provide informed judgment and advice on a range of problems that include (to choose at random) the adequacy of European troop contributions to NATO, the negotiation of military-base rights in Spain, the possible withdrawal of some part of the two U.S. Army divisions in Korea, and the possible sale of jet aircraft to Israel. It administers the world-wide Military Assistance Program and the corollary program of selective military sales. It plays a leading role in developing the U.S. position on arms control measures, e.g., the Nuclear Non-Proliferation Treaty, and preparations for U.S.-Soviet talks on limiting offensive and defensive nuclear weapons.

Reflecting its close and continuous relations with the

33

State Department, ISA is organized in geographical directorates for Europe, the Far East, the Near East-South Asia, Africa, and Latin America; and in functional directorates for Planning, Military Assistance, and Arms Control. Its effectiveness also requires day-to-day consultation and cooperation with the Joint Chiefs of Staff organization. In the foreign-military bureaucracy, ISA has inherent clout, but its influence during the Kennedy-Johnson period was perhaps magnified by McNamara's preeminent role in foreign affairs and military strategy.

The question is sometimes asked whether an organization like ISA is really a necessary feature of our policy-making process. Couldn't the JCS organization provide the Secretary of Defense with the desired advice and support directly, thereby obviating the need for this peculiar intermediary? The answer is no—for at least two reasons: First, the Secretary of Defense bears, together with the Secretary of State and the Joint Chiefs of Staff, the highest and heaviest responsibility for advising the President on matters affecting the national security. But the advice the President seeks from him, while of course grounded in the military aspects of the problem, is something apart from and above the undiluted military advice rendered by the professionals. The Secretary of Defense's advice must comprehend a broader context—by adjusting for political and budgetary realities, by verifying the validity of JCS assumptions with respect to nonmilitary factors, and, most importantly, by providing an independent judgment of what military power is likely to accomplish, and what its side effects are apt to be, in situations where its use is urged by the JCS, recognizing that the crucial factors are frequently almost unmeasurable and imponderable. The second reason is that the Joint Chiefs of Staff are not responsible to the Secretary of Defense alone. They also have a statutory responsibility for rendering military advice directly to the President and the National Security Council, and at times this may have to be discharged by means of a disagreement with the Secretary of Defense. For both of these reasons, every incumbent Secretary of Defense has felt the need for an alternative source of staff support in the consequential area of foreign-military affairs—an independent counterpoise able to test JCS positions and propose different ones.

Heading ISA in 1965 was Assistant Secretary of Defense John T. McNaughton, a lanky, intense, brilliant Harvard law professor who had won his governmental spurs since 1961, first as Deputy Assistant Secretary for Arms Control (in ISA), and then as General Counsel of the Defense Department. In the former capacity he had provided highly valued assistance to Ambassador Harriman in planning and negotiating the 1963 Test Ban Treaty. In an earlier governmental incarnation, following study at Oxford on a Rhodes scholarship, he had worked in the Marshall Plan organization in Paris for two years before returning home to run unsuccessfully for Congress in 1952. He had served a boyhood apprenticeship, and later a stint as managing editor, on his family's daily newspaper in Illinois, experience which added a sardonic crispness, apparent in both his conversation and his writing, to a strong and precise legal mind. When I joined ISA in January 1965, he had been there some six months, having succeeded William Bundy the previous summer. Bundy had moved across the river to become Assistant Secretary of State for Far Eastern Affairs, replacing the departing Roger Hilsman. I found McNaughton serious, able, engaging, possessed of a mordant wit, and more than slightly mesmerized by the McNamara mystique. We became warm friends and remained so until his tragic death in July 1967.

NESA AND MAP REAPPRAISAL

I was named Deputy Assistant Secretary for Near East-South Asian Affairs (NESA), a responsibility relating to a large and heterogeneous area stretching from Greece and Turkey on the southeast flank of NATO, eastward across the continent of Asia to the farthest boundaries of India. It thus included not only those states, but also Pakistan, Ceylon, Afghanistan, Iran, Syria, Jordan, Iraq, Saudi Arabia, Yemen, Lebanon, Egypt, and Israel. Consequential turbulence was endemic at three focal points—between India and Pakistan, between Israel and the Arabs, between Greece and Turkey (inscribing a photograph for me a year later, McNaughton wrote: "To Tim Hoopes—who manages more trouble than the rest of ISA put together").

In January 1965, however, McNamara and McNaughton were both anxious to have a thoroughgoing reappraisal of our military assistance to eleven "forward defense countries"; these bordered (or nearly bordered) on countries of the "Communist Bloc," were related directly to our global strategy of containment, and absorbed collectively almost 75 percent of our total military-assistance dollars. The countries were Vietnam, Laos, Thailand, Taiwan, Korea, Philippines, India, Pakistan, Iran, Greece, and Turkey. Anticipating both higher requirements for the support of the South Vietnamese Army (ARVN) and a continued decline in congressional support for the Military Assistance Program (MAP) as a whole, McNamara and McNaughton wanted a fresh assessment of rock-bottom future aid requirements in these key countries, as a basis for determining new priorities and thus a reallocation of limited MAP resources. I was asked to undertake this task and was soon launched upon it, supported by a small staff. McNaughton established two sensible conditions: (1) that we would omit Vietnam and Laos from the study because the war situation there was too fluid to permit a confident estimate of future requirements, and (2) that for the duration of the study (estimated at six months) the management of the NESA region would be left in the capable hands of Peter Solbert, who was McNaughton's Principal Deputy.

Accordingly, I had only a tangential relationship to the unfolding Vietnam conflict during the first eight months of 1965. Deeply engrossed in other matters, I viewed it from a respectable distance as a disturbing, but probably manageable, development. For like almost everyone else who claimed some measure of competence in foreign-military affairs during this period, I too was a child of the Cold War, fully accepting the need for the United States to assume a special responsibility for helping to contain the unruly forces of a revolutionary century in the interest of peaceful change, relative stability, and preservation of the United States. Moreover, I was one of those who had argued strenuously against the strictures of "massive retaliation" during the 1950s and had been, along with Henry Kissinger, a principal draftsman of the 1958 "Rockefeller Report," which constituted perhaps the pioneering effort to develop the concept of graduated deterrence and flexible military response. I thoroughly supported the Kennedy-McNamara efforts to strengthen our conventional forces and improve our capacity to fight effective limited actions across a broad spectrum of challenge to U.S. interests. In early 1965, and admittedly less than fully informed, I remained reasonably confident that the men directly responsible would pursue the problem of Vietnam with a sense of proportion. I thought they could hardly fail to recognize the broad reach of U.S. interests and obligations in other parts of the world and the clear fact that some of these were of far greater intrinsic importance than those in Vietnam. Above all, I assumed they understood that a power of universal interest cannot afford to become so deeply committed in one spot that it loses its ability to influence events elsewhere. As it turned out, my confidence could not be long sustained.

FINDING FUNDS FOR ARVN

Meeting in Athens on certain NESA problems in late September (the MAP reappraisal was completed), I was called home by McNaughton to prepare a "Draft Presidential Memorandum" (DPM) on military assistance, in time for the budget decisions in December. Such memoranda were not really for the President's eyes, but were rather a management tool of McNamara's for developing an authoritative statement of Defense Department policy on particular issues. There was a DPM on every major element of defense activity, e.g., strategic offensive forces, strategic defensive forces, general purpose forces, and airlift forces. Usually prepared by the Systems Analysis office under Assistant Secretary Alain Enthoven, the DPMs were circulated to the Joint Chiefs of Staff and the Services for analysis and comment, then revised and recirculated, and finally endorsed by McNamara. There had not previously been a DPM on military assistance, but it was now apparent why such a document was urgently desired. For as McNamara and McNaughton had anticipated, the escalation in Vietnam was rapidly pushing up the required level of equipment and other material support for ARVN; yet we were operating within a finite military assistance appropriation of about $1 billion. In 1964, for example, $215 million had been initially allocated to Vietnam, but $357 million had eventually been required. The additional $142 million had to be found by scaling down several other important programs—in Korea, Turkey, and Greece—where substantial military assistance was an integral part of our foreign policy relationship and therefore diplomatically (and perhaps militarily) damaging to reduce.

In late 1965, it appeared that support for ARVN would require something over $600 million, or about double the 1964 figure. But this was a *third* of our total MAP resources, programmed for some forty-three countries. It was thus quickly apparent that we could not meet the burgeoning Vietnam demands out of MAP funds without seriously dislocating our diplomatic-military relations with important allies and without weakening their military posture. It also came home to us, during this analysis, that the Military Assistance Program had not been designed to underwrite sustained hostilities anywhere, but only to provide deterrence against aggression, and a capacity for initial defense if deterrence failed. The solution, in essence, was to ask Congress to transfer material support for ARVN from the military assistance appropriation to the regular Defense Department budget. This would greatly simplify the growing logistical problem in South Vietnam by permitting support for both U.S. and ARVN forces to be handled through one pipeline, drawing on one budgetary source and being centrally managed. A similar arrangement had obtained during the Korean War with respect to U.S. and South Korean forces. Congress, acknowledging the precedent, agreed to the Vietnam proposal in early 1966.

THE INDIA-PAKISTAN WAR

Vietnam was not the only war in 1965. In September, the deep bitterness between India and Pakistan erupted in a burst of violence characterized by a series of thrusts and counterthrusts that could have served as a textbook example of classic escalation. In that conflict, too, I thought, the unmodified Cold War syndrome in the United States was an important contributing factor, for in our arms assistance policies we had too easily assumed that India and Pakistan both shared our view that the real enemy was Communism, embodied by Russia and China, and that all other antagonisms should and would be subordinated to that fundamental consideration. But we had failed to reckon with the profound changes in perception of the Communist military threat which had developed throughout the middle world since the Eisenhower-Dulles period.

Pakistan had been a military protegé of the United States since Secretary Dulles' moves in 1954 to develop a "northern tier" defense against a Soviet attack southward into the Middle East. The resulting CENTO alliance, which sought to bring together states sharing a historic concern with Russian imperialism, was aimed entirely at opposing Soviet expansion, and at persuading Pakistan to form the eastern anchor of a new Central Asian defense line, with Pakistani forces available for use in regional defense outside of Pakistan. While the U.S. did not formally join the alliance, it gave encouragement and military equipment to three of its four members—Pakistan, Iran, and Turkey (Great Britain was the fourth member; the U.S. was also allied with Pakistan through SEATO, and with Turkey and Great Britain through NATO). India, the far larger and more important country in South Asia, was excluded from the CENTO arrangement by mutual consent: the Nehru government was a proclaimed neutral in the East-West struggle, and in the Dulles period Washington looked upon neutrality vis-à-vis Communism as immoral.

CENTO was thus aimed primarily at deterring a Soviet military thrust southward, but, as the years passed, intelligence estimates and broader political appraisals told of the decreasing likelihood that the Soviets intended anything resembling a direct military movement. In a real sense, they had already leapfrogged the CENTO barrier by offering arms and economic aid to Egypt, Syria, and Yemen beginning about 1955, thereby gaining the substantial toehold in the Middle East that Dulles' alliance-building had sought to block. This development caused, however, no diminishment in U.S. arms aid to Pakistan; indeed the aid grew gradually larger as the equipment provided in the early years became obsolescent and thus called for replacement by more modern arms.

Also as the years passed, it was increasingly clear that Pakistan was not concerned with the military threat from Russia, but with the military threat from India, and that all of its urgent requests for help in achieving the enlargement and modernization of its forces were made with its massive Indian neighbor uppermost in mind. For a number of years, the United States thus gave military aid for one purpose and the Pakistanis received it for another. A few sophisticated U.S. officials were entirely aware of the polite deception and thought it was, on balance, good policy, but most of the U.S. military establishment simply considered arms aid to Pakistan a sound contribution to the containment of Russia and the solidarity of the Free World. This was also the rationale presented to Congress in the annual requests for military assistance funds.

In 1962, however, the arrangement was jolted by a Chinese-Indian border dispute on India's Himalayan frontier. The Chinese readiness to use force suddenly brought home to the U.S. government the truth that India was of great strategic weight and importance, not only for potential power reasons (physical size, location, population, and resources), but perhaps primarily because of the political dimension. Indian and Chinese developments were widely regarded as a competition between basically different political and economic systems, and it was believed that the winning or surviving system would exert a perhaps determining influence on the pattern of national development in Asia for decades to come. The U.S. image of China as an aggressive, expansionist military state was confirmed by this incident, even though analysis after the event suggested that Peking's aim was primarily to demonstrate stiff insistence on a question of boundary rectification and, not incidentally, to humiliate a weak and cumbersome Indian government.

The U.S. and Great Britain took immediate steps to shore up the shaky government in New Delhi and rescue it from the consequences of an illusory nonalignment. In military terms, the assistance was very moderate, the U.S. portion consisting chiefly of improved communications equipment for several mountain divisions and the loan of U.S.-manned cargo aircraft to improve the mobility and the resupply capability of the Indian Army. But this support for India had traumatic reverberations in Pakistan, and an erosion of U.S.-Pakistani relations followed steadily from that time, particularly after the U.S. gave evidence that it was developing a program of long-term military assistance to India. Frustrated over Kashmir, fearing Indian rearmament, and feeling suddenly isolated by the apparent U.S. shift of allegiance to its archenemy, Pakistan turned to closer political and military ties with Communist China. Three years later, in 1965, it was led to a series of provocations that produced the short but bitter September War.

Pakistan infiltrated several thousand armed soldiers (regular and irregular) into Kashmir where they carried out terrorist acts, anticipating no more than a localized Indian response. They reasoned that, while the conflict would be contained within Kashmir, it would hopefully raise enough dust to catch the notice once more of the United Nations and of world opinion. But the Indians, having been deeply humiliated by the Rann-of-Kutch incident earlier in the year, were under compulsion to prove they were not a military punching bag. They not only resisted in Kashmir with regular forces, but pressed across the cease-fire line to get at the sources of infiltration. This surprised Pakistan and led it to a powerful tank attack against a key road intersection for the purpose of cutting off the single Indian supply line through Kashmir. Again the Pakistanis were totally surprised when India responded by attacking across the international frontier at Lahore, revealing a clear superiority in manpower and in capacity for sustained fighting. President Johnson rapidly cut off military aid to both sides in an effort to bring the fighting to a halt and to curtail, insofar as possible, the embarrassment to the U.S. arising out of the use of American arms by both parties for purposes contrary to our military assistance agreements.

As the Pentagon official in charge of managing our foreign-military activities in the Near East-South Asian area, including our military assistance relationships with both India and Pakistan, I was fully absorbed, together with my State and AID counterparts (Phillips Talbot and William B. Macomber) in coping with the consequences, working for a cease-fire, and attempting to determine what kind of military assistance policy, if any, the U.S. should pursue toward the subcontinent in the wake of the war. My reappraisal study of

MAP programs for India and Pakistan, completed just before the outbreak of fighting, had uncovered the underlying flaws in our official thinking, that is, the fact that our rationale for military aid to Pakistan was out-dated, and the fact that our policy of aid to both parties was a high risk because they were far more dedicated to pursuing their own bitter enmity than to stabilizing the subcontinent against Soviet or Chinese encroachment. The study recommended giving future priority to India, both because it was the power of greater consequence and because it shared our interest in opposing China. It recommended sharply curtailing our military aid to Pakistan.

The atmosphere in the aftermath was not however conducive to rational choice. The Congress was appalled at our having furnished arms to both sides (and at the temerity of the combatants in using them against anyone but Russia or China). Moreover, the pro-Pakistan faction in the U.S. government, led by the military, insisted that only by continued military support of the Pakistanis could we hope to keep a fatal Chinese influence out of South Asia. The eggs had all been broken, but the squabbling cooks could not fashion even an omelet. Gradually it dawned on wiser heads that our military assistance provided far less U.S. influence and leverage in either country than did our economic aid, and that it would be helpful simply to remove ourselves from the role of military supplier to the subcontinent.

YEAR-END APPRAISAL OF VIETNAM

As 1965 came to an end, I had become a great deal more skeptical about the U.S. performance in Vietnam—about the validity of our stated purposes, the official assessment of the problems we faced, and our ability to control events. In the course of a brief holiday, which fell in the middle of the President's celebrated thirty-seven-day bombing halt and peace offensive, I wrote down my first considered impressions and sent them to McNaughton.

43

Memorandum for Mr. McNaughton
Subject: Vietnam

For better or worse, absence from Washington encourages reflective thought. Four days on a beach on the Florida Gulf have produced a few central thoughts on Vietnam, which I take the liberty of conveying to you. They were set down as rough notes . . . just before I heard about the President's wide-ranging peace effort, which I take it represents a significant shift of stance from the pre-Christmas plan to send Harriman to various places for pledges of additional support (troops and services) for the fighting.

US policy is clearly at a grave crossroads, and this is underlined by the President's peace overtures, constructed with apparent haste during the holidays. They seem to indicate his awareness that we stand at a new threshold, and his deep reluctance to plunge further into the morass if this can be avoided.

The continuing suspension of bombing in the North seems sensible and prudent because it will help the psychological climate in the neutral world, and even in those countries allied to us for other reasons (NATO); it should give Moscow a plausible excuse for attempting to moderate Hanoi's views; and it may, if continued long enough, enable Hanoi to resist the Chinese policy of no concessions. Equally important, we are not giving up much by the suspension except a psychological lift to the South Vietnamese Government, because bombing of the North has been singularly inconclusive. The basic simplicity of the North Vietnamese transport system, combined with oriental resignation, ingenuity and abundant coolie labor have neutralized the bombing effect. Infiltration of the South has not diminished, but has in fact increased; moreover, the bombing has served to stiffen North Vietnamese resistance, both directly and by giving the Chinese an added argument for a policy of no concessions. At the same time it has made it more difficult for the Soviets to play a moderating role.

The history of the Korean War also indicates the marginal effect of rear area bombing attacks on an undeveloped country. More extensive bombing would probably be equally

inconclusive in terms of bringing North Vietnam to the conference table. But destruction of Hanoi and of the irrigation
ditches would, on the other hand, put extreme pressure on
the Soviets to come in (perhaps with manpower stationed in
North Vietnam, in a deliberate attempt to foreclose further
US attacks by presenting the threat of a direct US-USSR
confrontation). It would also put very heavy pressure on the
Chicoms. In general, it is my view that an enlarged bombing
program would tend to unify, not to split, the Communist
world and would increase US diplomatic isolation in the
Free World.

Similarly, I see no rewards or gains to be reaped by a
further infusion of US manpower; this likewise looks to be
inconclusive. Even a doubling—from 170,000 to 350,000 men
—could be matched without great difficulty by North Vietnamese manpower and Chicom-Russian equipment. And
behind the North Vietnamese stands the Chinese Army. The
best we could hope to gain would be a further stalemate at
a higher level of effort, human sacrifice and risk.

There is apparently a belief, firmly held in certain authoritative quarters (Lodge, probably Westmoreland, and maybe
McNamara), that the war can end "in silence" rather than
through negotiations; that is, if the Viet Cong become convinced they cannot win, they will break off and simply dis-
appear. The outcome of the Huk rebellion in the Philippines, of the guerrilla insurgency in Malaya, and even of the
recent Communist Party demise in Indonesia are cited in
support of this thesis. The analogies all seem dubious to me.
In each case, Chicom support was physically remote; there
was no geographical contiguity. In the case of Vietnam,
China is just across the border, able to provide sanctuary and
an endless flow of manpower and equipment; also the political situation is complicated by the North-South split and
the fact of two established Vietnamese governments. In addition, the US is now so deeply committed in South Vietnam
that neither China nor the USSR could probably permit the
US to win a clear-cut victory there, and they clearly have
the means to drag it out. Chinese stubbornness on this issue
is suggested, I think, by a hypothetical reversal of the two

positions: if 150,000 Chicoms were in Mexico, it seems reasonable to believe the US would be determined to fight for decades and even generations to expel them.

Quite aside from the difficulties within Vietnam itself, the US must beware of unbalancing its whole global posture by giving too much emphasis—and too many resources—to Vietnam. The President's statement sometime ago that the Vietnam war will get "everything it needs" ought to be reviewed with great caution; for locking up 20-25% of our combat ground and air forces in an interminable stalemate is, in global terms, a maldeployment. Moreover, the expenditure of executive energy from the President and the Secretary of Defense/Secretary of State down to the desk officers is seriously disproportionate and unbalancing, taking our world position and responsibilities into account. This is particularly true, it seems to me, of the Secretary of Defense and ISA.

In this connection, both the military and political benefits of the "more flags" policy permit skepticism, particularly the effort to enlist European allies. It seems doubtful political and psychological wisdom to attempt to draw the former colonial powers back into Asia now that they have about completed their painful disengagement. This strains the political fabric of our relationships with them, which we need to maintain in good condition for other important purposes. In any case, their military contributions are bound to be negligible, because their own electorates don't want them back in Asia under any circumstances, because the Vietnam War lacks a moral imperative for them, and because (except for the FRG *) they cannot afford it. In this connection, the SecDef's lecture to the NATO Council on the Chicom threat seemed a curious initiative and was, as you know, received with particular coolness.

What do we do, then, if present peace overtures lead to negotiations, or if they don't.

1. In either case, I think we should moderate our objectives to avoid distorting and further unbalancing our global position, either by putting too much US energy and

* Federal Republic of Germany.

46

resources into Vietnam or by straining our relations with other nations who don't want to fight there.

2. We must put pressure on the South Vietnamese Government to moderate its own aims and be far more realistic. If it is true that all-out victory over the Viet Cong represents the moderate position in the South Vietnamese political spectrum, with some military leaders advocating outright war with China, then it is clear that we have some work to do.

3. I am drawn to the idea of limiting US military objectives in Vietnam to the holding and pacification of certain defined cities and ports which can be made secure at about the present level of US-South Vietnamese effort. This is a defensive, hedgehog strategy; it would attempt to contain the Viet Cong, to clear and pacify a respectable area within a chosen perimeter (Saigon, a string of ports on the eastern coast, and the intervening territory) and concentrate on governing this area. Even this limited strategy would require a continued US presence for a long time, but in the feasible tasks of holding and patrolling areas where our backs were to the ports, rather than in offensive forays deep into the interior of the country where durable pacification is evidently not possible without a scale of effort beyond anything that is proportionate to our global stance. I base this view on the belief that, without physical security, no economic or political program is worth a damn; and that we badly need a definable geographical area of recognized political-economic strength and stability, perhaps even as a prerequisite to negotiation.

4. All the choices are unpalatable, but the one least damaging to our total global position is a more limited military effort in Vietnam, aimed *not* at conclusive military victory (which is illusory) but at proving we are there to stay and must therefore be negotiated with. Ultimately, we may need something rather close to de Gaulle's concept of neutralization for SEA as a whole, guaranteed by decisive Soviet influence in Hanoi, decisive US influence in Saigon and Bangkok, and perhaps shared influence in Pnom Penh and Vientiane.

5. We should develop greater patience, and not allow ourselves to escalate the war even if, as seems probable, noth-

ing very tangible develops from the President's current peace overtures.

You will, I am sure, accept these rather intuitive, unsystematic judgments for what they are. If they are useful, it is because they come from outside the ambit of daily and technical concern with the problem.

Townsend Hoopes
Deputy

December 30, 1965

In a subsequent talk, McNaughton agreed with the general thrust of the memorandum and readily admitted the evidence of an emerging stalemate. But he remained implicitly confident that, in the end, the vastly greater weight of the United States would have to prevail. Like others who had participated in shaping the decisions of February, he was not yet prepared to acknowledge that the judgment of senior officials whom he respected, or his own judgment, had been mistaken in fundamental respects. This would come later, but in 1965 he was still a staunch supporter of Administration policy, a convinced and loyal member of the team.

THE DECEMBER BOMBING PAUSE

There had been an unannounced five-day halt of the U.S. bombing effort against North Vietnam on May 13, 1965. When the attacks were resumed on May 18, Rusk explained by analogy that the pause had been a phone call to Hanoi, but that they had failed to pick up the instrument at their end of the line. He did not explain why we did not let the phone ring a little longer, recognizing the possibility that the NVN government might have been in the basement taking cover from our earlier raids. But the first dramatic bombing suspension occurred on December 24; it lasted thirty-seven days and was combined with a spontaneous Johnsonian "peace offensive" that exploded like a sudden decision to hold a gargantuan Texan barbecue and prayer meeting.

48

It started at McNamara's urging, on a trip to the ranch in mid-December for discussion and decision on the next year's Defense budget. He had pressed for a pause several weeks earlier in Washington, arguing that it would help to neutralize rising international disapproval of the bombing, would be an acceptable military risk, and might produce negotiations. The President had put him off. Now, their budget discussions completed, the two men stood together along a cattle fence with one foot hooked onto the lower rung. McNamara put the case again, and this time the President approved the idea—and not only approved it, but promptly converted it into a massive "peace offensive" stamped with his own peculiar brand of messianic public relations. Harriman, who was scheduled to go foraging for troop contributions, found his mission changed and his itinerary lengthened. For seventeen grueling days he traveled to the heads of state in Poland, Yugoslavia, India, Pakistan, Iran, Egypt, Thailand, Japan, Australia, Laos, and South Vietnam. Rusk and Senator Cooper joined him for a brief descent upon the Philippines. Vice-President Humphrey was sent off to Japan, the Philippines, Taiwan, and Korea; and on January 13 he met with Kosygin in New Delhi where both were attending the funeral of Lal Bahadur Shastri, the Indian Prime Minister. Ambassador Goldberg went to Italy, France, and England; McGeorge Bundy went to Canada; Mennen Williams, the Assistant Secretary of State for African Affairs, covered thirteen African countries in four days. All of the hard-traveling envoys expressed the Administration's deep devotion to peace and urged their listeners to make a personal effort to impress this fact upon the recalcitrant North Vietnamese.

As a public relations effort it had dramatic scale and spontaneity; as a serious diplomatic effort it was a nullity. When I asked McNaughton how it had happened, especially how it had ballooned up out of all reasonable proportion, he slid his glasses down his nose and fixed me with a beady, professorial eye: "Well," he said, "I guess you would have to say it was about as quiet a peace offensive as a Texan could arrange."

THE NEXT TWENTY MONTHS

For the better part of the next two years (until October 1967), I was deeply immersed in the manifold problems and challenges of the NESA region: attempting to negotiate multi-year military aid agreements with Greece and Turkey (without actually committing U.S. funds), so that they could participate in the North Atlantic Council's decision to put NATO force planning on "a 5-year rolling basis" in response to a McNamara proposal; trying to preserve the integrity of King Hussein's moderate regime in Jordan by providing enough military assistance to meet the dynamics of Arab politics, but not enough to provoke Israel; monitoring Great Britain's painful withdrawal from East of Suez; telling the Shah of Iran, over a plate of watermelon on the afterdeck of his houseboat on the Caspian Sea, that the U.S. was not prepared to sell him high performance jet aircraft unless he receded from an apparent agreement to purchase sophisticated antiaircraft missiles from Russia; stonewalling the proponents of a resumption of large-scale military aid and sales to Pakistan and India; trying to discern and pursue the essential U.S. interest in the deepening Middle Eastern imbroglio that billowed up into major war on June 4, 1967, with all the suddenness of a summer thunderstorm.

I was of course fully and painfully aware of developments in Vietnam during this period—the conflict was casting an ever-lengthening shadow over U.S. relations in every other part of the world—yet at the same time not intimately involved or charged with any formal responsibility. The Vietnam problem was still being worked in a narrow channel. McNaughton, who had become McNamara's closest policy assistant on the subject, spent perhaps 70 percent of his time on Vietnam, ably supported by Richard Steadman, the Deputy Assistant Secretary for Far Eastern Affairs, and Steadman's hard-pressed staff. But no one else in ISA was closely informed. In a real sense, the arrangement was only a natural response to the need for a rational distribution of the total ISA workload. In the fall of 1966, I became McNaughton's Principal Deputy, while keeping the NESA portfolio, but this did not change my relationship to the Vietnam problem. Indeed, with McNaughton devoting so much of his time to Southeast Asia, it was imperative that the Number Two should take hold of the many other urgent problems demanding ISA's attention.

By the spring of 1967, it was apparent that McNaughton had become both physically exhausted and deeply disenchanted with the Administration's Vietnam policy. There had been almost from the beginning a detectable distinction between his public and private positions and, with the passage of time and the rising tempo of inconclusive destruction, the gap had widened. Punctilious in his public support of the Administration and personally devoted to McNamara who, he felt, was now earnestly trying to guide the war toward de-escalation and settlement (albeit within the strictures of a highly personal conception of loyalty to the President), McNaughton was by the spring of 1967 appalled by the catastrophic loss of proportion that had overtaken the U.S. military effort in Vietnam. "We seem to be proceeding," he said to me in barbed tones, after returning from a particular White House session, "on the assumption that the way to eradicate Viet Cong is to destroy all the village structures, defoliate all the jungles, and then cover the entire surface of South Vietnam with asphalt." He thought the odds were heavily against any basic improvement in the official perspective, and he concluded that, in any event, his own efforts were imposing little or no restraint on the gathering momentum of the U.S. war machine. He accordingly decided to leave government in early summer. McNamara, who was loath to lose him, persuaded him to consider the possibility of a different job within the Defense Department, one that would offer fresh perspectives and challenges and a new set of problems.

In June, Cyrus Vance, the Deputy Secretary of Defense and McNamara's closest associate, retired from office because of a painful back ailment that was forcing him to spend half of his Pentagon days lying on a couch. In the ensuing shift, Paul Nitze, the Navy Secretary, was named to succeed Vance, and McNaughton was in turn named to succeed Nitze. These were two thoroughly deserved promotions, which brought men of high competence and achievement to important posts. The breadth and depth of Nitze's experience in responsible foreign-military positions was unmatched by anyone then in government.

I was a plausible choice to succeed McNaughton as Assistant Secretary for ISA, but I viewed the prospect with mixed feelings. For one thing, I had by that time concluded that the Administration's Vietnam policy had become a quietly spreading disaster from which vital U.S. interests could be retrieved only if the policy were reversed or drastically altered. For another, I had a clear premonition that the policy was headed for a showdown—a fundamental knockdown, drag-out fight between its proponents and its detractors—which would be healthy, but which would at the same time increase the disruption and factionalism on the American scene. I was quite prepared, indeed eager, to apply the full extent of my energies to an attempt to change the policy, but, given the way in which the Administration had organized itself in respect of Vietnam, there seemed little opportunity for the opposition to get a hearing. To be effective at all, dissent and counterproposals had to be channeled into the inner group of advisers, and that was a gathering of homogeneous hawks—with the exception of McNamara.

At close range, McNamara was, and is, an immensely impressive and immensely attractive human being. To work with him was consistently an education and a pleasure. But his position on Vietnam in the spring of 1967 was disturbingly ambiguous. Accurately regarded by the press as the one moderate member of the inner circle, he continued to give full public support to the Administration's policy, including specific endorsement of successive manpower infusions and progressively wider and heavier bombing efforts. Inside the Pentagon he seemed to discourage dissent among his staff associates by the simple tactic of being unreceptive to it; he observed, moreover, so strict a sense of privacy in his relationship with the President that he found it virtually impossible to report even to key subordinates what he was telling the President or what the President was saying and thinking. He accepted occasionally, but rarely sought, advice from his staff. All of this seemed to reflect a well-developed philosophy of executive management relationships, derived from his years in industry; its essence was the belief that a busy, overworked chairman of the board should be spared the burden of public differences among his senior vice-presidents. Within such a framework, he could argue the case for moderation with the President—privately, selectively, and intermittently. But the unspoken corollary seemed to be that, whether or not his counsel of moderation were followed, there could arise no issue or difference with President Johnson sufficient to require his resignation—whether to enlighten public opinion or avoid personal stultification. It was this corollary that seemed of doubtful applicability to the problems and obligations of public office. McNamara gave evidence that he had ruled out resignation because he believed the situation would grow worse if he left the field to Rusk, Rostow, and the Joint Chiefs, but also because the idea ran so strongly against the grain of his temperament and his considered philosophy of organizational effectiveness. On the other hand, I strongly sensed that if I were given a specific role in Vietnam policy and if subsequent events showed my inability to influence the situation for the better, I would be impelled to resign; as things were going, it seemed likely that such a point of decision would be reached in the rather near future.

On balance, however, I was ready to risk these many uncertainties.

At is turned out, the matter was soon resolved when Paul C. Warnke was chosen to succeed McNaughton. As later events showed, it could not have been a wiser choice. Trained at Yale and Columbia Law, and for fifteen years engaged in practice with a distinguished Washington firm, Warnke was in 1967 the General Counsel of the Defense Department. In that capacity he had worked closely with McNamara on several involved legal and technical problems, especially those related to the controversial F-111 aircraft. Warnke had, as McNaughton once put it, that "special touch" with McNamara which was also a possession of Vance, McNaughton, and Harold Brown, the brilliant young Secretary of the Air Force. Warnke possessed a strong, lucid mind, bold in conception, rigorously disciplined in argument. He was tough, but always personally engaging, discriminating, and fair. Above all, he brought to stale interagency arguments on Vietnam the precious gift of candor, including a refreshing readiness to assert the increasingly obvious truth that the Emperor's policy had no clothes on.

I agreed to stay on as Principal Deputy of ISA, but McNamara graciously offered to propose me for the post of Under Secretary of the Air Force. I accepted this because it offered, after three intensive years in foreign affairs, a welcome shift of scenery and focus. The Air Force presented particular attractions. Only twenty years old as a separate military department, it was thoroughly modern in spirit and less encumbered than the older Services by those ritual encrustations that represent such serious obstacles to administrative clarity. Experimental, possessed of short lines of command and supple civilian-military relationships, the Air Force had grown to an impressive level of professional competence; in particular, it was a marvel of operational reliability. These factors suggested a stimulating environment for the practice of management; there would also be an opportunity to deal with the Vietnam War from a different vantage point.

On July 19, McNaughton, a veteran of innumerable long-distance flights to Vietnam, Europe, and other points on the globe, was killed in a domestic air accident near Asheville, North Carolina, when a small private plane rammed the Piedmont Airliner in which he, his wife, and younger son were riding. All were lost. It was a profound personal tragedy, and for the nation it meant the loss of a brilliant public servant who had only begun to realize his full powers. The next day, somewhat distraught, I wrote out the following memorandum to the ISA staff:

July 20, 1967

MEMORANDUM FOR THE ISA STAFF

JOHN T. McNAUGHTON

I doubt if there is such a thing as institutional grief. Each of us is responding in accordance with his own lights and his own perspective. Yet it may be possible, even useful, to set down certain common elements.

We have suffered a surpassing personal loss; and suffered it with the shock and disbelief that are themselves ironic and somewhat incredible for people who live amid daily reports of wholesale carnage across the world. How sharp and painful is the difference in impact between impersonal death and the irretrievable loss of a friend.

And the country has suffered a grievous loss of demonstrated leadership and high competence in public affairs. It can ill afford this. A brilliant career has been snuffed out in mid-passage. His was a driving, restless, extremely quick and far-ranging intelligence. He had a trenchant personality, saved from unvarnished bluntness by a sensitive imagination, an innate appreciation of nuance, and a graceful, if piercing, wit. There also remained a strong Midwestern strain (not quite residual isolationism) which rose out of his viscera, when the occasion demanded, to protect the country against fuzzy heads bent unwittingly on taking us down some new garden path or over some new brink. He took no wooden nickels. He was, I suspect, one of the most sophisticated minds in Washington. All of these great gifts he applied, with rare tenacity and zeal, to the immensely complicated and consequential problems of our disordered age.

His death was like the age, shot through with irony, profound tragedy, poignant contradiction. Almost his whole family was wiped out at a single stroke, leaving one poor son with neither mother, nor father, nor younger brother. It was characteristic of our era that there was not even time to say good-bye.

Townsend Hoopes
Acting Assistant Secretary

CHAPTER 3

Full-Throated War

BY OCTOBER 1967, 40 percent of our combat-ready divisions, half of our tactical airpower, and at least a third of our naval strength—the whole numbering some 480,000 men—were waging full-throated war on the Southeast Asian peninsula. The dollar coast of the effort was running at an annual rate in excess of $25 billion, and the number of Americans killed in action, which had totaled 6,500 for the six-year period through 1966, was nearing the 9,000 mark (plus 60,000 wounded) for 1967 alone. The Vietnam situation was, in truth, on the point of becoming the greatest American tragedy since the Civil War. It represented a serious and growing, yet officially unacknowledged, maldeployment of great but finite military strength, and an excessive drain on limited executive energies at the top of the government. The effect of these distortions was a neglect of intrinsically more important problems both at home and in other parts of the world. The war was seriously damaging the image of the United States as a nation devoted to justice and restraint, and was converting the image of a cruel North Vietnamese regime into something resembling "the brave little Belgium of international society." [4] Above all, through riots, protests, and the fateful merging of antiwar and racial dissension, it was polarizing U.S. politics, dividing the American people from their government, and creating the gravest American political disunity in a century.

The rather incredible disparity between the outpouring of national blood and treasure and the intrinsic U.S. interests at stake in Vietnam was by this time widely understood and deplored at levels just below the top of the government. But the President and the tight group of advisers around him gave no sign of having achieved a similar sense of proportion. All the President wanted, he said, was to give the people of South Vietnam a free choice, but his terms for political settlement left absolutely no room for substantive compromise with the other side; a clear-cut U.S. military victory was thus for him an implicit prerequisite. He was only acting, he said, to honor the nation's solemn commitments, but his conduct of the war implied a demand, if need be, for forces, dollars, lives, and time without limit. He and his advisers seemed to be operating on the implicit premise that every U.S. commitment is *ipso facto* a blank check, however devastating may be its impact on other national interests. Yet there was no evidence that the Administration had ever developed serious forward estimates of the ultimate cost of holding to this simplistic attitude.

During the autumn months of 1967, the President and his advisers believed, and were making concerted efforts to demonstrate, that we were in fact on the high road to victory. Rostow, who had by then succeeded McGeorge Bundy as principal foreign affairs adviser at the White House, was in the vanguard of this effort. Through the release of carefully packaged facts and figures, he sought to provide the press and the public with a feel for some of the basic reference points that had brought the President and other senior officials in both Washington and Saigon to "an honest belief that the war is being won": the "weapons loss ratio" was 4.7 to 1 in favor of the allies as opposed to an unfavorable 1 to 2 in 1963; enemy desertions were expected to reach 35,000 in 1967 as against 20,000 in 1966 and only 5,000 two years before; conversely, desertions from the Army of the Republic of Vietnam (ARVN) were down to about 75,000 as against

160,000 the preceding year; large-scale enemy attacks were declining in number, as were acts of terrorism and sabotage; the number of people under allied control had moved up impressively from 8 to 12 million, or to nearly 75 percent of the total population in the South.

What all of this showed, the Administration was arguing, was that the great weight of the U.S. effort, steadily applied, was having a cumulatve effect. It was wearing the enemy down. He was barely hanging on, aware that he was losing the fight yet unable to alter the inexorable odds against him. His losses in the South were extremely heavy, yet he showed an apparent unwillingness to commit substantially greater numbers of regular NVN troops to the South. Why? Because the U.S. bombing campaign made increased infiltration such a painful and costly effort. But this left him in the position of having to rely on the impressment of teen-agers in South Vietnam. Sooner or later his military structure would crack; indeed there were already signs of deterioration. "Captured documents," always a basic tool of Rostovian analysis, indicated that Viet Cong morale was very low. Granted the inherent difficulty of judging a war that had no front lines and no absolute standards of progress, a careful weighing of relevant indicators led, so the argument went, to a strong feeling of encouragement and optimism. There was no doubt that in the end we would prevail.

THE PRESIDENT'S MAN

By this time Rostow had become the channel through which President Johnson received almost all written communications on foreign affairs; he had, moreover, a large hand in determining who, outside the closed circle of advisers, the President would see or not see. He possessed great weight on Vietnam policy because he was both physically close and intellectually reassuring to the President. Rostow briefed him each morning, saw him several times a day, and selected the papers for his night reading. Astride the main channel, he could develop for the President all of the options, or some; could pass along all the views expressed by responsible department heads and their staffs, or some; could send them forward without comment, or with his own recommendations. It was a position of great temptation for a dedicated partisan whose mind automatically filtered out evidence that did not support his own established beliefs. And though, according to White House colleagues, he made from time to time sincere efforts in the direction of objectivity, he was altogether too much the compulsive advocate and true believer to be able to sustain these. The evidence leaves no doubt that he used his positional advantage to argue his own case—for a ground strategy of relentless pressure, for heavier bombing, even for invasion of North Vietnam—and that he was not scrupulous (as McGeorge Bundy, a man of colder mien, had been) about making certain that the President heard the full arguments on all sides of the issue. He shaped the evidence and maneuvered to set at discount with the President the views (of men like McNamara and Harriman) that were at odds with his own. Rostow's views were at times so wide of the mark as to produce reactions of total incredulity in thoughtful and experienced people—especially when he was revealing the stunning optimism to be found at the root of some new turn in the war that, to ordinary perceptions, seemed merely another failed prophecy or disappointed expectation. The evidence is however that his ebullient interpretations consistently reassured President Johnson. They did so by reinforcing the President's own bellicose instincts about the Vietnam War, his patriotic pride in American power, his belief in the inherent righteousness of the United States and its capacity to apply limitless power for good, his sense of moral duty to meet commitments undertaken, and his conspiratorial view of life and politics.

Rostow's burgeoning personal influence in 1967 was also explainable by the notable drop in stature of the other men on the National Security Council staff at the White House.

In an earlier period, that group had comprised a number of distinguished minds. But now McGeorge Bundy was gone to the Ford Foundation, Carl Kaysen to Princeton, Francis Bator to MIT, Michael Forrestal to law practice in New York City, Robert Komer to Vietnam, James Thomson to Harvard, and Chester Cooper to Harriman's office. They were succeeded by men of less independence and distinction who shifted papers, wrote speeches, and worked at the public relations aspects of shoring up the Administration's position on Vietnam. Rostow easily dominated such a group.

Rostow thus made a considerable contribution to the "credibility gap"—that general disorder and incongruity that characterized the interaction of ideas, policies, strategies, and personalities in the Administration's conduct of the war. He seemed exactly the wrong man for the job of helping a President to delineate the profound issues of the war and to identify with precision the hard core of U.S. national interest in Asia. As one senior official, who had worked closely with him over a period of years, put it: "Walt is vigorous and stimulating; he has all the trappings of intellect, but in the end no objectivity and no judgment." Rostow was no deliberate villain; he was a fanatic in sheep's clothing.

For the enemy the war remained fundamentally an internal insurgency boosted by infiltration, a seamless web of political-military-psychological factors to be manipulated by a highly centralized command authority that never took its eye off the political goal of ultimate control in the South. For the United States, however, the war had become by October 1967 a complex of three separate, or only loosely related, struggles: there was the large-scale, conventional war of U.S. armored brigades, massed helicopters, and unopposed tactical air support pitted against tough North Vietnamese regulars and Viet Cong main forces; there was the confused "pacification" effort, based on political-sociological presumptions of astronomical proportions, designed not only to break the Viet Cong stranglehold on the countryside, but to win over the villages to the Thieu-Ky government and establish "democratic institutions"; and there was the curiously remote air war against North Vietnam, designed to convince Hanoi that it must pay an unacceptable price for its interference in the South.

SEARCH AND DESTROY

As distinguished from the air war against the North, where control reached directly back to Washington, General Westmoreland enjoyed the broadest discretion in devising U.S. ground strategy in South Vietnam. The Joint Chiefs of Staff argued stoutly that both elements of the war should be left to the field commanders, but they gave way to presidential insistence on detailed White House control of the bombing. And tight control here was prudent, for the "Rolling Thunder" campaign, as it steadily expanded, carried an ever-present risk of military confrontation with Russia or China. Yet the President never insisted on a comparable overview of Westmoreland's operations, nor did McNamara—though he complained privately—ever press the point. The shooting war on the ground thus proceeded with full autonomy, subordinating by its sheer weight (and undermining by its sheer destructiveness) the political efforts aimed at pacification, reform, and nation-building. In the circumstances, which revealed a peculiarly American set of priorities, a serious attempt to relate the military effort on the ground to the political aims of the struggle in the South was scarcely possible. The preferred military doctrine dictated the strategy and the strategy determined the policy. Though not officially acknowledged, nor even planned that way, military victory became an end in itself.

Westmoreland was a thoroughly decent, moderately intelligent product of the Army system, long on energy and organizational skill, short on political perception, and precluded from serious comparison with the leading generals of World War II and Korea by an unmistakable aura of Boy

Scoutism. Like those predecessors, however (and like his contemporaries who had moved instinctively to discourage and dilute the development of counterguerrilla formations, like the Special Forces, within the U.S. Army), Westmoreland was a Big Corporate Military Executive, geared to large-scale, fast-moving, modern operations supported by maximum firepower. He relished the challenge of searching out and destroying the NVN regular forces, but was essentially indifferent to the fighting capacities of the ARVN, asking only that it get out of his way; and he gave lowest priority to pacification, indeed seeming not to see the relationship between aggressive search and destroy operations in the populated countryside and the stream of refugees (some 900,000 by October 1967) who were forced from their land by the terror of artillery and air strikes, by burned out villages and ruined crops; and who, pressed into crowded, unsavory camps along the southern coast, were now sullenly anti-American.

It remained a miracle, and in the last analysis a major failure of leadership, that during nearly three years of steadily rising combat and casualty levels, Washington did not seriously question or modify the Westmoreland strategy of attrition. For the strategy rested on the belief that the U.S. could inflict losses on the enemy that he would be forced to regard as intolerable, while the U.S. suffered losses that we would find quite acceptable. In the context of all Western experience with land warfare in Asia and of the known readiness of Asian Communists to die in large numbers, it was an astonishing belief, particularly when applied to a war of supposedly limited objectives. But more astonishing still was the fact that it was never subjected to critical analysis by the authorities in Washington. Westmoreland was the field commander and, in accordance with traditional dictates of professional courtesy, Washington would not attempt to second-guess him. The difficulty was that an absence of critical analysis obtained in the Saigon headquarters as well; the trouble may have been, as Sir Robert Thompson, the British counterinsurgency expert, remarked, that "with the introduction of a seven-day sixty-hour week in all American headquarters, no one was given any time to think." Applying his chosen strategy with fidelity, Westmoreland sought to arrange the conflict in ways that would produce maximum attrition of the enemy, acknowledging, if pressed, that his methods involved serious casualties for his own forces as well. Companies, battalions, and regiments were set out in remote places rather like lures, their activities designed to provoke NVN-VC attack; then U.S. artillery and air strikes moved in for the kill (U.S. Army commanders were quite right that the best way to kill VC in large numbers was with artillery and air strikes).

As late as the fall of 1966, following operations in War Zone C, a certain aura of optimism surrounded this strategy. Some were ready to believe that, in its unprecedented mobility and massive firepower, American forces had discovered the military answer to endless Asian manpower and Oriental indifference to death. For a few weeks there hung in the expectant Washington air the exhilarating possibility that the most modern, mobile, professional American field force in the nation's history was going to lay to rest the time-honored superstition, the gnawing unease of military planners, that a major land war against Asian hordes is by definition a disastrous plunge into quicksand for any Western army.

But in the spring of 1967, the enemy sent large numbers of troops across the Demilitarized Zone, and it became apparent that U.S. forces were not engaged in a mopping up exercise. American casualties rose above those of the ARVN. By October, Marine officers in I Corps were saying that casualties in that zone had been one-for-one all year long. Westmoreland called for and received more American soldiers; also additional Koreans. But it was soon evident that North Vietnam was matching the allied buildup almost battalion for battalion. There was a significant improvement in the enemy's firepower and he showed a greater willingness to sacrifice troops. People like Rostow might rejoice in such indicators as an improved "weapons loss ratio," but this rather ignored the larger fact that the enemy's logistical capacity had now grown so large that he no longer needed to steal our weapons. Russia and China were supplying plenty of new ones. Moreover, while VC morale might indeed be low, this was the pervasive psychological condition of all Vietnamese: VC, ARVN, peasant. It didn't seem to mean much.

All Vietnamese were tough and incredibly stoic in the face of appalling catastrophe; fatalistic, they were also remarkably resourceful and effective when well led. Because two-thirds of the NVN-VC casualties were suffered in self-initiated actions, the enemy retained the option of slowing down his attacks if we really began to hurt him. Meanwhile, he was prepared to press on. At the heart of the U.S. military problem were the intractable realities that the enemy had a cause in which he believed, a remarkable capacity for organization, a manpower pool that was for practical purposes bottomless, and a clear will to exploit all of these assets. An American brigade commander said in November, "let us not forget that the Vietminh lost an estimated half million dead in the struggle against the French. The Viet Cong are better organized and they have lost nowhere near that number in this war." By the midsummer of 1967, no one should have doubted that Hanoi could and would go on raising the ante.

Westmoreland showed, however, little inclination to rethink his strategy, and there were no significant admonitions from Washington. U.S. initiatives thus continued to produce sanguinary, inconclusive battles in remote border regions. In November, U.S. paratroopers, after being pinned down by withering fire for four days, attacked fixed enemy positions on a rise of ground known as Hill 875, near Dakto in the barren Central Highlands. They suffered 135 dead and 150 wounded. A sizeable portion of the enemy force was killed, but much of it disengaged and slipped away. A few days later the paratroopers abandoned the hill, which was of no intrinsic value, and after a month the jungle growth had largely reclaimed the scene. As opposition to this stupidity hardened in a growing segment of the foreign-military bureaucracy, grounded in a deepening certainty that the strategy of attrition applied to Asia had never been in touch with reality, Westmoreland asserted that, "we have achieved all of our objectives while the enemy has failed dismally." He also told reporters that the notion of a "military stalemate" was the "most ridiculous" explanation of the current situation he had ever heard.

PACIFICATION

From my vantage point, the American-guided pacification program had become by the fall of 1967 a transparent monstrosity, an example of American optimism and messianic zeal gone off the deep end. Conceivably, it might have had a fighting chance in 1962 or even later, if there had been a really serious U.S. determination to centralize control of all political and military efforts in a single proconsul, to subordinate military activity to clearly perceived political purpose, and to press the Government of South Vietnam (GVN) much harder for basic reforms. Rostow and Hilsman had developed in late 1962 a "strategic concept for counterinsurgency" that embraced these principles and that was also sensitive to the truth that protection for the people against Viet Cong terror had to be achieved by means that did not themselves alienate the people by causing heavy civilian casualties and wanton physical destruction. The concept argued for static defense of villages supplemented by small, counterguerrilla bands spotted throughout the area to be cleansed of Viet Cong. The crucial fact was that the Viet Cong lived off the countryside, that the guerrilla bands were almost wholly dependent on food and other supplies coming from the villages. The weak link in the insurgency chain was the neces-

66

sary contact between the VC political cadres in the villages (who extorted the supplies) and the guerrilla platoons (that operated in the surrounding area). Effective counterinsurgency required population control measures within the villages as a means of forcing the exposure of the VC political cadres, who would have to violate curfews and other controls in order to link up with the guerrillas. The principal military action would be to fight the Viet Cong guerrillas with their own tactics of harassment and ambush. Similarly, the infiltration trails (which in 1962 were of small importance, since VC logistical requirements were being met almost wholly from within the South) would be plotted and booby-trapped, and NVN infiltration parties would be ambushed and chewed up by counterguerrilla patrols. Within the frame of such carefully moderated protective measures, the vital political efforts —to provide land reform, agricultural and health services, education, and greater participation in the political process —would be made.

But the concept was never applied. The U.S. Army strongly resisted the proposed emphasis on simple, counterguerrilla forces, and the military establishment as a whole opposed the subordination of military judgments to a high political authority located in Saigon. Nor did the State Department rush forward to assert proconsular authority. Frederick Nolting, who became Ambassador in Saigon at a date early enough to have tested the concept, was disinclined to assume any military responsibility, and in 1962, Rusk thought Vietnam was primarily a military problem in which U.S. diplomacy ought not to become too deeply enmeshed. There were other major difficulties: since 1954, U.S. military advisers had trained and equipped a 175,000-man South Vietnamese Army along purely conventional lines. Even if the U.S. Army had been more flexible in outlook, it is doubtful whether the GVN and the ARVN commanders could have been persuaded to dismantle their divisional and regimental paraphernalia and convert to less glamorous, lower-silhouetted counterguerrilla formations. The fact of an over-large, mal-organized ARVN was in the broadest sense a fundamental obstacle to progress both before and after 1965, for by burdening the South Vietnamese economy with an armed force far beyond its capacity to support, it ensured indefinite dependence on the United States. Worse still, the size of the force inevitably shifted the locus of political power inside Vietnam to the military, and this distorted natural political and economic development by, among other things, drawing all the ablest and most ambitious young men into military careers. Finally, although the United States had assumed the major burden of the fighting, the most important political levers in Vietnam were allowed to remain in the hands of the GVN. But neither Diem nor his successors showed any readiness to subordinate their own political imperatives to an American "strategic concept of counterinsurgency," to the view that the root purpose of pacification was to gain the positive allegiance of the people, or indeed to any other American objectives. And by its large-scale military inter-vention in 1965, the U.S. lost its leverage with the GVN. From that point forward, Thieu and Ky knew we would fight their war no matter how incompetent or corrupt their performance.

By late 1967, pacification thus seemed to me a program beyond retrieval by American resources and personnel. If it proved anything, it was that U.S. policy having said *A* could not avoid saying *B*. We were trapped by logic, for pacification was the undeniable corollary of the military effort. Finding the GVN incapable of defending its territory, convinced of the domino theory, and fearing for our own prestige and security, we had taken over the military side of the struggle. But this led only to the rediscovery that regaining control of the villages and hamlets was a deep-seated political problem. Until the Viet Cong infrastructure was rooted out of the countryside and the population persuaded to acknowledge and support, if not quite to love, the government in Saigon, large-scale victories over NVN forces would be inherently inconclusive. Moreover, large-scale victories involved artillery and air strikes, which killed civilians and thus inhibited political persuasion.

Pacification involved nothing less than political counter-revolution in the interests of democracy. Precisely for this reason, it could not be planned and carried out by foreigners, and particularly not white men. Probably, it had no chance of success at all so long as the country was being physically destroyed by large-scale warfare. The dilemma facing the Administration was of course that the GVN lacked both organizational drive and reforming zeal, and that its operatives did not commend themselves to the villagers as self-evident, authentic apostles of justice and democracy, or even of modest land reform; too often they were looked upon, accurately, as simply a different form of repression and exploitation. But the U.S. could not escape identification with the GVN. The anguish and moral confusion of the villagers, whose allegiance, voluntary or forced, was the ultimate prize in the deadly struggle, was poignantly expressed by a young ARVN major in late 1967. He saw the cities of South Vietnam increasingly taken over by foreigners, which created a gravitational pull upon the native elites—political, economic, and intellectual. He saw this was leaving the great mass of peasants in the countryside leaderless, except for the Viet Cong. Moreover, he saw these developments creating a sharp suspicion between city and village, manifest in a progressively harsh approach to pacification in the countryside by city-based GVN officials. He said, "There will soon be islands of Americans, Australians, Koreans and Thais, all hostile and suspicious toward Vietnamese [in the countryside], because they . . . believe every Vietnamese is a communist . . . Everyone is a communist under the criterion the police use. Using the police way, every Vietnamese [in the countryside] would have to be killed and our villages repopulated with Americans if the war was to be won . . . If we can't close the huge gap [of suspicion and misunderstanding], then only the communists can benefit, because the people will have no one else to turn to." [5]

Facing the knowledge that pacification was the ultimate reason for the military effort, but recognizing the GVN's fundamental inability to make it work, the U.S. had belatedly focused on the necessity of giving the pacification effort more attention, more resources, more horsepower. For several years the program had been handled by Deputy Ambassador William Porter, who was also burdened with myriad other duties. But in the spring of 1967, Robert Komer had gone out from the White House staff to serve as Westmoreland's full-time deputy for pacification, with the personal rank of Ambassador. Having said A we said B. The President and his advisers, confident in their ability to handle and resolve the military problem, were able to persuade themselves that success in pacification was also a reasonable expectation, given enough resources, organization, effort, and time. As in the case of the military campaign, they calculated that it was a matter of the rational application of means; with an input of X you could expect a result of Y. They seemed unready to acknowledge the very marginal influence that foreigners can exert on the intimate, complicated, political processes of another people, particularly a people in revolutionary ferment. It was another example of that troublesome American belief that the application of enough resources can solve any problem; if no solution is forthcoming, it means the resources were inadequate and the answer is to apply more. David Halberstam once wrote, only half in jest, that during the days of the strategic hamlet program the province chiefs were afraid to stand out on the local airstrips "for fear of being buried alive by resources tumbling out of the sky: barbed wire, bricks, pigs, rat killers, pig fatteners, mosquito killers, snow plows . . ." [6]

Americans could not get to the heart of local politics in Vietnam, because the Vietnamese would not permit the necessary intimacy, and because it was beyond U.S. capability to provide enough operatives with the knowledge and skill to break through the formidable barriers of language and cultural difference. Even those U.S. personnel especially trained for pacification can understand only a smattering of Vietnamese, and most Vietnamese interpreters know only a few hundred words of English. A more fundamental problem is that villagers usually tell the Americans and their interpreters only what they think they want to hear, this bland accommodation having become a first law of survival in a country where warring factions of lethal consequence for peasants have crossed and recrossed the land for the past twenty-eight years in a seemingly endless tug of war for the body and soul of the people. Thus earnest American questions are often imprecisely repeated by interpreters, peasant answers may or may not bear any relation to the facts, and the final English rendering may further distort the peasant's reply. As William J. Lederer once put it, it was through such "daisy chains of misinformation" that data were compiled for feeding into Ambassador Komer's computers, which in turn produced official reports on the status of the pacification program.

In October of 1967, the Komer computers claimed that the GVN exercised effective control over 67 percent of the people of South Vietnam (this was down from the 75 percent figure used by Rostow in September, presumably owing to refined calculations). Even the lower figure, however, included the so-called Category C hamlets, representing 4.3 million people, or about one-half of those claimed to have been effectively pacified. But in the typical Category C hamlet, conditions were so precarious that the Revolutionary Development Team frequently took to the safety of the district headquarters at night, as did the hamlet chief. Such villages were really secure only by day, and then only if friendly regular troops were nearby. Komer, an able, ebullient, and hard-driving man, was quite aware of the dangerous imprecisions in his reporting system, or indeed in any system that could be devised to measure pacification. He would have preferred to apply it simply as an internal measure of progress for official use only, for he recognized that if the public figure grew from 67 percent to 80 percent or 90 percent, as he thought it might, the American people would want to know why the war hadn't already been won. But like others in Saigon, he was the victim of relentless White House pressure to show dramatic progress in the war; to some extent, he was the victim of his own compulsive optimism.

He had favored, for example, the strong U.S. initiative in April 1967 to establish the new South Vietnamese constitution and the later public relations effort to point up the significance of the presidential and senatorial elections in October. These actions were of a piece with the underlying, only half-veiled, determination to press for a military victory, for U.S. endorsement of a constitution that specifically barred all Communists from participation in the GVN could only greatly narrow our military and political options. In the eyes of the world, such an endorsement transferred our commitment from the people as a whole to a particular form of government and a particular group of men. Moreover, the carefully drawn electoral laws and the Thieu-Ky group's full use of its inherent leverage on behalf of its own cause precluded anything but a victory for the existing military government. Some candidates were barred because their advocacy of peace was considered to be evidence of Communist sympathies (one man thus eliminated had been the GVN Finance Minister until 1966). No militant Buddhist could be a candidate, and no run-off elections were permitted, as it was feared that these might produce a "civilian victory." Several oppositionist newspapers in Saigon were closed down during the campaign. As Robert Kennedy later wrote: "it was in these and many similar ways, and not in the crude stuffing

72

of ballot boxes, that the election ... was such a disappointment." [7]

The result was to legitimize military rule in a way that tended to push civilian nationalist groups, like the Buddhists, toward the only viable opposition, the NLF. Moreover, the energies expended on establishing the importance of the electoral process were energies unavailable for a serious attack on the mundane but crucial problems of improving the quality and discipline of government administration. The indiscipline, unresponsiveness, and corruption of the bureaucracy were at the heart of the GVN weakness. But these grave defects were unfortunately not corrected, and may have been aggravated, by the somewhat contrived creation of an "instant parliament."

Our strong endorsement of these particular elections appeared also to create practical future difficulties for U.S. policy. For on the assumption that serious negotiations on the war would have to involve political compromise in the South and thus to bring forth something like a coalition government, it seemed to me that, by creating structural barriers to compromise, the U.S. was painting itself into a corner. Only if one could assume total eradication of the Viet Cong and the long-term survival of the Thieu-Ky group could one piece together a plausible rationale for these U.S. actions. Komer confirmed on a trip to Washington in November 1967 that such assumptions underlay official thinking in Saigon. He favored American support for these new institutions, he said, because "it reassures the Vietnamese that the U.S. has a real stake in seeing to it that these processes work," i.e., that the U.S. was specifically committed to the exclusion of all Communist participation in the government of South Vietnam. Komer thought this was a feasible posture because the United States "is winning and will win the war." On the other hand, the *New Yorker*'s Far East correspondent, Robert Shaplen, wrote early in the same month that "The assumption—primarily an American one—that the Vietnamese elections ... have had, or are likely to have, any salutary effect on the war or on the internal political situation here [Saigon] is regarded by most Vietnamese as unwarranted and unrealistic."

If one fed on official cables and reports alone, one could not easily escape involuntary enrollment in the conspiracy of optimism, or entanglement in the maze of irreconcilable statistics. Fortunately, an occasional shaft of piercing light from outside this enclosed system was enough to rekindle the skepticism on which balanced judgment depended; and such revealing shafts were increasingly available. I came across in the month of October the transcript of a TV interview out in the Vietnamese countryside with four U.S. enlisted men, specialists assigned to pacification duty. The question put by the TV correspondent was "How is pacification going and how are your relations with the Vietnamese?" The answers seemed to me eloquent testimony to the prospects for our success:

First GI: Some of them hate us over here. Of course village reaction to the RD [Revolutionary Development] program is a part of it ... you get hate, stares; it's really ..."

Second GI: This is the biggest part of the war. We have to gain the confidence of the people. We have to show them that we want to help them, and then make them understand what we are trying to do in this country.

Third GI: We are trying to win these people over to us. But you get these South Vietnamese and they think that we are trying to do something to them that they don't want to do. This is definitely wrong. We try to help these people and they don't realize it.

Fourth GI: I think the big thing is the illiteracy ... It's really hard to get anything over to these people because education-wise, they are just not ... there is no comparison between themselves and the American soldier, even on the lowest level.

CHAPTER 4

Bombing North Vietnam

TECHNICAL FACTORS

IN OCTOBER 1967, the bombing campaign against North Vietnam presented a number of different aspects. It was, first of all, being conducted with professional zeal and ingenuity, and exemplary human courage, combined with a scrupulous adherence to the restrictions on targets and target areas imposed by the highest political authorities. It was also my impression, during my first month at the Air Force, that the limited nature of the air war's objectives was firmly understood, if reluctantly accepted, by the military men—that is, to impede and hopefully to reduce the flow of manpower and supplies across the North-South boundary, and to impose upon North Vietnam a high and cumulative price for its subversion-aggression against South Vietnam, but not to destroy the government or the population of North Vietnam.

General William Momyer, Commander of the 7th Air Force in Saigon, a highly intelligent and meticulous professional airman, clearly grasped the differences between the circumstances facing him in Vietnam and the classical textbook conditions of war. In military theory, effective air interdiction requires an ability to attack the enemy's warmaking capacity at the source, to attack the movement of supplies from the source to the battlefield, and then to force the rapid consumption of supplies on the battlefield itself by maintaining a high intensity of ground combat. Momyer understood, if some others did not, that North Vietnam was simply a conduit for the through-put of Russian and Chinese supplies and not in any sense an independent source of war-making power; moreover, that the elusive NVN-VC forces in the South possessed the option to stand and fight or to disengage, thus denying the U.S. command a reliable influence over the rate at which they expended the supplies that came down the trails from North Vietnam. In the circumstances, the main air effort had to be applied against the middle element—the movement of supplies from import point to battlefield—and Momyer acknowledged that this was inherently the most difficult target system, made more so by the remarkable ability of the North Vietnamese quickly to repair roads, bridges, and transfer points.

In addition, U.S. airmen had to fight their way into the northeast targets (Hanoi and the approaches to Haiphong) through very heavy missile and gun defenses, which continued to improve in density and accuracy. By the end of 1967, the Air Force, Navy, and Marine Corps had lost about 950 aircraft to enemy action over North Vietnam, and about 450 in the South; the Army had lost 420 (mostly helicopters) in the South. Of the air crews lost over North Vietnam, 33 percent had been recovered by skilled and courageous rescue operations. Forty-six percent of the airmen downed in the South had been similarly recovered. Accidents and other operational failures unrelated to enemy action accounted for the loss of about 1,200 additional aircraft for all services, the total amounting to approximately 3,000 planes and a cost of $2.9 billion. These were cumulative losses since February 1965.

Notwithstanding these difficulties, the military leadership was optimistic. The past year had brought forth improved electronic countermeasures to confuse and neutralize enemy gunners, better tactics had driven the few harassing North Vietnamese MIGs from the sky, the number of sorties was up, aircraft loss rates were down in relation to number of sorties flown, and more efficient munitions were in prospect. The steady application of mounting pressure was thought to be having a cumulative effect. To me the foundations of this optimism were not, however, self-evident, for there existed in the calculus of bombing effectiveness at least four adverse and intractable factors. The first (which McNamara had analyzed brilliantly in August and which will be discussed in a moment) concerned the relatively small volume of supplies required for NVN-VC operations in the South, in relation to the relatively large import capacity of North Vietnam. The others were the bad weather problem, the inherent inaccuracy of conventional dive-bombing, and the Hanoi regime's amazing ability to maintain an adequate flow of supplies while under relentless bombardment.

A fundamental, but soft-pedaled reality was that the northeast monsoon covered the whole of coastal Vietnam for nearly eight months of every year—from late September to early May—with drenching rains and heavy fog, producing conditions of such poor visibility that visual bombing attacks were possible on the average of only five days per month, and were frequently precluded for from two to three weeks at a time. The standard criteria for visual bombing were a 10,000-foot cloud ceiling and a five-mile horizontal visibility. Under such conditions, U.S. aircraft employing a diving technique and releasing the bombs at 6,000 feet could, against defended targets around Hanoi and Haiphong, expect to strike within 400 feet of the aiming point, on the average. Against less heavily defended targets farther south, the accuracies were somewhat better, but in bad weather the bombs fell, on the average, between 1,500 and 1,800 feet from the target center. Moreover, neither the Air Force nor the Navy possessed in 1967 an operationally ready "all-weather" fighter-bomber—that is, an aircraft with sufficiently refined and integrated navigational-targeting equipment to achieve visual bombing accuracies while flying through rain, fog, or darkness. The

F-111A was such an aircraft, but it was not yet in service, and its subsequent introduction into Vietnam was marked by painful misfortune and disappointment.

During the Korean War, the problem of inaccuracy had similarly frustrated the American air effort. Beginning, for example, in the late summer of 1951, the Commanding General of the Far East Air Force had commenced "Operation Strangle," a major campaign to interdict railroads, bridges, marshaling yards, and storage points in an effort to prevent the Chinese and North Koreans from supplying their troops at the front. Averaging 9,000 sorties a month, the U.S. fighter-bombers imposed relentless pressure on the enemy lines of communication and for a time appeared to be destroying rail transport faster than it could be repaired. Yet the effects were limited. The enemy in fact continued to bring up supplies in quantity, even though these frequently had to be carried on foot. Darkness and long stretches of bad weather hindered the U.S. effort and gave the enemy additional time for recovery.

It was also a little-publicized fact that bombing accuracies had improved hardly at all in the period between Korea and Vietnam. Shrouded in professional embarrassment, the explanation was traceable to the Eisenhower-Dulles era and the strategy of "massive retaliation." Throughout that period most of the Air Force money, operational energies, and creative research was applied to the development of strategic nuclear forces (B-52 bombers and Intercontinental Ballistic Missiles), while tactical aviation was starved and neglected. Even the few tactical fighter-bombers developed in those years were built and programmed as nuclear weapons carriers and, since pinpoint accuracy is not a necessity with nuclear weapons, no one devoted much attention to advancing the art of precision delivery. Not until our several tactical air arms were actually involved in Vietnam and forced to operate under political restrictions that, in one form or another, are an integral element of limited war, did they really face up to the acute requirement for far greater accuracy. But research, development, and procurement take time.

Chronic bad weather and the relative inaccuracy of our bomb delivery were thus advantages for North Vietnam, but apart from this the Hanoi regime had clearly demonstrated a superior capacity to cope with the effects of the bombing. A senior U.S. Army officer in Vietnam said, "In particular, the American military mind cannot really comprehend the adaptability of the North Vietnamese because they compare it instinctively with that of their own people. But the North Vietnamese, like the Chinese, can round up a whole town in an hour and use it for portage, if necessary for a period of days or weeks." He went on to cite a case he knew of through prisoner interrogation. U.S. aircraft had knocked out a small railroad bridge outside of Hanoi. The whole population of the nearby village was herded together and each person was told to fill his rice bag with dirt. One by one the 1,000-odd bags were piled up to fill the bomb crater. New railroad tracks were laid on top and trains were moving again within twenty-four hours. The officer added, "Caucasians cannot really imagine what ant labor can do."

In the circumstances, it was perhaps not surprising that neither Admiral Sharp, the overall Pacific Commander (CINCPAC), nor the Air Force and Navy staffs in Washington had ever produced a meaningful assessment of our bombing effectiveness over North Vietnam. Data were in profusion, but they added up to nothing coherent, and the professionals instinctively fought shy of definitive evaluation, preferring to address their analytical efforts to the operations themselves—that is, to the questions of how to improve bombing accuracy, achieve a higher sortie rate, or expedite the development of new weapons. They came to the problem, in short, with a built-in predisposition to avoid the hard question whether airpower could be efficacious in the particular circumstances where its application had been ordered by higher authority; their instinct was to assume that it was or could be, and they preferred to concentrate their energies on developing the means and techniques that would prove them right. As a general rule, such a "can do" attitude is eminently desirable in executive agents of military policy, but this corollary reluctance to submit their *raison d'être* to searching examination only underlined the vital need for wise and disinterested civilian direction and control of the policy.

The military belief that attacks on Haiphong could be decisive had always been, for example, something of a mystery. The conviction apparently started with Admiral Sharp, who was not the wisest or most perceptive military mind, but it had spread quickly to the Joint Chiefs of Staff and the Senate hawks. In the spring of 1967, Sharp, on a trip to Washington, urged McNamara to see the logic and benefit of such attacks, but McNamara politely rebuffed him, remarking that every piece of intelligence he had read made clear that no military equipment was entering through Haiphong; he thought, therefore, that attacks on Haiphong could have no *direct* effect on the NVN war effort in the South, and could have an indirect effect only if one could believe they would force Hanoi sharply to increase food imports via the northeast railroads at the expense of weapons. He, McNamara, was skeptical.

Determined to make his case, Sharp returned to his headquarters at Pearl Harbor and called for Major General John Vogt, the young and very able deputy for operations of the Pacific Air Force (PACAF). He told Vogt he was convinced the North Vietnamese were bringing military equipment into Haiphong at night, but that U.S. intelligence had no evidence of this because all of the photoreconnaissance missions were flown during daylight hours. He wanted PACAF to lay on a night photographic mission. Skeptical, but intrigued, Vogt conferred with his Air Force superior, General John Ryan, the PACAF Commander, and the mission was duly planned and ordered. A single reconnaissance aircraft made a high-speed run at Haiphong harbor, coming in low from the sea in pitch darkness. Nearing the target, it pulled up sharply, exploded its flash bulbs, and raced away. The mission produced pictures of exceptionally high quality. What they captured was a scene of total inactivity—ships lying at dockside, hatches open and holds empty. The subsequent undiminished drum-beating for attacks on Haiphong, by Admiral Sharp, General Wheeler, and others, reaffirmed the human truth that conviction is often more a matter of faith than of fact.

THREE REALITIES

But beyond these debatable technical-professional considerations, three points were abundantly clear in October. One was that the bombing of North Vietnam over a period of thirty-two months had neither stopped nor reduced the infiltration. Defenders of the effort were forced back on the argument that without the bombing the infiltration would be much worse, an argument that might be true, but was entirely hypothetical and somewhat sophistic. The cold, unhypothetical fact remained that the flow of men and supplies from North Vietnam to South Vietnam had definitely increased in absolute terms.

The second abundantly clear point was that the bombing campaign against the North had become the focus and catalyst for most of the opposition to the war, both at home and abroad. It was progressively isolating the U.S. from its friends throughout the world, including the major nations of Asia: Japan, India, and Indonesia. In the UN, over thirty non-Communist nations, among them several NATO allies, had called for cessation with essentially no conditions. Korea, Thailand, Australia, New Zealand, and the Philippines—which had committed fighting forces to South Vietnam—were of course notable exceptions. Honest and dedicated American officials, long accustomed to broad acceptance of the United States as the shield and buckler of the Free World, were shocked at the thought that their country's military actions could be regarded with moral suspicion. Yet as a result of the protracted, gradually stepped-up bombing campaign against the North, the U.S. was acquiring a "bully image" in many parts of the world—the most powerful nation on earth pounding the daylights out of a tiny little backwater, pouring bombloads on cement plants, bicycle factories, petroleum storage, footbridges, and miscellaneous supply points in an endless string that now equaled and would soon exceed the vast tonnages dropped on Germany, Italy, and Japan in World War II.

For those Americans who were aware of the Viet Cong's systematic assassinations, kidnappings, and related savageries, and who had never been bombed, the air war was not much of a moral issue, though it did seem an imprecise and highly disproportionate form of reprisal. The citizens of many smaller, weaker countries, especially those that had themselves suffered bombing, and also antiwar groups in the United States, tended however to identify morally with North Vietnam. The bombing program thus raised the emotional temperature of the war in ways that made it far more difficult for the Administration to handle, politically at home and diplomatically abroad; it produced however little compensating military advantage, and, in terms of public opinion, it shifted the moral onus from Hanoi to Washington. Had there been no bombing of North Vietnam, had the allied countereffort been confined to South Vietnam, it is probable that dissent at home and abroad would have proved far more manageable, for no one could argue that a tenacious, measured defense of one's own territory was immoral. The deepest irony of all was imbedded in the fact that, in the end, the bombing program and its implications forced not Hanoi, but Washington, to seek the conference table.

It had to be said, too, that President Johnson's rhetoric did not help matters. For while he showed himself in fact a man of ultimate restraint, his articulation of the bombing policy was devoid of any sense of proportion or magnanimity. His words showed little or no awareness of the vast disparity between the size and strength of the United States and that of its adversary. As Senator Fulbright had put it in a private, pungent moment, "we go ahead treating this little piss-ant country as though we were up against Russia and China put together." [8] Johnsonian insensitivity to a factor that was central to the observations of many at home and abroad meant that the United States projected to them a meanness of spirit.

The third unmistakable reality in October was that, notwithstanding the evidence of the first and second points, President Johnson was resolutely determined to continue and indeed to step up the bombing effort against North Vietnam. Ignoring the rising chorus of public dissent, he took a series of decisions that widened the pattern of authorized targets and made the rules of engagement progressively less stringent.

McNAMARA AND THE BOMBING ISSUE

Another significant aspect of the autumn of 1967 in Washington was the growing evidence that McNamara's power and influence were in serious decline. Since midsummer, his friends and supporters, who felt him to be the only moderate within the inner circle and thus the one real hope for arresting the escalation and gradually winding down the war, had been treated to the embarrassing spectacle of McNamara publicly opposing or expressing reservations about proposed actions that promptly became official policy. Would American casualties in the South be increased if the bombing of North Vietnam were curtailed? McNamara said no; the military leaders and the Senate hawks said yes, and the President publicly adopted their view as a central argument in his defense of continued bombing. Should the Chinese buffer zone be ruled out of bounds to U.S. bombing because of the risks of an incident with Communist China? McNamara said yes; the military leaders said no. Targets in the buffer zone were added to those authorized for strike. Should the U.S. commit itself to build without delay an anti-ballistic missile system against Russia's nuclear missile force? McNamara had strong reservations; an entire host of advocates who would fall comfortably within the term "military-industrial complex" had none.

In September, McNamara himself announced the decision to move forward with actual construction and deployment of a "thin" ABM system designed not against Russia, but to offset the possibility of an irrational attack by China. The announcement came at the end of a speech that argued brilliantly the basic case against the wisdom and utility of any ABM system. To all but the most sophisticated and informed listeners, who understood that McNamara's espousal of the Chinese rationale was an attempt to deflect pressures for a "thick" anti-Soviet ABM, the announcement seemed a clear *non sequitur*. As it was known that the President had definitely decided there had to be some ABM deployment, as a means of relieving pressure from the Senate hawks on the bombing campaign and a range of other war-related matters, the impression was left that McNamara had yielded to the President on ABM in order to preserve his effectiveness on other issues.

There were other evidences of subtle and not so subtle depreciation. Joseph Alsop, who regularly provided journalistic resonance to the line Walt Rostow was currently putting about, wrote that McNamara was of course a splendid "Defense Minister," but perhaps lacked the innate toughness required in a "War Minister." And his fellow columnist William S. White wrote, in the same vein and very probably from the same source: "Perhaps the best way to put it is that McNamara is a brilliant manager—but more bookish than martial in spirit and attitude."

McNamara himself seemed to me, during that summer and early fall, increasingly tired and depressed. Always a man of incredible physical and mental resilience, he now appeared to stay thin and tired. He also seemed increasingly alone in the cavernous Pentagon. It was the aloneness of a man in deep doubt, a man whose intelligence and integrity forced him to accept the realization that, in the major decisions of the war, rigorous logic and quantification analysis had conspicuously failed. They had failed because of Ho Chi Minh's "irrational" determination that North Vietnamese, by reason of their readiness to die in great numbers, could in fact outlast U.S. firepower. But owing to his own strict conception of loyalty to the President, McNamara found it officially necessary to deny all doubt and, by his silence, to discourage doubt in his professional associates and subordinates. He was also, almost surely, more affected than he showed by the loss of his two closest associates, Vance and McNaughton, the one through physical disability, the other through tragic death. These had been serious, sudden, deeply personal deprivations that could not be quickly made good in the best of circumstances, and the autumn of 1967 was a period of gathering storm.

The result of McNamara's ambivalence, however, was to create a situation of dreamlike unreality for those around him. His staff meetings during this period were entirely barren affairs: a technical briefing, for example, on the growing strength of air defenses around Hanoi, but no debate on what this implied for the U.S. bombing effort, and never the slightest disclosure of what the President or the Secretary of State might consider the broad domestic and international implications to be. It was an atmosphere that worked to neutralize those who were the natural supporters of his concerns about the war. Meanwhile he and they were being dragged in the wake of events and other men's wills toward what both perceived as dangerous shoals on which the Great Leviathan of the United States might well run aground, and perhaps even break up.

Yet in the end McNamara's doubts were not suppressed. To a sympathetic observer not privy to his inner thoughts, it seemed that an innate candor, a deepening appreciation of the largeness of the issues at stake, and a troubled conscience gradually, and to a large extent unwittingly, betrayed his deliberate decision to confine his moderating proposals to private executive channels and his firm intention to spare an already beleaguered President the added burden of a public split in the Cabinet. The doubts had cropped up, obliquely, as early as May 1966 when he delivered in Montreal a brilliant and original speech on the causes of and likely remedies for world violence and disorder—an analysis that raised eyebrows among traditional believers in the ultimate efficacy of military power. The doubts had appeared, increasingly in 1967, in off-the-record talks with certain journalists and in reports of anguished conversations with close friends in Georgetown, notably Robert Kennedy. One story, attributed to his wife, indicated that in the early spring he had been "at war with himself," up half the night debating the question of whether he ought to resign.

A more definitive expression of his doubt, and the one which set him explicitly at odds with the Senate hawks, the military leaders, and (as it turned out) the President, was his statement before the Stennis Committee (formally the Preparedness Investigating Subcommittee of the Senate Armed Services Committee) on August 25, on the pivotal issue of the air war against North Vietnam. The members of that Committee were deeply frustrated by the glaring fact that a war effort of great scale and cost was producing an obviously inconclusive result, and they bore a natural sympathy for those who were charging that "civilian restrictions and interference" were inhibiting the natural unfolding of military logic. Deciding to ventilate the bombing issues, the Committee heard testimony during August from ten military leaders and one civilian—McNamara. The military leaders unanimously endorsed a policy of wider, heavier bombing (in greater or lesser degree) and expressed their distaste for restrictions that were "contrary to military principle." McNamara was thrust into the position of defending the Administration's past policies and justifying their continuance. It was a difficult task, complicated by the crucial uncertainty as to whether the President in fact desired continuance or an intensified and escalated effort.

In a powerful and lucid statement, tightly reasoned, supported by facts and figures, McNamara said in effect that, unless the United States shifted to an indiscriminate bombing campaign aimed at annihilating the population of North Vietnam, the air war against the North could not be expected to accomplish more than "to continue to put a high price tag on North Vietnam's continued aggression." He saw nothing in the record to indicate that Hanoi "can be bombed to the negotiating table." His case rested essentially on a finding that North Vietnam, although a primitive agricultural society offering few industrial and military targets, possessed nonetheless a highly diversified transportation system. It had a capacity to import 14,000 tons per day, but was in fact importing only 5,800 tons. Of this, the remarkably small sum of under 100 tons per day was all that was needed to sustain NVN and Viet Cong forces in the South. He argued that this requirement in the South was too small in relation to the capacity of the system to permit belief that we could, by bombing, prevent North Vietnam from sustaining combat operations at the 1967 level. In reaching this conclusion he assumed the continued willingness of Russia and China to maintain a steady flow of military and war-supporting equipment, and the continued tenacity of the people of North Vietnam who "are accustomed to discipline and are no strangers to deprivation and to death."

In conclusion, he insisted that the limited objectives of the bombing "were soundly conceived and are being effectively pursued." He added: "The tragic and long drawn out character of that conflict in the South makes very tempting the prospect of replacing it with some new kind of air campaign against the North. But however tempting, such an alternative seems to me completely illusory. To pursue this objective would not only be futile, but would involve risks to our personnel and to our nation that I am unable to recommend."

87

The statement rang with intellectual authority, and courage. It was also a personal testimonial, for McNamara had not cleared it with either Rusk or the White House. Probably beyond his intention, it had the effect of polarizing opinion on the bombing. The moderates suddenly possessed not merely a rumored, but a proclaimed, champion within the citadel; the hawks were more certain than ever of their adversary's identity. For not only did McNamara's testimony adhere tenaciously to limited objectives and limited means; it showed a willingness to accept an inconclusive military result in preference to the wider dangers of continued escalation. Such precepts were not well received by the nation's military leaders. All of them were sensitive about their reputations, which the Vietnam War was not enhancing; many, particularly the older and less sophisticated officers, were temperamentally unable to acknowledge any substitute for clear-cut victory. To aging, hard-bitten warhawks in the Senate, like Stennis and Thurmond, McNamara's views were pure heresy.

The Committee's summary report, issued on August 31, was primarily an attack on McNamara. A slapdash, emotional polemic, it drew a far sharper line between the military and civilian views than in fact existed, and it urged with dangerous imprecision a bombing campaign that would meet the Committee's hope for "a successful end to the war as quickly as possible." While it admitted the existence of "important policy and political considerations over and above the pure military requirements," its argumentation and conclusions totally ignored these. The report faithfully recorded the frustration of both the Senators and the military leaders, but did no credit to the Committee's ability to weigh evidence and produce considered judgments. The report stated in part:

> The top military leaders of this country are confident that the Port of Haiphong can be closed, the land lines of com-

munication to China interdicted, and Hanoi's receipt and distribution by sea and land routes of war-sustaining materiel greatly reduced by Air Force and Navy aviation if they are permitted to do so ... The Secretary of Defense testified that he does not believe that such a campaign can stem the flow of supplies and goods sufficiently to prevent support of North Vietnamese and Viet Cong combat activity in South Vietnam at its present level. The Joint Chiefs and other military experts believe it can accomplish more—much more.

As between these diametrically opposed views, and in view of the unsatisfactory progress of the war, logic and prudence requires [sic] that the decision be with the unanimous weight of professional military judgment.

It is not our intention to point a finger or to second guess those who determined this [current] policy. But the cold fact is that this policy has not done the job and it has been contrary to the best military judgment. What is needed now is the hard decision to do whatever is necessary, take the risks that have to be taken, and apply the force that is required to see the job through.

Greatly to his credit, McGeorge Bundy, who by then had moved out of government to the presidency of the Ford Foundation, weighed in with a letter to the *Washington Post* that effectively pierced the Committee's pretensions to objectivity. He said: "First, the Senators appeal not to evidence but to authority. They set up a group of generals and admirals against Secretary McNamara, and their position is that the generals and admirals are right simply because they are professionals. The Subcommittee does not demonstrate the military value of the course it urges; it simply tells us that the generals and admirals are for it ... Nothing is less reliable, in hard choices of this sort, than the unsupported opinion of men who are urging the value of their own chosen instrument —in this case military force. We must not be surprised, and still less persuaded, when generals and admirals recommend additional military action—what do we expect them to recommend?" [9]

It was a brave try, but it changed nothing at the time. The issue was drawn, the trend was set. The President was jolted and displeased by McNamara's statement before the Stennis Committee. One reason for his displeasure was the feeling that McNamara was depreciating the bombing publicly in a way that increased Hanoi's bargaining power. Venting his annoyance to a member of his staff, he drew the analogy of a man trying to sell his house, while one of the sons of the family went to the prospective buyer to point out that there were leaks in the basement. The analogy itself was richly revealing of Lyndon Johnson.

The press story on November 28 that McNamara had been nominated to be president of the World Bank was, at first reading, a stunning surprise; on reflection it seemed inevitable. No doubt the President's decision was fashioned out of complex motives, an intuitive mix of seemingly contradictory considerations. He admired McNamara greatly and recognized that his performance had been exceptional; he noted McNamara's fatigue and wished to preserve him for further service to the country; the World Bank job had been discussed between them and McNamara had expressed serious interest in it. On the other side stood the President's growing determination to drive on relentlessly to a military victory that would disarm his critics and assure his reelection (or the election of his chosen heir) in 1968; there was unrest among the military leaders and vague hints that one or two top military advisers might resign over McNamara's "interference with the conduct of the war." In that context a doubting Secretary of Defense could be a political liability. Moreover, Lyndon Johnson was strongly allergic to opposition within the bosom of his official family, he disliked and probably suspected his cabinet officer's continued intimacy with the Kennedys, and he had made to at least one senator the sarcastic complaint that "that military genius, McNamara, has gone dovish on me."

One White House aide saw the President's decision as "an

act of real compassion," but related the embarrassment of the press leak to the President's "inept way of handling people." The awkward fact remained that there was no urgent need to settle the question of the World Bank presidency in 1967; the Bank's directors had already extended George Wood's term for one year, until December 31, 1968. Certainly McNamara gave every evidence of planning to stay on at the Defense Department through 1968. When all factors were duly weighed, one was left with the irreducible feeling that the most Byzantine of American presidents had given McNamara a fast shuffle, and had gauged his man's character, inner ambivalence, and fatigue well enough to be confident that he would go quietly and suffer the indignity in silence.

CHAPTER 5

Official Optimism—Public Doubt

THE WASHINGTON autumn of 1967 was sunny and hot, presenting an unbroken string of benign and lovely days, suffused with warm, harmonious color and stretching to a seeming infinity. The glorious weather could not, unfortunately, conceal a political climate grown more harsh, a debate on the war grown more belligerent and less coherent, and a deepened private pessimism. The mood of the country as a whole, though not so abrasive as Washington's unrepresentative concentrate, was clearly one of moral unease and practical doubt.

For by October the war's major incongruities were being intellectually understood, or at least intuitively sensed, by a growing number of Americans. More penetrating, more urgent questions were being asked about the disparity between the limited nature of our stated objectives and the ever-rising, apparently unlimited, level of our military involvement. Debate raged in the public press, on television, and in angry demonstrations in large cities and great universities; a crowd of twenty thousand marched on the Pentagon; there were stirrings of dissent and rebellion in the halls of Congress. For by October the mounting scale and toll of the war were rapidly washing out the Administration's basic rationale—the argument that it was simply honoring a commitment of two predecessors to help anti-Communist Vietnamese protect themselves against the depredations of their northern kinsmen. That slender statement of purpose could no longer bear the crushing weight of the U.S. military effort as it then existed, and there seemed the predictable certainty that the effort would grow larger and heavier still—without benefit of consultation with Congress and with no prospect of a national referendum on the war until late 1968. The Administration was officially optimistic, but the public was no longer able to accept official optimism at face value. Few seemed ready to believe that further graduated increases in military pressure, such as the President had recently authorized and made known, would be able to produce any dramatic breakthrough. No one expected early negotiations. The only clear prospect was for more and heavier fighting, and the American people were increasingly asking why and to what end?

RHETORICAL ESCALATION

It was in this climate of opinion, on October 12, that "the real Dean Rusk stood up" (as Chalmers M. Roberts of the *Washington Post* put it) and pointed to Communist China as the true expansionst menace and the underlying reason why an open-ended commitment in Asia and a tenacious fight to the finish in Vietnam were imperatives of U.S. security. Earlier in his press conference he had sought to characterize the national debate on Vietnam as merely "variations on a theme," on the valid, unexceptionable ground that all would agree we should defend our vital national interests. But this stance begged the question whether we had vital interests in Vietnam. Asked by John Finney of the *New York Times* why he thought the security of the U.S. was directly at stake in Vietnam, Rusk replied that "Within the next decade or two, there will be a billion Chinese on the mainland, armed with nuclear weapons, with no certainty about what their attitude toward the rest of Asia will be." He said, "We are not picking out Peking as some sort of special enemy.

93

Peking has nominated itself by proclaiming a militant doctrine of the world revolution and doing something about it.
This is not a theoretical debate; they are doing something
about it." He added that in such circumstances, "it gets
tough . . . we are tested, and we find out what kind of people
we are."

To those of us who considered our country already over-
committed in Vietnam—politically, materially, and emotionally—the Rusk press conference, which was passionately rendered and showed evidence of careful preparation, was disheartening in the extreme. And because they were so at odds
with the best available evidence, the Secretary's assertions
represented yet another defeat for reasoned proportion and
institutional expertise. Leading Far Eastern scholars, close
observers in Hong Kong, and specialists within the State Department did not believe that Communist China loomed as
the powerful menace Rusk described. Broadly speaking, they
saw China as a clumsy, backward country whose primary focus
was of necessity on domestic problems so awesome that they
threatened to engulf its government and its people. That
Mao's regime was prone to shrill, even hysterical, propaganda
no one denied, but the corollary fact was an operational policy
of extreme caution. Mao combined polemical ferocity with
actionary prudence. Both elements were reflections of China's
weakness. The Chinese nuclear development was a reality,
but not on a scale that could pose a significant threat to the
United States for many years to come. The possibility that
China would try to employ nuclear blackmail against her
smaller neighbors was also a matter to be reckoned with, but
the effective counter was not to fight a land war in Southeast
Asia; rather, it was to formulate a carefully defined American
(or American-Russian) warning that nuclear threats could
not be made with impunity, that they would bring into play
counterthreats by powers of far greater nuclear weight. The
idea of such guarantees by the nuclear Great Powers was a

corollary of the Non-Proliferation Treaty and had already been seriously discussed with such countries as India.

These considerations, necessary to any balanced assessment of China and the threat it posed, were ignored by Rusk at his press conference; he thus conveyed an inaccurate and misleading impression. Yet the fears he so dramatically raised carried an even graver implication: they threatened to lift the sensible restraints that the U.S. had, with difficulty, managed to impose on itself during the long emotional bout with its China policy since 1947. To invoke the specter of a billion Chinese with nuclear weapons, to imply that the Viet Cong and North Vietnam were primarily agents of a coordinated plan for Chinese expansion was to eliminate any logical basis for a compromise settlement in Vietnam. If China constituted a direct threat to the United States and if the Vietnam War was really a testing of the U.S. ability to resist Chinese expansion that would, if unchecked, roll on across the Pacific to Hawaii and the California coast, then the only logical U.S. objective was to bring about a change in the character and purposes of the government in Peking by whatever means were necessary—and without delay, while the clear preponderance of military power lay with us.

Rusk declined to acknowledge such an apocalyptic consequence of his vision, but the disclaimer could not alter the logic his words had set in motion. They amounted to dangerous rhetorical escalation. Moreover, by playing to the felt situational need of the moment, he mortgaged the future. For exaggerating the Chinese threat could only make it harder to move U.S. opinion toward the prospect of a rapprochement with the less fanatical, more pragmatic Chinese leaders who seemed likely to succeed the aging despot, Mao. Lastly, and not incidentally, it was hard to believe that Rusk had made it easier to persuade Japan and India to renounce nuclear weapons, which was of course the purpose of the Non-Proliferation Treaty.

Vice-President Humphrey soon provided the kind of authoritative reinforcement that showed that the Rusk press conference had not been an aberration. Speaking in Doylestown, Pennsylvania on October 15, he asserted that "the threat to world peace is militant, aggressive Asian communism, with its headquarters in Peking, China." He added, "Communist China has failed in its attempt to overrun Southeast Asia because we are there resisting aggression. . . . We have proven in Europe that resistance to aggression . . . serves the cause of peace and our own security. The threat to our security is [now] in Asia. And we are fighting there not only for the Vietnamese, but for ourselves and the future of our country."

There was in all this a kernel of truth, a vast disproportion, and a poignancy. True it certainly was that containment of Soviet power had served the cause of peace in Europe, but we and our West European colleagues had possessed the prudence to understand where containment had to begin. It could not extend into Eastern Europe, even though freedom was clearly ravaged there, for, notwithstanding our sense of repugnance, there were limits to the reach of American political and military power. We could stand solid in Western Europe because there was a base of underlying strength and community to stand upon; and we could, by re-creating a military balance and fostering economic recovery in Western Europe, gradually exert attractions upon Eastern Europe that would rekindle the suppressed national spirit of the satellite peoples. It was a painfully slow and disheartening process, subject (as the 1968 invasion of Czechoslovakia later showed) to serious regressions, suffered on the very threshold of apparent success. But in the meantime, U.S. vital interests, including the security of Western Europe, were preserved.

It was also true, as the Vice-President said, that we faced in Vietnam "not handbills, but hand grenades . . . one more communist apparatus trying to seize the land and people by brute force." But in the context of Rusk's press conference, the question was what the Vice-President's remark had to do with China and the U.S. strategic interest. The watchful containment of Chinese ambitions had been a prudent and valid U.S. policy since 1949, but one that we had conducted primarily from strong positions offshore—from Japan, Taiwan, Okinawa, the Philippines. What the Vice-President was unable to explain was why U.S. vital interests in Asia required the presence of nearly 500,000 Americans in a bloody war in which the Chinese Communists were not even engaged. There could be only one sustainable rationale—that North Vietnam was China's agent, that the struggle in Vietnam was a proxy war, that China would be the direct beneficiary of any outcome except an American victory. But this was Rusk's leaky thesis that could not stand the test of historical analysis. It ignored, among other truths, the historical enmity between Vietnam and China and the fact that Vietnam's principal foreign policy problem throughout history had been how to cope with Chinese encroachment.

The poignancy lay in the wonder that sincere and able men could put forth positions so utterly lacking in proportion. And it seemed to me it was this lack of proportion, more than any other single deficiency, that was rendering the solemn words of Administration spokesmen so increasingly unconvincing.

THE SHIFT IN PUBLIC OPINION

The Rusk-Humphrey efforts did not convince and, as the war grew in scale and intensity, so did the opposition to it. By November, the Gallup Poll showed that 57 percent disapproved of the President's handling of the war, while only 28 percent approved—an astonishing relationship between a democratic society and its leaders in the midst of a major military conflict. In the Senate, three moderate Republicans (Case of New Jersey, Morton of Kentucky, and Cooper of Kentucky) all blamed the President for "irresponsible escalation" of the fighting and expressed the conviction that there was no hope for negotiations until the U.S. took the first step of stopping the air war against the North. Senator Morton, reviewing his earlier support of the war, said candidly, "I was wrong." Senator Robert Kennedy followed suit. Representative Morris Udall, brother of the Secretary of the Interior, told his constituents that "We are on a mistaken and dangerous road . . . I refuse any longer to accept a tortured logic which allows little mistakes to be admitted, but requires big ones to be pursued to the bitter end, regardless of their cost in lives and money." Senator Eugene McCarthy said the Administration's Vietnam policy was rooted in a number of "unsubstantiated assumptions"—which was possibly the understatement of 1967.

A striking aspect of the public reaction to these shifts of position by public men of stature was the silence, even the approval, of moderate and conservative groups that had hitherto formed the backbone of respectable support for the war. A number of bankers, businessmen, even military officers on active duty wrote private letters of approbation to the dissenting senators and congressmen. In the conservative state of Arizona, the mail reaction to Udall's shift was reportedly 40 to 1 in favor (although some of it no doubt came from superhawks who reasoned that, if LBJ wouldn't go all the way with the bombing, the only alternative was to pull out). This remarkable lack of fire from the Right was, as I judged it, the first real evidence of a consequential shift in public sentiment on the war. But if such it was, President Johnson and his inner circle did not see, or did not choose to see.

THE ADMINISTRATION VERSUS THE PRESS

November also brought to a head the irreconcilable differences between the Administration and the press on the issue of how the war was going. The Administration continued to insist it was being gradually won, that there was no stalemate; more roads were open to safe travel; aircraft now landed unscathed at Tan Son Nhut airport on the outskirts of Saigon; the people in the South were being brought progressively under GVN allegiance and control through the pacification program; the ARVN was becoming a tough, cohesive army. The current phrase for all this progress was "at last we begin to see light at the end of the tunnel."

The roughly five hundred newsmen covering Vietnam appeared to be reporting a different war. They found no evidence that North Vietnam's will or fighting capacity was being weakened, that any real headway was being made in pacification, or that the GVN was any less corrupt or more efficient. They thought the Administration's chosen indicators of progress were either superficial or irrelevant, and they noted a marked disparity between the optimism of high American officials in Saigon and the gloomy assessments emanating from lesser officials posted in the provinces. Reports from the latter group indicated an increasing tempo of VC terrorism and a deepening pessimism among the peasantry, even a feeling that U.S. obstinacy on the question of a bombing halt was deliberately prolonging the war against the interests of the people of South Vietnam. The *New York Times* Bureau Chief in Saigon had said as early as August, "In the opinion of most disinterested observers, the war is not going well. Victory is not close at hand. It may be beyond reach." Peter Arnett, a New Zealander and Pulitzer-Prize-winning reporter, wrote in the late fall: "The South Vietnamese Army is sick. Like the society which created it, it is riddled with factionism, nepotism, corruption, inefficiency, incompetence, and cowardice . . . It often lacks the will for combat and is increasingly prone to let Americans do the fighting."

Individually and collectively, the journalists ascribed to themselves a broader and deeper knowledge of the situation than they thought could be possessed by any but a durable handful of American officials in Vietnam—for most of them lived and worked "in-country" for several years at a stretch, moved freely from province to province and corps to corps, and talked with Vietnamese scholars and priests, businessmen and peasants, as well as soldiers and politicians. They thus achieved, in their view, a broader and more accurate synthesis than most American officers, enlisted men, diplomats, or economic aid administrators who were largely confined to the perspectives of one regiment, one air group, one district capital, or one province, and who moreover were rotated back to the United States after a short tour of duty (twelve months for most military personnel and eighteen months for civilians). This journalistic claim to superior knowledge was not at all unfounded, but the basic conflict over the issue of how the war was going had also to be seen in the broader context of the fundamental difference in outlook between Government and Fourth Estate. The former, being burdened with full responsibility for ongoing programs of consequence, always has a strong vested interest in accentuating the positive and de-emphasizing the negative; the latter, being responsible primarily for its own integrity (for presenting the truth as it sees it), is far more inclined to let the chips fall where the facts seem to be. The press inevitably functions as a critic of governmental policy and operations unless it is censored.

The President's reaction to this critical broadside was to wrap himself in the mantle of War Leader and stand forth as defender of the faith, a legitimate heir of those giant predecessors—Lincoln, Theodore Roosevelt, Woodrow Wilson, Franklin Roosevelt—who had defied the public opinion of their day and who, though castigated by their contemporaries, were later proclaimed by historians for their perception, wisdom, and courage. James Reston of the *New York Times* wrote, "Make no mistake about it. The President is being told by a shrinking company of intimates that the communist aggression in Vietnam is the same as the Nazi aggression in the Rhineland, Austria and Czechoslovakia, and he is holding the line; as Churchill defended freedom in Europe, so Johnson is holding the bridge in Asia..." It was my impression that this presidential stance was not empty posturing, but that Lyndon Johnson believed in both the War President and the European analogies. For the information and prognoses coming to him from his Ambassador in Saigon, his military commanders, his pacification chief, and the several intelligence agencies seemed to provide grounds for sober optimism. All of these men insisted that gradual, steady progress was being made on all fronts and that the great weight of the U.S. military-political effort was having a cumulative impact that could not be indefinitely resisted. The word out of the White House staff was that, "In a few months, everybody—even the most cynical and skeptical reporter in Saigon—is going to have to admit that we are definitely winning this war." Yet press criticism remained relentless and adamant, and support for the war was crumbling at the edges. A special effort in persuasion seemed necessary; in mid-November the President called Ambassador Bunker, General Westmoreland, and Ambassador Komer to Washington to make it.

Bunker, speaking to the Overseas Press Club and later on television, expressed quiet optimism, asserted that progress was being made, but refused to predict an end or even a turning point. Westmoreland was, on the other hand, more forthright and incautious. To the National Press Club, he said, "I am absolutely certain that whereas in 1965 the enemy was winning, today he is certainly losing." He called to his support the assertion that the U.S. had at last reached the long-awaited "crossover point" at which more of the enemy were being killed than were being replaced by recruitment and infiltration. He called the bloody battle then shaping up around Dakto "the beginning of a great defeat for the enemy." The bombing of North Vietnam, he said, had "retarded infiltration of men, equipment, and supplies . . . and tied down about 175,000 men to air defenses and another 500,000 to maintain the transportation system." In a joint television appearance with Bunker, he was led to predictions that, in the subsequent enemy offensives of Tet, were to cost him his remaining credibility. He said, "I think it is conceivable that within two years or less the enemy will be so weakened that the Vietnamese will be able to cope with a greater share of the war burden. We will be able to phase down the level of our military effort, withdraw some troops." He added that the final mopping up would take "several years." If read carefully, these were rather sobering statements. But his manner of presentation and the main thrust of the remarks portrayed a high confidence that the war was going well, and in the brisk style befitting a modern corporate military executive, he set forth a "plan" involving a procession of surprisingly detailed steps, all neatly packaged in four phases. In November 1967, he found the U.S. war effort moving nicely into phase three "when the end begins to come into view."

At a press conference the same week, the President, in response to a question as to why there was so much confusion, frustration, and division in the country concerning Vietnam, wrapped the cloak of history about him and replied, "I don't need to remind you of what happened in the Civil War. People were here in the White House begging Lincoln to concede and to work out a deal with the Confederacy when word came of his victories. . . . I think you know what Roosevelt went through, and President Wilson in World War I. . . . We are going to have this criticism. We are going to have this difference. . . . No one likes war. All people love peace. But you can't have freedom without defending it . . . We are going to do whatever it is necessary to do to see that the aggressor does not succeed."

The *Washington Post* later described this major effort as "nine days of statistics old and new, of intelligence estimates revised and unrevised, of prediction, evaluation, opinion, conjecture, fact, rumor and logic . . . it was the Administration's most ambitious public relations campaign to date, an adroit hard sell." Most observers thought the net effect was to strengthen the hand of the hawks in both the Administration

102

and the Congress. The President had reaffirmed beyond doubt his determination to drive the Great Leviathan through turbulent waters to ultimate victory—whatever the cost—counting on the tested formulae of other embattled War Leaders: warnings of blood, sweat, and tears coupled with the promise of certain, if distant, victory. The air was suddenly thick with indications of a greater military effort. Joseph Kraft wrote that "once again Washington is going through the familiar, tell-tale agony which precedes a decision to escalate the war in Vietnam."

The bombing campaign was immediately stepped up, featuring heavier attacks against the Hanoi-Haiphong complex. One report from a diplomatic observer in the North Vietnamese capital said: "For the past four days, Hanoi has experienced an almost uninterrupted series of alerts, bomb explosions, antiaircraft barrages, falling planes and missile bursts." The seaport city of Haiphong had been struck for the first time on November 15, and a "doughnut campaign" against that target area was now pursued. Eighty percent of North Vietnam's seaborne imports entered through Haiphong harbor, and intelligence indicated that the civilian population of the port city had long since been evacuated. The aim of the "doughnut campaign" was to cut the bridges and rail lines leading inland, and then destroy the besieged stockpiles of supplies burgeoning in the streets, parks, and other public places, but without striking close enough to the dock area to risk hitting Soviet shipping. Those who believed North Vietnam could be bombed to the conference table had long considered Haiphong the single most important target in North Vietnam, and the President's decision, although it fell well short of an authorization to attack the shipping itself, represented a definite intention to increase the military pressure. The campaign was pressed for a short time with naval carrier aircraft; then for reasons never quite clear to Washington, it was quietly dropped. Perhaps Admiral Sharp had developed higher priorities, or the aircraft loss rate proved too high, or the weather turned too bad. Whatever the reason, the campaign died away inconclusively after a few weeks.

The Administration's special effort to fortify the faithful and reassure the country suffered a similar fate. After a brief rise, the President's poll ratings fell again, and the glum, unchanging realities of the war seemed only to deepen the national divisions. The press and public appeared to be seeking firmer answers and predictions than they had got. Senator Hartke of Indiana said, "With due respect to General Westmoreland, more people have been killed in Vietnam while he was here telling us about the great victories in that war." There was a rising complaint that the President "seemed to be responsible to nobody," that out of blind pride, willful stubbornness, and a misplaced concern for the national prestige, he was arbitrarily pressing the war beyond the bounds of reason and the country's tolerance. The *Saturday Evening Post* said editorially, "The war in Vietnam is Johnson's mistake and, through the power of his office, he has made it a national mistake. More and more Americans have come to see this; that is the message of the polls that the President now ignores." On November 30, Senator Eugene McCarthy announced his decision to challenge the President for the Democratic nomination, saying, "I am concerned that the Administration seems to have set no limit on the price it is willing to pay for a military victory."

It was a moment of deepening trouble. No doubt a majority of the country wanted to stand behind their chosen leaders and their fighting men, as in all times past. But what seemed to prevent this response was the pervasive sense, boring through the smog of irreconcilable statistics, that the official assessments did not add up, that the leaders had either badly miscalculated or were not leveling with the people, or both—that something was fundamentally wrong.

The central question at issue was "are we really winning the war and is military victory really possible?" The judgments of the senior U.S. representatives in Vietnam, the men who were running the war, who were in daily touch with the strengths and weaknesses of the situation, could hardly be dismissed out of hand. They were honest men, and they had marshalled their arguments with some coherence and force. Fact and impression were interwoven in the rich-textured fabric of their careful optimism. Yet as November passed into December, a wide variety of source materials both official and unofficial, including political reports, intelligence studies, prisoner interrogations, scholarly articles, and the oral reflections of first-hand observers began to cast serious doubt on almost every critical point in the official assessment.

For one thing, the manpower situation in North Vietnam indicated neither imminent nor ultimate success for Westmoreland's strategy of attrition. Within a total population of about 19 million, there were 4 million males in the 15–49 age group, of whom about 2 million were physically fit for military service; there were probably 1.2 million fit males in the 17–35 age group, considered prime for military service. Probably not more than 25 percent of the larger group nor more than 40 percent of the prime group had as yet been inducted into the armed forces; moreover, this manpower pool was augmented by at least 200,000 physically fit seventeen-year-olds each year. The regular armed forces of North Vietnam had been increased from about 250,000 in 1965 to perhaps 470,000 at the end of 1967, but only 55,000 had been sent to South Vietnam and another 18,000 to Laos.

The NVN regulars plus the Viet Cong main forces in the South numbered about 118,000, supplemented by a purely guerrilla force of perhaps 75,000 and administrative support units (including "political-motivational" elements) of another 40,000. Although the estimates were extremely rough, it thus appeared that the enemy's total military-political strength in the South approximated 235,000 men, of which less than a quarter were regular troops of North Vietnam. Moreover, attesting to a faith in its future viability, Hanoi continued to send several thousands of young men abroad each year for technical and other educational training. (In round numbers, the combined U.S.-ARVN forces totaled 1.2 million, supplemented by 65,000 troops from Korea, Thailand, Australia, New Zealand, and the Philippines.)

The bombing had inflicted heavy damage and strain on NVN's economy and society as a whole—perhaps $400 million in measurable destruction and the diversion of 300,000 people to air defense, road repair, and transporting supplies to the South. But Russia and China had more than made good the material losses, providing perhaps $1.6 billion in military and economic aid (or about four times the estimated bomb damage) since 1965, with the greatest gain being in the quantity and quality of military equipment. Of the total, Russia supplied about 75 percent of the value, including almost all of the modern equipment; China supplied mostly food and small arms. The diversion of several hundred thousand people from normal economic tasks was an undoubted social and administrative strain, but there was thought to be considerable slack in NVN's primitive agricultural economy, particularly with China supplying an increasing part of the food requirements. This situation suggested that the actual cost of the manpower diversions was in fact quite small. An underemployed coolie labor force, subject to the harsh discipline of an authoritarian regime in wartime, could be moved from place to place at will and at a cost to the regime of little more than rice rations and minimal shelter. Moreover, certain supply and engineering tasks were being performed by a few thousand Chinese labor troops stationed in North Vietnam. They could no doubt be increased, although that would present a political problem that Hanoi would surely prefer to avoid.

In the four months since the Stennis Committee's call for heavier bombing of the North, almost every one of the remaining targets of military and economic significance (except a few points in Hanoi and the dock and harbor areas at Haiphong) had been struck and restruck. About 55,000 sorties had been flown and 100,000 added tons of ordnance dropped on North Vietnam during the period, yet the sustained intensity of the new effort had made no measurable impact on Hanoi's ability or determination to support military operations in the South. The fact had to be faced that enemy forces in South Vietnam were at least four times larger than when the bombing started in 1965; moreover, they possessed more and better weapons and equipment of all kinds (especially automatic rifles, large mortars, rockets, trucks, and communications gear). The bombing had enlarged NVN's already versatile transportation system by stimulating the construction of new roads, bridges, and barge routes, and by increasing the number of supply depots while reducing their average size.

On the point of NVN determination to fight on, evidence suggested that the bombing had re-created in Hanoi something rather like the spirit of London during the 1940–41 Blitz. A society under siege was being drawn closer together by a clear and present danger in ways that emphasized common interests and subordinated factional differences and grievances. A psychological climate was being created in which the government in charge could extend and reinforce tough decrees by effective appeals to the patriotism, loyalty, and readiness for sacrifice of all citizens. The bombing seemed to be strengthening the social fabric of North Vietnam. Unlike the situation in Saigon, Hanoi seemed to be free of labor absenteeeism, draft dodging, black market operations, and prostitution (all of which were later reported in evidence and on the rise following the partial bombing halt of March 1968 and the complete cessation in October 1968). Moreover, the sustained nature of the bombing inspired ingenious approaches to the problems of protecting people, transporting goods, and supporting the war effort in the South.

Diligent study of these factors made it difficult to avoid certain conclusions: that (1) available NVN manpower was for practical purposes inexhaustible; (2) Russian and Chinese supply of weapons, equipment, and food had made good the material losses caused by both the bombing in the North and the fighting in the South; (3) such supply was contributing to a measurable strengthening of NVN military power; (4) Russia and China could maintain the present level of material support, and Russia could provide even more sophisticated weapons; (5) the bombing had neither stopped nor slowed down the rate of infiltration; (6) in the circumstances, the rate of infiltration seemed to be a matter within Hanoi's control within broad limits, i.e., the spigot could be opened up or cut back within a range of "effort levels" chosen by NVN; (7) the important constraints on infiltration were not factors in the North (e.g., limits on manpower, supplies, trucks), but rather factors in the South, especially the limited capacity of the VC infrastructure to accept, distribute, and manage additional troops and supplies.

Unless such conclusions were seriously in error, the United States was not winning the war in the final months of 1967, even slowly and gradually. Moreover, if the intangibles of political reaction in the United States were added to these essentially quantitative measurements, e.g., reaction to American casualties, to the war's cost, to world opinion, I thought the reasonable result was to reinforce the basic judgment by a factor of at least 2. For example, what Westmoreland regarded as an optimistic prognosis seemed to involve domestic strains that the American people were unlikely to be willing to bear. Westmoreland was saying we were in for at least two more years (and possibly more) of large-scale battles with the North Vietnamese main force units, to which would have to be added "several years" of mopping up. At the 1967 casualty rate of about 9,000 killed and about 60,000 wounded, this suggested that we faced a minimum of another 18,000 American dead plus 120,000 wounded before ARVN could "conceivably" begin to take up the slack (the record turned out to be 15,000 U.S. dead and 92,000 wounded in 1968, plus 6,300 dead and 55,000 wounded in the first six months of 1969). This was the Westmoreland plan. It contained no hint of negotiated settlement. Yet the Administration was operating on the unspoken assumption that the American people would stay the course and pay whatever the price turned out to be, and that it was clearly in the national interest that they do so.

Beyond the question of whether the United States was winning the war stood a more fateful, less quantifiable one: "*Can* we win the war?" Or stated conversely: "Will Moscow and Peking allow North Vietnam's insurgency to be totally defeated?" Suppose the American optimists were not deluded, suppose the great size and weight of the U.S. effort really began to break up the enemy's cohesion, suppose NVN really started to lose the war. What then? Would Moscow or Peking stand by and accept a clear-cut American victory in South Vietnam? I thought that, within broad limits, the answer was rather clearly no. Moscow might not fully relish the role into which it had been thrust, and Peking was on record as insisting that each country must fight its own national-liberation war with, at most, encouragement from China. Yet neither could wholly ignore the fact that Ho Chi Minh and his colleagues, in their efforts to gain material and political support from other Communist countries, had dramatized themselves as the cutting edge of Communist world revolution. (General Giap was, for example, on record as having said, in the "reverse-English" style of the Communist dialectic, "South Vietnam is the model of the National Liberation Movement in our time. If the special warfare that the United States imperialists are testing in South Vietnam is overcome, this means it can be defeated everywhere in the world.") The Communist movement was in fact badly splintered and its ideology was a broken Humpty-Dumpty that could probably never be put together again. Still, there was a felt need to preserve appearances in revolutionary situations. Both Russia and China had to recognize that their own zeal for the revolutionary cause was being tested under conditions of public scrutiny.

I doubted very much whether Moscow would allow events to get so out of control that its choices were narrowed down to a direct military intervention in order to save the Hanoi regime. Conceivably this could happen if the U.S. invaded North Vietnam. Neither did there seem a great likelihood of direct Chinese intervention, unless the U.S. invaded North Vietnam. But major military intervention was, in any event, a final choice at the end of a rather long flight of stairs. What gave the question, "Can we win?" such relevance and cogency was the abundant evidence that Moscow and Peking could take many steps short of confrontation with the United States that would, in all probability, continue to frustrate our stated objectives. It was clear that they could continue to sustain Hanoi at about the present level of hostilities without undue strain. In addition, the Soviets could provide more sophisticated weapons, as well as more trucks, railroad cars, and barges; China could provide more labor troops or coastal defense forces, either of which would permit Hanoi to send larger regular NVN forces to the South. If past experience was a useful reference, such measures would neutralize those U.S. advantages that the optimists assumed were developing. They would raise the level of the war's intensity, cost, and casualties; they would re-establish the condition of stalemate. Moreover, to achieve these results, NVN need not win large battles; it would be enough to force the U.S. to fight and take casualties.

The official optimism in Washington and Saigon thus appeared to leave out of account a heavy platter of unpalatable facts.

The final month of 1967 also brought forth two notable reports from informed, independent, extra-governmental groups who sought to modify and moderate what seemed to them the extremist tendencies of the Administration's Vietnam policy. They did not seek to repudiate the commitment in Vietnam, but rather to restore to it a sense of proportion.

On December 12, a group of scholars and former government officials centered on the Carnegie Endowment for International Peace (including General Matthew Ridgway, former UN Commander in Korea, Army Chief of Staff and NATO Commander; Roger Hilsman, former Assistant Secretary of State for Far Eastern Affairs; Charles Yost, former U.S. Ambassador to Laos; Marshall Shulman, Director of the Russian Institute at Columbia; George Kistiakowsky, former Special Assistant to President Eisenhower for Science and Technology; Adam Yarmolinsky, former Deputy Assistant Secretary of Defense for International Security Affairs; and Harding F. Bancroft, Executive Vice-President of the *New York Times*) produced a short paper, known as the "Bermuda Statement," [10] intended for the private consideration of the highest U.S. officials. Publicity was deliberately spurned on the sound tactical theory that Lyndon Johnson's rationality quotient was higher if he didn't consider that he was being pressured. Inevitably, however, the paper leaked. Noting that "There now appears to be serious danger that the momentum of the Vietnam conflict may carry hostilities to disproportionate and even perilous levels," the paper urged the United States to modify its strategy "so that it can defend South Vietnam without surrender and without increasing the risks of a wider war." It emphasized that "United States policy should not be dependent on Hanoi's decisions."

The group urged U.S. action in four areas: (1) Make every effort to reduce violence in the South to levels at which a sustained effort can be maintained with the support of both

111

the American and Vietnamese people. "The emphasis should not be on the military destruction of communist forces in the South, but on the protection of the people of South Vietnam and the stabilization of the situation at a politically tolerable level." (2) Stop the bombing of North Vietnam unconditionally, a step that "should not be made contingent upon an immediate military *quid pro quo* nor taken in the expectation that it would lead to early negotiations." (3) Press the GVN "to assume greater and greater responsibility, both political and military, for the defense and pacification of the country." And (4) recognize the National Liberation Front as "an organized factor in the political life of South Vietnam" because the risks of such recognition are "less than the risks for the United States of persisting in an infinitely prolonged attempt to destroy the NLF or to exclude it by American military force."

On December 20, fourteen "moderate" American scholars issued a long statement on Asia as a whole.[11] Through it they expressed the conviction that "the decision of the United States to maintain a presence in Southeast Asia has been of crucial importance," and indirectly they credited the U.S. effort in Vietnam with giving the Indonesian military leaders the confidence to depose Sukarno and the opportunity to destroy the Indonesian Communist Party without serious interference from China. They said that U.S. withdrawal from Vietnam under conditions of Communist victory would be "disastrous for free people everywhere," but that an escalation of the war into a regional or global conflict would be "equally ruinous." Their principal advice to the Administration was couched in these words: Vietnam is "a crucial test of whether we can stay the course with a limited war involving extremely important but limited objectives. It is a part of the broader test of whether in this nuclear age we have the wisdom, maturity, and patience to avoid totalistic policies. . . . Nothing would do more to strengthen American support for our basic position than to show a capacity for innovation of a de-escalatory nature, indicating that there is no inevitable progression upwards in the scope of the conflict."

THE LONE RANGER

The President was made aware of these studies, but they appeared to have little effect. Buoyed by the stream of glad tidings coming from his advisers, he seemed also temperamentally incapable of admitting error. Playing the role with a kind of heavy gusto, he was the Lone Ranger—embattled in the cause of freedom and justice which, being absolute virtues, must be pursued without allowing the doubts of timid men to circumscribe the grandeur of one's methods. Stubborn and bellicose, he plunged ahead. On December 4, he lashed out at critics who "are looking for fire escapes and ways out," which, he said, was what people had done in Mussolini and Hitler's time. On December 8, he announced that 10,000 additional Army troops for Vietnam would be swiftly airlifted from Fort Campbell, Kentucky. This represented an acceleration of the scheduled buildup, and the President was personally on hand to bid God's speed to the departing troopers. The arrival of these fresh brigades would mark that point at which U.S. forces in Vietnam exceeded the number sent to fight in Korea.

On the bombing of the North, the President remained adamant. A few days before Christmas, on the eve of departure for Canberra to attend the funeral of his friend, Harold Holt, the Australian Prime Minister, he said at a press conference: "We are not going to be so soft-headed and pudding-headed as to say that we will stop our half of the war and hope and pray that they stop theirs. We have tried in some instances . . . every time we have, they have escalated their efforts and they have killed our soldiers. . . . a burned child dreads the fire."

From Australia he flew to Thailand where 50,000 U.S. airmen on seven of the world's most modern air bases were daily carrying the war to North Vietnam. At Korat, he cast into the predawn darkness words of praise that symbolically underlined his determination to continue the bombing. He said, "Through the use of air power, a mere handful of you men—as military forces are really reckoned—are pinning down several hundred thousand—more than half a million—North Vietnamese. You are increasing the cost of infiltration. You are imposing a very high rate of attrition when the enemy is engaged, and you are giving him no rest when he withdraws." The words were a thoroughly deserved tribute to men of high professional competence and exceptional courage; they begged the question whether the mission assigned them was worth the candle.

From Thailand the President moved to Cam Ranh Bay in Vietnam to extend Christmas greetings to the troops. As he later reported it to the American people, "I told them that I wished I could bring them something more—some part of the pride you feel in them, some more tangible symbol of your love and concern for them. . . . I decorated 20 of them for gallantry in action. . . . In the hospital, I spoke with those who bore the wounds of war. You cannot be in such a place, among such men, without feeling grief well up in your throat. . . . That was Christmastime in Vietnam—a time of war, of suffering, of endurance, of bravery and devotion to country."

Having thus struck the strident chord of military determination and the muted note of private anguish, he flew across the world to Rome, for a pre-Christmas audience with the Pope, to pluck the gentle strings of peace. "I had flown thousands of miles from Vietnam to Rome," he reported, "so that I might receive the counsel of this good man—this friend of peace. . . . I wanted to promise him—as I have promised you, my fellow Americans—that the disappointments we had known in the past would not deter us from trying any reasonable route to negotiations. . . . I told His Holiness that America welcomed his efforts to bring an end to the strife and sorrow."

It was a virtuoso performance. He had gone full circle in both geography and policy, and left the U.S. position exactly where it had been—bent upon military victory whatever the cost, if that were necessary to achieve the stated objectives; open to a negotiated settlement on U.S. terms at any time Hanoi wanted to admit it was beaten.

Nineteen sixty-seven thus ended in a strange dissonance of point and counterpoint—official optimism, determination, and blind faith versus unofficial pessimism, disbelief, and a felt need for policy changes. On the distant battlefields of Southeast Asia, no decision was in sight. The enemy was hurting, but was still quite capable of fighting on a large scale—indeed the final months of the year had revealed his ability to coordinate attacks over wider geographical areas. Heavy infiltration continued, and the scale of the ground fighting strained U.S. troop resources. The ARVN's improvement, if any, was something one had to take on faith, as it was impossible to form an independent judgment on the basis of reports reaching Washington. "Yeah," said a tough and skeptical Army colonel newly returned from his second tour of fighting, "they've been improving every year for the past seven years." At the Demilitarized Zone, both sides were bogged down in the cold mud and slush of the winter monsoon. U.S. aircraft carried their death-dealing, inconclusive bomb-loads through leaden winter skies to drop them on targets obscured by rain and fog.

American public opinion, troubled and uneasy, was puzzled by unaccountable disparities in the situation. Here was the country, on the threshold of what ought to have been its most mature and creative period, experiencing self-doubt on an unprecedented scale. Never had America possessed so much power or enjoyed such rich material blessing; never had it been more unsure of its purposes and its goals. Much of the sense of disconnection, alienation, and simple distrust enshrouding the Vietnam war seemed to derive from the irreconcilability of a political policy described as one of strictly limited objectives and a military policy of ever-increasing, apparently unlimited, means.

The President himself, sustained by a shrinking circle of true believers, still seemed confident that his goals and methods would ultimately be vindicated. Yet he was a poignant figure: prideful, bellicose, unpopular, a man who could no longer be certain of a friendly audience except at a military installation; beleaguered by an incredulous press, an alienated youth, and an uneasy general public. Shielded by Rostow, he was probably unaware that his subcabinet group and an influential segment of the foreign-military bureaucracy were increasingly disenchanted with his leadership, frustrated by their own impotence, and incipiently rebellious.

CHAPTER 6

The Strains of January

As 1968 OPENED, the Administration continued to be principally occupied with the problem of holding together domestic support for the war and presenting to the world an image of confidence (an image of composure seemed beyond hope of achievement). A wide range of actions was worked out and pursued, not with programatic planning or cool efficiency, but more in the manner of a distracted mother cat faced with the unending task of keeping her large, squirming, and elusive litter of kittens in the basket. One would slip out; she would run to fetch it; meanwhile two more would get away.

A mixed strategy was employed to mitigate the increasing doubts and complaints. On the one hand, the air war against the North was further intensified to relieve pressure from frustrated Senate hawks, coupled with an implicit assurance that no more troops would be added to the ground war until after the 1968 elections. On the other hand, the GVN was pressed hard to draft into the ARVN the entire layer of young Vietnamese, eighteen to twenty, who were seen nightly on American television riding their motorscooters and drinking at bars in downtown Saigon. Westmoreland announced his expectation that 1968 would see the ARVN carrying a major share of the combat at the Demilitarized Zone, where the fighting had been fiercest and the casualties heaviest during most of 1967. The GVN also began a "new" and highly publicized drive against corrupt officials within its ranks. None of these gestures was particularly novel or convincing; and the suggestion that the GVN was about to move with ruthless efficiency against corruption was transparently incredible. For that deep-seated cancer in the South Vietnamese body politic had long since passed the boundaries of Asian normalcy; it now dominated and paralyzed the whole society, fed by the billions in aid that poured untold quantities of every conceivable commodity into a simple, fragile economic system, and aggravated by the presence of a half million Americans spending money on necessaries and pleasure. ARVN corps commanders typically took a cut on everything in their jurisdictions from important jobs to beer and prostitution; division commanders collected taxes on behalf of absentee landlords, for a substantial percentage; petty functionaries, pressed to the wall by appalling inflation, demanded bribes for the issuance of a driver's license, an import license, or permission to take a job with the Americans.

These moves in Washington seemed to reflect the fatigued minds of Administration officials so long under siege that they had lost the capacity not only to produce fresh and imaginative perspectives, but even to distinguish reality from unreality. Massive doses of optimism continued to pour forth in speeches, briefings, progress reports, and studied leaks to the press. The President continued to see light at the end of the tunnel and, from the deck of an aircraft carrier, predicted "not many more nights of war." But the mood of the country was shifting steadily against the war.

Foreign Minister Trinh of North Vietnam had stated in early 1967 that a U.S. bombing halt "could" bring about negotiations. On December 31 he made a similar statement, but changed the "could" to "would," and this diplomatic signal was underlined by NVN representatives in Paris. It fell to William Bundy, the Assistant Secretary of State for Far Eastern Affairs, to explain why this apparently encouraging shift in the NVN position should be dismissed. Bundy's real convictions about the war remained to the end a carefully guarded enigma, but in the manner of a professional public servant he lent his considerable diplomatic and legal skills to the support and advocacy of the Rusk position. In response to a reporter's question relating to the significance of the Trinh shift, Bundy replied "I'm not sure they are anywhere near the point of being ready to yield." He feared, he said, that the enemy would use a bombing cessation not merely to get talks started but also to strengthen their military position. He thought they would then move the war to a "fighting and negotiating" stage from which only they could benefit. Accordingly, he implied, Hanoi was still too determined and unyielding to justify the risks inherent in a U.S. bombing pause.

Beneath these views, so rational and proportioned on the surface, lay at least three tendentious assumptions. One was that the bombing was really preventing the enemy from supplying his forces in the South at a level determined by him; a second was that the enemy's continued resupply of his forces during a bombing halt would be flagrantly unreasonable, whereas our resupply of U.S. and ARVN forces would be reasonable; a third was the implicit belief that a steadfast pursuit of the present U.S. course would bring the military situation to a point at which the enemy *would* be ready to yield, following which negotiations could proceed favorably because they would amount essentially to the ratification of his surrender.

THE DILEMMA OF LIMITED OBJECTIVES

There was almost universal agreement that a bombing halt was the key to a negotiated settlement of the war, but to state that premise was merely to open Pandora's box. The U.S. military leadership was absolutely against it on the grounds that, by facilitating the flow of enemy supplies to the battlefield, it would lead to heavier American casualties. The argument was tenuous, but it achieved powerful emotional and political resonance among Senate hawks and those elements in the country who are life members of the There-is-No-Substitute-for-Victory Association. On the other hand, there were strong arguments in support of a halt. One was the evidence that military victory in Vietnam was no more than a tenacious illusion, and that the consequences of continuing to press for it included the gravest social and political cleavages at home and in our other alliance relationships.

There was a growing general fear that frustration and disillusion in Vietnam would lead the American people into a new period of irresponsible isolationism characterized not alone by a lack of enthusiasm for military interventions, but by a general indifference to the fate of struggling young nations everywhere. It was curious how the views of hawks and doves converged around this point of the war's ultimate effect on the country and on world opinion. The hawks perceived that a failure to stay the course in Vietnam would, by eroding America's faith in freedom and in itself, lead to a repudiation of commitments elsewhere, to isolationism, and finally to unopposed Communist expansion. The doves perceived that further pursuit of military victory (assuming it did not produce general nuclear war) would lead to deeper frustration, followed by repudiation of the war policy, disorderly pullout from Vietnam, and lapse into mindless isolationism. In the one case, our friends and allies would be frightened into neutrality by a loss of confidence in America's courage, steady purpose, and capacity for leadership; in the other, by an unrestrained American imperialism.

The root difficulty about a serious bombing halt seemed to lie in Hanoi's adamant insistence that the bombing had to be stopped "unconditionally" before it would come to the conference table. Much effort over a long period of time had been applied to ascertaining just how hard Hanoi's position was on that point. Of particular interest and significance had been the Ashmore-Baggs mission of January 1967. These two

American journalists, traveling to Hanoi to seek North Vietnam's participation in a conference at Geneva called "Pacem in Terris II," sponsored by the Center for the Study of Democratic Institutions, were encouraged by the State Department to sound out the NVN leaders on the prospects for serious negotiations. In private talks with Ho Chi Minh, they discerned that Hanoi might be willing to restrain the buildup and resupply of its forces in the South if the U.S. stopped the bombing and also ceased introducing additional U.S. troops. It appeared that a secret contact might be made to arrange reciprocal restraints with respect to the question of additional troops and supplies, *before* a bombing halt actually took effect. Based on these favorable soundings and the close consideration of them in the State Department, Ashmore and Baggs wrote a letter to Ho Chi Minh in early February 1967, expressing the serious interest of "senior officials of the State Department" and emphasizing that "the U.S. remains prepared for secret discussions at any time, without conditions...." The letter went on to say "They [the senior officials] expressed particular interest in your suggestion that private talks could begin provided the U.S. stopped bombing your country and ceased introducing additional U.S. troops into Vietnam. They expressed the opinion that some reciprocal restraint to indicate that neither side intended to use the occasion of the talks for military advantage would provide tangible evidence of the good faith of all parties ... they expressed great interest in any clarification of this point that you might wish to provide through a communication to us." [12] With the knowledge and approval of Katzenbach, Harriman, and William Bundy, the letter was dispatched from Washington via Moscow on February 2.

British Prime Minister Wilson was concurrently persuaded to take advantage of a scheduled London visit by Kosygin to pursue the prospect of Vietnam talks. To guard against any misunderstanding of the U.S. position, Chester Cooper, an expert on Vietnam and a principal assistant to Harriman, was dispatched to London on February 6 to brief Wilson. He presented a "Phase A–Phase B" scenario. Under Phase A, the U.S. would *announce* a bombing halt, but this would not take effect until Phase B talks had been held to arrange a mutual de-escalation of the ground war. The U.S. would however have taken the "first step" by the public announcement that it had stopped the bombing. Wilson laid out the A–B proposal to Kosygin who responded that North Vietnam "would" come to the conference table if the bombing were stopped. He repeated this remark on British television on February 9. For a brief moment, hopes were raised throughout the world.

But the White House had had second thoughts. Though the President had told a press conference on February 2 that "just about any step" by North Vietnam could produce a cessation of the bombing, Rusk briskly dismissed the Kosygin statement as part of "a systematic campaign by the Communist side" to generate pressure for a bombing halt without even "elementary reciprocity." In a far more categorical act, the President dispatched a hard letter of his own to Ho Chi Minh, reversing the Phase A–Phase B scenario and thus of course both destroying the Ashmore-Baggs effort and profoundly embarrassing the British Prime Minister. The U.S. could not, he wrote, take the first step while merely hoping that mutual de-escalation on the ground could then be worked out. Hanoi had to act first. Talks could begin "as soon as I am assured that infiltration into South Vietnam by land and by sea has stopped." It was a letter guaranteed to produce a resoundingly negative response, and Ho Chi Minh promptly released it to the public together with his own contemptuous reply which said in part, "The Vietnamese will . . . never accept talks under the threat of bombs."

Ashmore later wrote that "this conciliatory feeler was effectively and brutally canceled before there was any chance to determine what response Hanoi might have made. . . ." He and Baggs both charged the State Department with double dealing. My own impression was that the incident merely served to illuminate the fundamental split in the U.S. government on our national objectives and policy in Vietnam. Katzenbach, Harriman, and Bundy had given encouragement to the Ashmore-Baggs mission and to the related effort in London. However, when it began to look as though the effort might succeed, as though talks might really begin and the U.S. might really have to stop the bombing, it got too close to the bone for Rusk and Rostow and they moved to quash it, relying on their positional advantage with the President, on his strong visceral preference for "nailing the coonskin to the wall," and on his known reflexive susceptibility to suggestions that some canny Communist was trying to pull the wool over his eyes.

Six months later, in the autumn of 1967, President Johnson had once again swung the pendulum back toward a more moderate public approach to negotiations. In the course of a long speech, delivered in Texas and devoted to a review of the war, he asserted the U.S. willingness to stop all air and naval bombardment of North Vietnam "when this will lead promptly to productive discussion." He then set out the famous noncondition that was to become known as the "San Antonio formula." He said, "We of course assume that, while discussions proceed, North Vietnam would not take advantage of the bombing cessation or limitation." While this seemed a hopeful augury, there were soon evidences of hard U.S. probing to find out precisely how Hanoi would respond, which indicated something less than a genuine willingness to "assume" no trickery until it was proved after the fact of a bombing halt. But Hanoi was wary and evasive, and Rusk continued to spread upon the record the sort of statements that seemed calculated to chill the prospects. He said, for example, in early October, "I have yet to hear anyone tell us that if we did stop the bombing they could definitely deliver Hanoi to the conference table. I have asked a number of governments, 'All right, if we stop the bombing, what can you deliver?' I get no response."

Clark Clifford, at that time a private citizen who had just returned from a mission to Asia for President Johnson, was encouraged by the San Antonio formula, which seemed to him an honorable way to de-escalate the war and get talks started. He was however "greatly depressed" by the subsequent official interpretations, for these seemed to insist that North Vietnam must stop *all* resupply of its forces in the South before the U.S. would judge that Hanoi was "not taking advantage" of a bombing halt. Such a position seemed unreasonable to Clifford and calculated to produce a negative response from Hanoi. In his confirmation hearing before the Senate Armed Services Committee in January 1968, Clifford ventured his own interpretation of the San Antonio formula. He said that Washington would not consider that Hanoi was exploiting a bombing halt if it continued a "normal" resupply. He took this position entirely on his own authority without consulting anyone. His statement caused a serious flap at both State and the White House, but after two days the President decided to avoid a public difference with a new Cabinet officer and publicly endorsed the Clifford interpretation. There was to be in the months ahead further evidence of Clifford's strength of purpose and independence of mind.

In fact, the fundamental aversion of the hardliners to a bombing halt and to any negotiations in 1967 (and later) derived from the coldly perceived reality that achievement of our "limited objectives" in Vietnam depended upon a clear-cut military victory. For the nation's purposes, as these men had defined them, admitted of no compromise with the enemies of the Thieu-Ky government, but instead required a total frustration of the purposes of Hanoi and the Viet Cong. Progressively committed, by a combination of misguided ideological zeal and careless perception of the national interest, to the preservation and anchoring of a narrowly

124

based government in the South, which could not survive without a large-scale U.S. military presence, whose constitution ruled out all political participation by the main adversary, and which was diligently throwing in jail even those non-Communists who advocated opening a dialogue with the National Liberation Front, President Johnson and his close advisers had become squarely impaled on a central dilemma: the basic U.S. rationale for the war turned on "limited means," "limited objectives," and "honorable negotiations"; moreover, the maintenance of minimal support for the war at home and in the world community required the firmest adherence to that posture. But to move in fact toward serious negotiations and political settlement while the Viet Cong remained even a residual military-political power in the South required acceptance of compromise. In this context, compromise could only mean some Communist participation in the government. But that seemed to risk Communist takeover, which in turn threatened to undermine the "free choice" for South Vietnam to which the United States had committed itself and for which Americans had died in significant numbers since 1965. (As Rusk had put it in 1966, "If the Viet Cong come to the conference table as full partners, they will in a sense have been victorious in the very aims that South Vietnam and the United States are pledged to prevent.")

In short, President Johnson and his close advisers had so defined our national purposes and so conducted the war that a compromise political settlement would be tantamount to a resounding defeat for U.S. policy and prestige. Accordingly, it could not be faced. Military victory was the only way out, unless some sudden, miraculous *deus ex machina* could infuse the Thieu-Ky group with the necessary vigor, competence, and popularity to stand alone. Small wonder that in moments of crunch the President's men shied away from negotiations as "premature," and fell back upon a resolute pressing of the military struggle as the only hope for their deliverance.

Bundy's dismissal of the Trinh signal reflected the Administration's strong tendency to feel and to present the war as fundamentally a test of wills. In his State of the Union Message of January 17, the President said of Vietnam, "it is our will that is being tried not our strength... the enemy has been defeated in battle after battle." This theory rested on the assumption that the United States, being by far the stronger party, must surely win in the end, provided only that the American people stayed the course. It argued that the North Vietnamese were in fact already beaten, but continued to fight on chiefly because Hanoi perceived weakness of purpose in America. General Wheeler said at this time, "The single most important factor in prolonging the war is Hanoi's calculation that there is a reasonable possibility of change in U.S. policy before the ultimate collapse of the Viet Cong manpower base and infrastructure.... We are winning the war in Vietnam, but Hanoi is still not ready to give up—the major campaign of the war is being fought here in the United States."

It was mildly astonishing to me that the inner group's assessment could be so consistently wide of the mark, but this fallacy, as so much else, flowed from the Rusk-Rostow view that the war in Vietnam was for Communism a global testing of the liberation-war doctrine, and therefore had to become for the U.S. the war to end all wars of national liberation. Within that context it was vital to disabuse Asian Communists, once and for all, of any notion that the United States was indecisive or unwilling to make a total effort to defeat them, at any time or place. But this view seemed to obscure the truth that was right under our noses. North Vietnam was fighting *primarily* to achieve an unfulfilled national purpose. While it was, to be sure, fully aware of the implications for the wider application of the Mao-Ho-Giap insurgency doctrine, it was fighting not an abstractly ideological war, but a very particular war—in a particular place, characterized by a particular kind of terrain and weather, peopled by a particular breed of men and, above all, conditioned by a particular history. What really drove Ho's sacrificial legions was not the dream of world conquest, nor even the notion of generating a new momentum for Communist advance and triumph throughout Asia. What motivated Hanoi and enabled its leadership to hold 19 million primitive people to endless struggle and sacrifice against odds that were statistically ludicrous was the goal of national independence. That goal, almost gained at the end of World War II, had been callously denied by an absentminded U.S. acquiescence in the return of French military forces and French colonial interests; almost gained again in 1954 after a grim, protracted war of attrition against the French, it had been frustrated once more by John Foster Dulles, SEATO, and the willingness of all the Great Powers, including Russia, to look the other way when Diem refused to hold the promised all-Vietnam elections in 1956; almost won a third time in 1964–65, it had been denied yet again by large-scale U.S. military intervention.

National aspiration was the historical imperative that explained Ho Chi Minh. The international Communist overtones were real enough, but secondary. Maintaining a broad base of support for the war over several decades; instilling the Army cadres with tenacity, ingenuity, and readiness for sacrifice in the face of enormous odds; nurturing resiliency in the face of repeated disappointment; reorganizing the economy and distribution system under the heavy pressure of U.S. bombing—in short, defeating one renowned military power and holding at bay the most powerful nation in the world—these were achievements which, viewed objectively, would cause Ho Chi Minh to go down in history as an extraordinary leader. But they were explainable primarily in terms of nationalism; ideology was a fuel of insufficient octane rating. But if nationalism was the principal driving force, it followed that the war in Vietnam was not a test of wills between two parties—Hanoi and Washington—with equal interests at stake. For North Vietnam it was a fundamental struggle, the priority task that embraced all others, a matter of survival. To the United States, it was far more peripheral, necessarily competing for attention and resources with the other manifold interests and commitments of a global power. Yet this was a fact of life which neither the President nor his inner advisers seemed to understand.

There was also something deeper in the Administration's misunderstanding—an unexamined assumption buried at the very center of the theory of deterrence and graduated military response as applied to Asia: namely, that we and the North Vietnamese shared a common understanding of what constitutes victory and defeat. As William Pfaff of the Hudson Institute had perceptively noted, both sides in World Wars I and II understood what it would take to bring the fighting to an end; victory and defeat were similarly defined by Nazis, Western democrats, and Russian Communists. But in Vietnam both we and the enemy were prone to claim victory in the same battles, and this seemed not the result of mere propaganda; rather, it seemed to derive from the reality that each side was fighting in the context of a quite separate set of values and expectations.

The strategy of the strong, as Pfaff noted, confronts the strategy of the weak. We use firepower and wealth to achieve impersonal objectives: democracy, liberal government, the containment of Communism. The enemy practices defiant and personalized violence, stoically accepting the destruction of wealth and the loss of lives. We believe the enemy can be forced to be "reasonable," i.e., to compromise or even capitulate, because we assume he wants to avoid pain, death, and material destruction. We assume that if these are inflicted on him with increasing severity, then at some point in the process he will want to stop the suffering. Ours is a plausible strategy —for those who are rich, who love life and fear pain. But happiness, wealth, and power are expectations that constitute a dimension far beyond the experience, and probably beyond the emotional comprehension, of the Asian poor. For them there may be little difference between the condition of death and the condition of unrelieved suffering in life. Indeed the Buddhist belief in reincarnation tends to create a positive impetus toward honorable death because the faithful discharge of moral and civic duties in this life are the understood passports to a higher station, greater comfort, and less suffering when one next returns to earth. And it is through such a series of trials on earth that the soul makes its slow and painful advance toward eventual unity with God.

The strategy of the weak is therefore the natural choice of ideologues in Asia, for it converts Asia's capacity for endurance in suffering into an instrument for exploiting a basic vulnerability of the Christian West. It does this, in effect, by inviting the West, which possesses unanswerable military power, to carry its strategic logic to the final conclusion, which is genocide. We project on Asians our own values; we believe the threat of steadily enlarged destruction will force them to seek a "reasonable" end to the war. But the weak defy us by a readiness to struggle, suffer, and die on a scale that seems to us beyond the bounds of humanity. Prisoner interrogations repeatedly revealed this phenomenon. An NVN officer, or a half-naked, ill-fed Viet Cong, would be asked what would happen if, contrary to the assurances of his leaders, the Americans continued to come endlessly, in ever-increasing numbers, bearing heavier artillery and bigger bombs. The answer very often was fatalistic and unimpassioned: "Then we will all die." Such defiance forces the West to confront the necessity of carrying out the threat of ultimate escalation: to bomb them into the stone age. At that point we hesitate, for, remembering Hitler and Hiroshima and Nagasaki, we realize anew that genocide is a terrible burden to bear.

Sir Robert Thompson said in January, "Now obviously

withdrawal means losing, but massive escalation equally means losing. If I may put it very bluntly, it would mean losing stinking. . . . If you escalate massively, it would mean that the rest of the world would want to have very little to do with you as a people. And I think that, quite possibly, the U.S. as a result of all this would have lost its soul and would tear itself apart."

It was my impression that these inner truths tugged at Americans on at least two levels—their sense of morality and their sense of the practical. The fact that the killing in Vietnam was growing steadily larger in scale, more efficient, more impersonal, more remote from any connection with meaningful political objectives was an increasing source of moral unease. Also, there was wider acceptance of the fact that the U.S. performance appeared ruthlessly imperialistic to many of America's friends in other parts of the world, and that this reaction was tarnishing our national reputation for justice and restraint, which was judged (when it seemed in jeopardy) to be a highly valued heritage. On the practical side, if there was no real prospect of sharing with the enemy an understanding of what constituted victory or defeat, then there was no logical point at which the war and the killing would stop—particularly not if Russia and China continued to provide a steady flow of food and guns. Moreover, it was beginning to be recognized that the marginal utility of destructive action diminishes, both psychologically and practically, as more destruction is carried out. The enemy has less and less to lose by fighting on, as the lessons of Britain in 1940 and of Germany in 1945 should have taught us.

THE BOMBING-CASUALTIES LINKAGE

The dilemma of the bombing remained at the forefront of the war debate in official circles and in the press. The Bermuda Statement and the Report of the Fourteen Asian Scholars had reinforced the arguments of the moderates, and to these was added on January 16 a public report by the

Citizen's Committee for Peace and Freedom in Vietnam. Its membership comprised an impressive array of names, including former presidents Truman and Eisenhower, General Omar Bradley, and Dr. James B. Conant. Some of them were notable hawks. But in a paper entitled "Balance Sheet on the Bombing," they came down firmly on the limited efficacy of that effort, and were quite clear about its importance relative to the conflict in the South. They said in pertinent part:

> We disagree with those who call for a sharp or unlimited escalation of our air attacks in the North. . . . Bombing of the North can hinder but cannot prevent the enemy from securing supplies from China and Russia and infiltrating some of them into the South. Bombing can impede but not prevent the infiltration of men. Nor is bombing alone the way to break the will of North Vietnam. . . . The war cannot be won from the air in the North; it can be lost on the ground in the South.

Using this new report as a point of departure, I sent McNamara a memorandum on January 18. It was in part a renewed argument for a bombing halt, citing both the Citizen's Committee report and the December statements as reflections of "a growing, informed awareness that the bombing campaign is making, at best, a marginal contribution to the war effort—an awareness not confined to careful students of military affairs, but shared in varying degrees of explicitness and certainty by journalists, diplomats, and leading citizens of many countries." McNamara was of course familiar with this argument and agreed with it. My primary purpose, however, was to illuminate the invidious political linkage that had been allowed to develop between the level of the U.S. bombing effort in the North and the level of U.S. casualties in the South. Admiral Sharp, who ran the air war against the North from Honolulu, held the view that there was an actual linkage. In mid-January, the senior Marine commander in Vietnam told the press in categorical terms, "There is a direct relationship between the number of American troops killed and the bombing—there is no argument about that. When the bombing stops, more Americans are killed." (He was referring to the bombing of North Vietnam; no one had ever suggested curtailment of bombing and other air activity in close support of ground forces.) Other military leaders expressed the relationship in some variant of the phrase that a bombing halt would force U.S. troops "to fight with one arm tied behind their backs." The President seemed entirely persuaded by these arguments and was indeed inserting them into speeches and Medal of Honor ceremonies with increasing frequency.

While the idea of linkage possessed an attractive simplicity, any serious analysis showed that the number of Americans killed varied directly with the level of our ground operations in the South and was almost unrelated to our air activity in the North. But so long as the bombing-casualty linkage remained a palpable political fact, it constituted a perhaps insuperable obstacle to a bombing halt under any conditions short of a total cessation of North Vietnamese resupply activities (which was an unrealistic expectation). My memorandum was accordingly aimed at pointing out the fallacy of the linkage and the inflexibility it imposed on our diplomacy. I argued:

There appears to be, in military reality, only the most tenuous relationship between bombing in the North and U.S. casualties in the South. This is the express or implied conclusion of each of the studies and statements cited herein (and of earlier CIA analyses as well). Infiltration has continued at a steady rate through three years of bombing attacks. A bombing halt would relieve pressure on NVN resources, but this would not necessarily lead to increased infiltration, and it might lead to talks. In particular, there is no reason why it would lead to an increase in U.S. casualties. Present U.S. casualty levels in the South are not a function of the bombing attacks against the North. They are a function of the U.S. ground strategy in the South.

A decision to halt the bombing would accordingly seem to require a corollary decision to alter the ground force strategy—away from hyper-aggressive "search and destroy" operations . . . toward what have been called "seize and hold" operations in the populated areas, where the people of South Vietnam actually live. I am aware of the political difficulties. Abandonment of the extreme aspects of the present strategy of attrition would require a more explicit acknowledgement than now exists that military victory is not in the cards; it would require a shift to the task of providing maximum protection to the people of SVN and to that portion of SVN territory that can be brought and held under allied control.

To the charge that such a de-escalatory shift would yield control of large pieces of territory to the Viet Cong, the answer must be that much territory now claimed by the allies is in fact held so fleetingly and superficially as to constitute no control . . . minimal security is an absolute prerequisite of any political and social development; it seems . . . clear that the Westmoreland strategy, given either the present or foreseeable magnitude of U.S. and allied forces, is unlikely to provide this.

My primary purpose is . . . to point out that, owing to the political linkage between the bombing of the North and U.S. casualties in the South, . . . our highly discretionary ground strategy is a major obstacle to a bombing cessation; that, therefore, if the USG * wishes to be free to decide the bombing issue on its merits, it cannot avoid coming to grips, concurrently, with the need to arrest and reduce U.S. casualties through a significant scaling-down of the ground war.

Whether McNamara agreed with these arguments and whether he pressed them with the Joint Chiefs or the President, I do not know. It was not his habit to respond to unsolicited memoranda. Moreover, he had only a month re-

* United States government.

maining of service at the Pentagon and this of course militated against new initiatives.

THE PUEBLO SEIZURE

On January 23, Washington received word that North Korean patrol boats had captured the U.S.S. *Pueblo* with eighty-three crewmen aboard and had forced it into Wonsan Harbor. It was a hammer blow to an Administration already struggling to balance its commitments and resources, and to hold together declining public support for its actions in Vietnam. The initial Congressional reaction was angry. Senator Russell, Chairman of the Senate Armed Services Committee, called the seizure "almost an act of war" and his House counterpart, L. Mendel Rivers, hoped the President "will take all necessary steps to restore this ship to our fleet." Senator Mansfield called the seizure "a clear violation of international law." Senator Fulbright took the opportunity to comment that the American commitment in Vietnam had allowed other countries to move against the U.S. with impunity.

The reasons for the seizure were not entirely clear, but seemed to be connected with a basic North Korean effort to build up a domestic war psychology by increasing the state of tension with South Korea and its United States protector, as a means of carrying out the "lofty national duty to force the U.S. imperialist aggressors out of South Korea." In retrospect, one could see that the government at Pyongyang had given several warnings of a possible seizure. On January 6, North Korean naval ships had moved in on a fleet of seventy South Korean fishing boats and captured five; on January 11, they had intruded upon a group of two hundred South Korean fishing craft and had sunk one by collision. On January 21, two days before the *Pueblo* seizure, North Korea's delegate at Panmunjom formally protested to his American counterpart that the United States had "infiltrated into our coastal waters a number of armed spy boats...together with a group of

South Korean fishing boats." Moreover, just a few days before the *Pueblo* incident, a thirty-one-man North Korean commando team had infiltrated the DMZ and made its way to the very gates of the "Blue House" in Seoul (the official residence of the President of South Korea) for the purpose of assassinating President Park. All members of the commando group were killed or captured, but the incident profoundly shook the South Korean government.

Behind these events lay the curious but important fact that the North Korean premier, Kim Il Sung, was approaching his fifty-eighth birthday. It is a basic tenet of Korean philosophy that a man should accomplish his life's work by the age of sixty, and Kim Il Sung had set himself the ambitious task of unifying Korea. In Seoul, Ambassador Porter and General Bonesteel, Commander of U.S. and United Nations forces in South Korea, took this matter seriously and considered that the next eighteen to twenty-four months could be critical—that is, could be characterized by Kim's willingness to commit rash acts and to run risks of war, even though unsupported by Russia or China. Their assessment was that both Russia and China desired North Korea as a buffer against the northward projection of U.S. power, but that neither was interested in supporting an invasion of South Korea. The two larger powers would accordingly provide money and equipment to maintain a strong buffer, but would act to restrain Kim Il Sung's adventures, recognizing that they might not possess decisive influence. According to Bonesteel, both powers had stated this position of restraint, obliquely but publicly, in their Asian propaganda broadcasts. Porter and Bonesteel accordingly believed that a full-scale invasion was unlikely; what they feared most was a serious North Korean provocation which would trigger a major South Korean response.

The South Korean government was deeply concerned by the *Pueblo* seizure, in part because it coincided with and seemed to reinforce the "Blue House incident." They saw it correctly as an intensification of the hard, cruel subwar of infiltration and subversion that North Korea had been waging against the South—a war marked by almost daily incidents at the DMZ, attempted landings on the southern coast by northern guerrillas, casualties among both South Korean and American troops, and 179 dead infiltrators in 1967. They warned on January 26 that unless the United States took "stern action" to recover the *Pueblo,* either another Korean War would break out, or American leadership in Asia would be seriously threatened. Said Premier Chung Il Kwon, "If the United States does not treat North Korea firmly, the Communists will repeat such incidents, requiring more U.S. sacrifices." All evidence suggested that the seizure had been at North Korean initiative without the knowledge or support of Russia or China. The first comment out of Peking was a cautious statement that "the Chinese people . . . are watching the development of the situation with close attention." The Soviet reaction was equally restrained. These indicators notwithstanding, Rostow opined, on the basis of no visible evidence, that Russia had very probably instructed North Korea to seize the *Pueblo,* and that accordingly our best countermove was to arrange to have South Korea seize a Soviet trawler!

Fortunately, it was painfully clear to others that the U.S. was in no position—politically, psychologically, or militarily— to be drawn into another inconclusive war of murky purposes in Asia. The Administration made two countermoves, both primarily psychological. One was to send a sizable mix of fighter-bombers, interceptors, and reconnaissance aircraft to Korea (about 150 planes) to reassure the South Korean government. This was a buildup accomplished with swiftness and precision by regular squadrons of the Air Force and the Marines. The second move was to call up just short of 15,000 reservists, mostly from the Air Force, primarily to replace the squadrons sent to Korea. To some, the mobilization of reserves called to mind the Tonkin Gulf incident and its aftermath; and there was a suspicion that President Johnson would again use this crisis as an opportunity to obtain a reinforcement of his Congressional mandate with respect to Vietnam. The *Washington Post* observed that the *"Pueblo* affair has given the Administration a comparable justification for tapping the military reserves on a scale which would have been difficult to justify solely in terms of the highly controversial conflict in Vietnam."

But the President made, on January 27, a very low key statement putting the *Pueblo* seizure in the context of North Korean attempts "over the past 15 months" to "interrupt the growing spirit of confidence and progress in the Republic of Korea" and to intimidate the South Koreans. He stated that the "best result would be for the whole world community to persuade North Korea to return our ship and our men. . . ." Later the same day, Ambassador Goldberg made a similar statement in the UN Security Council. It was clear that the United States would not go beyond diplomatic means in its attempts to redress this painful humiliation. The decision was disquieting to the South Korean government, notwithstanding the buildup of tactical air power, and it was later necessary to send Cyrus Vance to hold President Park's hand. The incident itself and the carefully modulated, half-uncertain U.S. response it produced revealed the poignant truth that the country's military, but even more its psychological, resources had been stretched taut and thin by the malaise of the Vietnam involvement.

THE KHESANH SIGNAL

Two days before the *Pueblo* seizure, an event in the central highlands of South Vietnam signaled the beginning of the agonizing seventy-day seige of the U.S. Marine garrison at Khesanh. Nearly a year before, in February 1967, small units of U.S. Marines had begun patrolling in the Khesanh valley, which is at the junction point of five infiltration routes from North Vietnam. In April, the Marines had been reinforced to a strength of two battalions, and in twelve days of

137

fighting had killed 600 North Vietnamese while losing 138 of their own men. Reduced once more to small patrol units during the summer and early fall, the garrison was restored to a strength of 3,000 men in December, after aerial reconnaissance showed large NVN forces moving into the valley.

On January 21, a North Vietnamese probe in battalion strength was directed against the GVN district headquarters at Huong Hoa, just a mile from Khesanh. On January 23, the same day as the *Pueblo* seizure, there were suddenly 35,000 North Vietnamese soldiers in the immediate vicinity of Khesanh, and daily shelling commenced. The Marine garrison was reinforced to a strength of 5,000 men, and the siege began in earnest. Elsewhere along the northern rim of South Vietnam near the DMZ, another Marine regiment encountered large enemy forces.

These events sharply etched the somber prospects facing the United States in the Far East in the first month of 1968. The Tet offensive was about to begin.

CHAPTER 7

The Tet Offensive

ON JANUARY 31, in a surprise offensive that burst with the suddenness of a giant bombshell all over South Vietnam, the enemy launched a wide range of powerful, simultaneous attacks against dozens of key cities and towns. A commando unit of nineteen Viet Cong infiltrated the compound of the U.S. Embassy, made their way into several buildings, but were unable to get into the Embassy itself. After six hours of fighting with Embassy guards and reinforcements, including thirty-six U.S. paratroopers landed by helicopter on the Embassy roof, the entire Viet Cong unit was wiped out.

But the Embassy raid was only the political spearhead of a massive political-military assault on the entire U.S.-GVN structure. Saigon was attacked and partially occupied by several thousand enemy troops who had arrived in civilian disguise on bicycles and public buses. There were 1,000 enemy soldiers in Hue, 2,500 in Ben Tre. NVN forces seized large sections of Kontum in the central highlands, and of Mytho, Cantho, and Soc Trang in the Mekong Delta. In Washington the first reports were confused and fragmentary, but even these gave unmistakable shape to the truth that South Vietnam was experiencing a spreading disaster.

Westmoreland was quick to conclude that "the enemy's well laid plans went afoul." He and his spokesmen dismissed the enemy's tactics as suicidal, and pressed the suggestion that we were witnessing "a last desperate push," a final NVN effort to redress a military balance that had been moving inexorably against Hanoi by reason of the great weight of the U.S. effort. Ambassador Bunker provided a similar assessment. Taking his cue from Saigon and adding his own brand of hyperbole, the President reported to the nation on February 2 that the Viet Cong's offensive had been "a complete failure" militarily and psychologically. Speaking at a news conference, he said the Communist drive was the first phase of a campaign whose main objective was "a massive attack across the frontiers of South Vietnam by North Vietnamese units." He expressed confidence that the allied troops would "give a good account of themselves. . . . The enemy will fail and fail again because we Americans will never yield." As Commander-in-Chief, he could hardly have spoken otherwise in the heat of the first assault, for reassurance was called for in the face of ominous appearances. In fact, his words were premature and optimistic in the extreme, for even the first phase of the Tet offensive swept on for another two weeks with mounting casualties, destruction, and irreversible political consequences for the allied war effort.

THE SITUATION IN VIETNAM

The enemy was carrying out a carefully calculated three-pronged drive—one prong directed against Saigon and the major cities and a second against U.S. forces at Khesanh and other outlying posts; the third was designed to fill the vacuum left in the countryside by government troops who were drawn back to defend the cities. By occupying large rural sections abandoned by the government, the NVN-VC not only dealt the whole pacification program a grievous blow, but threatened to strangle the towns by cutting them off from normal sources of supply. Three to four weeks later, a number of towns were still surrounded and dependent on airlift. Very heavy fighting continued in Saigon and its suburbs through February 20, with action centering in the

Cholon district. An estimated 11,000 U.S. and ARVN forces were committed to battle against 1,000 Viet Cong. In an effort to dislodge the enemy, artillery and air strikes were repeatedly used against densely populated areas of the city, causing heavy civilian casualties. An additional 4,000 U.S. troops were brought in on February 9, part of them being helicoptered to the Pho Tho racetrack where a large Viet Cong force was entrenched. On February 11, two ARVN battalions were locked in battle with 400 VC near an ammo dump along the Ben Cat River.

Everywhere, the U.S.-ARVN forces mounted counterattacks of great severity. In the delta region below Saigon, half of the city of Mytho, with a population of 70,000, was destroyed by artillery and air strikes in an effort to eject a strong VC force. In Ben Tre on February 7, at least 1,000 civilians were killed and 1,500 wounded in an effort to dislodge 2,500 VC.

The effort to recapture Hue, the cultural and religious center of Vietnam, met fierce resistance from the 1,000 NVN troops who had captured it on January 31. After ten days of bitter street fighting, U.S. Marines finally penetrated the inner city, an area of two square miles known as the Citadel, to which the enemy force had withdrawn. On that same day, the Mayor of Hue found the bodies of three hundred local officials and prominent citizens in a common grave several miles from the city, slain en masse by the enemy. The fierce house-to-house fighting gradually exhausted the small contingent of Marines, and reinforcements were called for on February 21 "because the steam has gone out." Not until February 24 did U.S. forces achieve reoccupation of the city as a whole and ARVN forces capture the Imperial Palace. The enemy had gradually been driven to the southern part of the Citadel. There he did not put up a last ditch resistance, but slipped away one night to the southwest, with a sizable part of his men and equipment. The guns fell silent on a devastated and prostrate city. Eighty percent of the buildings had been reduced to rubble, and in the smashed ruins lay 2,000 dead civilians (apparently more civilians died than soldiers). Three-quarters of the city's people were rendered homeless and looting was widespread, members of the ARVN being the worst offenders.

David Douglas Duncan, a famous combat photographer who had covered all of the world's major battlefronts since World War II, including Korea, Algeria, and the French struggle to keep Vietnam, was appalled by the U.S.-ARVN method of freeing Hue. He said, "The Americans pounded the Citadel and surrounding city almost to dust with air strikes, napalm runs, artillery and naval gunfire, and the direct cannon fire from tanks and recoilless rifles—a total effort to root out and kill every enemy soldier. The mind reels at the carnage, cost, and ruthlessness of it all. Wouldn't a siege-blockade have been a more effective and less wasteful military tactic?" He contrasted this response with Henry Stimson's intervention in World War II to save Kyoto, the religious heart of Japan, which had been marked for destruction by allied airforces, and with John J. McCloy's similar rescue of classic Rothenburg in Germany. "Poor Hue, it had no friends or protectors. Now it is gone."

On February 12, the National Liberation Front made a statement which said in part, "in two weeks we have completely upset the enemy's combat arrangements and taken over the complete initiative. Not only are we masters of the mountainous regions, but we are attacking inside the cities and big bases. . . . The pacification program is a shambles."

On February 14, Westmoreland's headquarters estimated that 33,000 of the enemy had been killed and 6,700 captured. Of the allied forces 3,400 were killed and 12,000 wounded, of which the American toll was 1,100 killed and 5,500 wounded. That same day, South Vietnam began to mobilize an additional 65,000 troops, which President Thieu said were needed because the current Communist offensive has "enabled us to realize even more clearly the urgent problems that must be resolved."

A second round of enemy actions began about February 18, featuring coordinated rocket and mortar attacks on U.S. and ARVN installations, and to a lesser extent on the cities. In most cases, these were not followed up by ground assaults. Ton Son Nhut Air Base, near Saigon, was the target of sporadic firing. Six Americans were killed and sixty-seven wounded on February 19, four aircraft were set on fire, the base chapel was destroyed, and the control tower and several buildings were damaged. On the same day, 500 Viet Cong stormed into Phan Thiet, the capital of the province ninety miles east of Saigon; they released several hundred prisoners from the jail, and took over the provincial hospital. They were driven out the next day. On February 20, Viet Cong troops seized a village only two miles north of Ton Son Nhut and began setting up mortars. They were driven out eight hours later by national police and ARVN units. But on February 24, Ton Son Nhut was subjected to more rocket and mortar attacks in which four U.S. servicemen were killed and twenty-one wounded. Westmoreland reported record U.S. casualties for the third week of the month—543 killed and 2,500 wounded.

Meanwhile, Khesanh came under intensified siege. On February 4, the Joint Chiefs of Staff, in response to an explicit request from the President, expressed in writing their judgment that Khesanh "could and should be defended." On February 7, the enemy overran the Special Forces camp at Langvei, a few miles from Khesanh, killing 316 of the defenders including eight Americans. Another 200 members of the garrison escaped to the Marine base at Khesanh. By February 16, two NVN divisions were moving into position for an assault on Khesanh in the face of a heavy U.S. bombing and strafing effort to break up the enemy troop concentrations. U.S. intelligence expressed a fear that the enemy had transported enough steel matting into eastern Laos to build a runway for MIG-21s within a hundred miles of Khesanh.

On February 23 the enemy carried out a major probe of the base's defense perimeter following an extremely heavy Communist barrage; 1,300 rounds of artillery, mortar, and rocket fire fell on the Marines during a five-hour period. On February 26, a Marine patrol came under heavy fire about 800 yards outside the Khesanh base, and a Marine rescue platoon was also heavily mauled. Exact American casualty figures were withheld under a new directive announced by the U.S. command.

The Administration's decision to defend Khesanh was based in great part on Westmoreland's assessment that the attacks on the cities were "a diversionary effort" to distract our attention from the "invasion" of the northern part of South Vietnam. The official rationale was that the enemy was clearly aiming at a big victory at Khesanh—as at Dien Bien Phu—as a prelude to peace negotiations on terms favorable to him. This latter diagnosis was quite possibly true, but it did not seem to some of us a compelling argument for standing at Khesanh. A self-initiated tactical withdrawal would have got our foot out of a bear trap and provided nearly 7,000 combat troops to assist in the recovery of the cities and the adjacent countryside, which were being ransacked in the rear of Khesanh. Moreover, the enemy had options: he might attack Khesanh; he might, on the other hand, content himself with teasing, torturing, and tying down the garrison for an indefinite period. By committing ourselves to hold Khesanh, we preserved Giap's options and forfeited our own. The Administration's rationale seemed little more than another fig leaf for the defiant pride of the President and his military advisers, a blindness to fundamental misjudgments which stubbornness and lack of perception were now compounding.

Sir Robert Thompson expressed a view in early February that reinforced my own. He said: "These battles within the cities are the decisive ones and the larger-scale battles which have been, and are being, fought in the Annamite Mountain chain are the diversions." He thought the American tendency to believe that the Tet offensive was a desperate decision to "go for broke" showed "a complete lack of understanding of the strategy of the war and the stage it has now reached"; he believed the pacification program would have to start from scratch "in a time frame of at least 20 years."

On February 25, Westmoreland conceded that the Tet offensive "does not seem to be a go-for-broke effort," but he insisted that the enemy had "suffered a military defeat" despite his having gained "some temporary psychological advantage." He expressed the need for "additional troops" in order that he might "more effectively deny the enemy his objectives and capitalize on his recent defeats. . . ." The Communist onslaught made it clear to him that "the time has come for debating to end, for everyone to close ranks, roll up their sleeves and get on with the job," but he maintained there would be no change in basic strategy.

THE SITUATION IN WASHINGTON

Washington was in a posture of troubled confusion and uncertainty for the first two weeks in February. No one had a reliable assessment of the situation in Vietnam for, as usual, the official reporting was larded with an optimism that could not be reconciled with press reports of continuing enemy momentum, of U.S.-GVN confusion, and especially of the vast destruction being carried out by the allied forces in their determined efforts to recapture the cities and towns and villages. But the action was all in Vietnam. No initiatives to review or change policy were proposed in Washington; indeed no one seemed to have any clear idea of what should be done next.

In the Pentagon, the Tet offensive performed the curious service of fully revealing the doubters and dissenters to each other, as in a lightning flash. Nitze suddenly spoke out on "the unsoundness of continuing to reinforce weakness," and wrote a paper that argued that our policy in Vietnam had to be placed in the context of other U.S. commitments in the world. Warnke thought Tet showed that our military strategy was "foolish to the point of insanity." Alain Enthoven, whose Systems Analysis office had remained curiously on the outer edges of Vietnam policy, confided that, "I fell off the boat when the troop level reached 170,000." In various ways, the Under Secretary of the Army, David McGiffert, the Assistant Secretary of Defense for Manpower, Alfred Fitt, the Deputy Assistant Secretary for Far Eastern Affairs (ISA), Richard Steadman, and other influential civilians expressed their strong belief that the Administration's Vietnam policy was at a dead end.

One thing was clear to us all: the Tet offensive was the eloquent counterpoint to the effusive optimism of November. It showed conclusively that the U.S. did not in fact control the situation, that it was not in fact winning, that the enemy retained enormous strength and vitality—certainly enough to extinguish the notion of a clear-cut allied victory in the minds of all objective men. Nor could we take seriously the view that the Vietnamese were stepping up their operations out of despair, out of a certain knowledge that time worked against them. On the contrary, the Tet offensive seemed to proceed from an NVN assessment that the situation presented a number of ripe opportunities: the garrison at Khesanh was surrounded and under increasing pressure; another sizable portion of U.S. combat forces in northern I Corps was pinned down by heavy Communist artillery fire from across the DMZ; the cities were vulnerable to attack and the surrounding countryside to recapture. In general, the doctrine of search-and-destroy had resulted in scattering U.S. combat forces all over uninhabited border lands; the Tet offensive had made blindingly clear the fatuousness of Westmoreland's ground strategy. What seemed imperative now was a shift that would de-emphasize search-and-destroy, concentrate on the protection of population centers, and curtail American casualties; otherwise, I thought, domestic support for any form of long-continued effort could not be assured. Even the staunch and conservative *Wall Street Journal* was saying in mid-February, "We think the American people should be getting ready to accept, if they haven't already, the prospect that the whole Vietnam effort may be doomed, that it may be falling apart beneath our feet."

But modifications of strategy ran counter to Westmoreland's every instinct, and there was no will in Washington to bell that particular cat. It is quite possible that the idea of a strategy change never occurred to the President; that is, that either he never understood the incompatibility of Westmoreland's ground strategy with his own stated political objective, i.e., to gain the political allegiance of the people of South Vietnam—or that he regarded the political aim as mere words and the need for military victory as the only governing reality. McNamara, though he complained privately of the error and waste inherent in search-and-destroy operations, could not get his hands on the levers without explicit presidential support; and the Joint Chiefs of Staff, although some of them were disquieted by the attrition strategy, were unwilling to *direct* changes. In the particular circumstances, continued JCS deference to Westmoreland seemed an extreme form of professional courtesy, but it was a cold fact that in February 1968 the men and the means did not exist in Washington to change our military strategy in Vietnam.

THE PRESIDENT REACTS

The President's basic reaction to the Tet offensive was to convince himself anew that the war was a test of wills between parties of equal interest. While pressure rose on every side for a reexamination of America's prospects and strategy, he and his closest advisers gave the unmistakable impression that all the big questions had been long since resolved—and that the answer was to plunge onward. He spent much time in February visiting U.S. military bases. He announced to the world he was in no mood to compromise. He defended

Westmoreland. He urged total firmness on the war. About mid-February, Harry McPherson, the President's Special Counsel and principal speech writer, sent him a memorandum urging a bombing halt on grounds of practical domestic politics. McPherson argued that the "average middle-class American" who had hitherto supported the war was coming to believe that the President had made Vietnam "LBJ's personal war," that the bombing was being pressed so unreasonably as to appear an obstacle to talks and, therefore, to de-escalation and a satisfactory settlement. The next day McPherson received a call from Rostow who told him the President had read the memorandum and wished McPherson to know that the President had no intention of halting the bombing; indeed Rostow had been instructed to enlist McPherson's assistance in developing new arguments in support of continuing the effort.

At the same time, the President was cautious about further manpower commitments. About February 13, he dispatched the 27th Marine regiment and one brigade of the 82nd airborne division on "temporary duty" to Vietnam. This force package totaled 10,500 men and the temporary nature of the deployment reflected growing concern at the inadequacy of our strategic reserve to meet the requirement of NATO contingency plans and other possible crises. These units were important combat elements in that dwindling reserve, and the JCS was most reluctant to denude the forces at home in the absence of new presidential decisions that would assure a larger pool of available manpower. The JCS in fact put forward in mid-February a proposed "mobilization package" asking for an immediate call-up of two National Guard divisions and some Army reserve units (totaling 50,000 men) plus the Fourth Marine division and its companion air wing (totaling another 40,000 men). The proposal also called for alerting 130,000 additional guardsmen and reservists for later call. Privately, the Tet offensive had shaken even the military chiefs.

Thus a sort of debate sprang up on the reserve issue. Some elements in Congress urged the President to move quickly to mobilize at least three National Guard divisions, but the idea ran into stern opposition from Senator Richard Russell, the seasoned and prestigious chairman of the Armed Services Committee. Russell let it be known that he could no longer approve "piecemeal escalation" of the ground war, and would therefore oppose troop additions unless the President agreed concurrently to a drastic increase in the weight of the bombing effort against North Vietnam—by which he seemed to mean at least Haiphong harbor, the instrumentalities of government at Hanoi, and the rail lines in the Chinese Buffer Zone. Another straw in the wind was the reluctance of certain governors to see their National Guard units federalized and shipped out of state, for they were seriously concerned at the prospect of further urban rioting in the coming summer. The President remained cautious and uncommitted.

Some of course had no doubts. Joseph Alsop, who always wrote *ex cathedra* and seemed at times to have invented the Vietnam War, decreed throughout February that the meaning of the Tet offensive was "quite simply" that the Hanoi war-planners had concluded they couldn't stand the gaff of a protracted war and had decided to go for broke, in order to drag the United States to the negotiating table on Hanoi's terms. But, said Alsop, echoing Rostow, "As the captured documents continue to pour in . . . it becomes clearer and clearer that the Tet-period attacks on the cities were a major disaster for General Giap, if measured in terms of his planned goals." An unprecedented opportunity was thus at hand! With a quick infusion of fresh troops, Westmoreland can "launch a decisive counter-offensive." Accordingly, "The President will be feckless, foolish, and derelict in his duty (and he will also be acting against his own practical, long-range interests) if he fails to call up the reserves in order to insure negotiations on our terms." If it did nothing else, this kind of fustian trumpeting provided some comic relief during a bad month.

Discussing the general situation with Warnke about this time, I argued that, unless the situation could be turned around, some one was going to have to resign, "with drama," for at least two simple reasons—as a matter of personal integrity, to avoid being dragged any further in the wake of a policy one felt to be fundamentally wrong; and as a means of breaking the deceptive façade of supposed governmental unity, and thus of contributing new force and substance to the public debate. I was increasingly aware, I said, that the upper reaches of government were honeycombed with people who were not merely discouraged and disenchanted, but deeply angered by the enduring stupidity and the self-protective tenacity of the inner circle. I thought one resignation might produce a modest chain reaction of perhaps a half dozen, and I was perfectly willing to be the first. Warnke was thinking along similar lines, but he put the choice of resignation farther down the road. He preferred, first, a vigorous renewal of the effort to turn the situation around, in the context of the Tet offensive. He said, "If we wade in with both feet, we can perhaps make a difference; and if we fail, maybe they will do us the honor of firing us."

The chances of producing any dramatic change of policy seemed remote in mid-February. Control of the war effort remained tightly held by the inner group, and they were, with the exception of McNamara, united both in their conviction about the rightness of present policy and in the fact that all were implicated in the major decisions since 1964. Worse still, as it seemed, McNamara's designated successor was not only a close friend of LBJ, but an eloquent hawk with no doubts about the war. In all respects, Clark Clifford seemed to fit the President's temperamental requirement for harmony within the inner group. *Newsweek* called him "loyal, well-seasoned and, more important, determined to hold the line in Vietnam." Still, I was not without hope.

I had been at Aspen, Colorado, for a seminar and some skiing when Clifford's appointment was announced in mid-January, and there had been some discussion of what it portended. Professor Brzezinski, Director of the Research Institute on Communist Studies at Columbia, ticked off the circumstantial facts and professed to see small chance for any change. Granting this view was plausible, I argued that the facts adduced didn't add up to anything conclusive. I had known Clifford over a number of years, particularly during the Truman period when he was at the White House, and had been impressed, then and later, by the steely independence beneath the velvet charm. He was, I thought, above all his own man. Moreover, he was too intelligent, too much the trained lawyer, with too firm a sense of proportion and too strong a passion for reasoned answers, not to grasp the galloping distortions that now dominated the conduct of Vietnam policy. I did not foresee the full measure of his courage and tenacity that the ensuing months would reveal, but I was encouraged. In any event, Clifford was the only remaining hope for restoring some sense of proportion to our national position at home and abroad. If he couldn't be persuaded, then there was no alternative to resignation.

On February 13, two weeks before Clifford took office, I wrote him a personal letter:

Dear Clark:

I have concluded that it would be useful, before you take office, to put before you a certain perspective on aspects of the Vietnam problem. I do so in the belief that these aspects involve critical nuances unlikely to come through clearly in formal briefings or even in supplementary talks. I put them to you with more candor than discretion, believing you would prefer this, but believing in any event that candor and clarity are needed at this juncture of our affairs.

I am concerned with two subjects: (1) the intrinsic value of our bombing in the North; and (2) the relationship of our ground strategy in the South to a pause or cessation of bombing in the North. The bleak events of recent days may have temporarily pushed these subjects into the background, but they will recur, for they are among the central elements of the problem.

Let me acknowledge at the outset several personal premises: first, the idea of a US military victory in Vietnam is a dangerous illusion (primarily because both the Soviets and the Chicoms have the capacity to preclude it—probably by supply operations alone, but if necessary by intervening with their own forces); second, if events in Vietnam are ever to take a turn toward settlement, definitive de-escalation is a prerequisite; and third, admitting all the uncertainty and risk, the most promising approach to negotiations and thus settlement continues to involve a cessation of the US bombing effort against North Vietnam as one of the first steps.

The letter then turned to a discussion of the air effort against North Vietnam, cited the absence of a meaningful official assessment of effectiveness, and provided the following composite of my own conclusions and the judgments of others, including outside study groups:

—Since the beginning of the air strikes in early 1965, the flow of men and materiel from NVN to SVN has definitely increased.

—The rate of infiltration is not limited by factors in NVN— i.e., available manpower, LOC capabilities, available transport carriers, or available volume of supplies. Rather, the constraints on infiltration relate to the war situation in the South—i.e., the VC infrastructure and distribution system in the South have a limited capacity to absorb and manage additional materiel and troops.

—The bombing has inflicted heavy damage on North Vietnam's economy and society as a whole ($400 million of measurable damage and the diversion of up to 300,000 people from agriculture to road repair, transport and air defense). But NVN's allies have provided economic and military aid substantially in excess of the damage, and the cost of the manpower diversions may be quite small, owing to the considerable slack in NVN's underemployed agricultural labor force.

—NVN has gone over to decentralized, dispersed and protected modes of producing and handling essential goods and safeguarding the people. It has made a durable adjustment to the bombing.

—The NVN regular army, the VC main forces, and the VC local forces now have better equipment and more effective weapons than in 1965, and the Soviet Union could provide them with even more sophisticated weapons. Only a moderate fraction of the 1.2 million fit males in the prime age groups (17–35) have as yet been inducted into the armed forces.

—On balance NVN is a stronger military power today than before the bombing began.

The letter went on to argue that these conclusions "are as essentially undeniable as they are unpalatable," that "bombing targets in the North did not prevent the current buildup at Khesanh, nor notably hinder the recent coordinated VC attacks on the cities. . . . The air war over Hanoi and Haiphong in particular seems increasingly a techno-electronic contest between the U.S. and the Soviet Union with diminishing relevance to the struggle in the South. We seem to have in the bombing campaign an instrument of some modest, but indeterminate, value which plays an essentially psychological role in the struggle and whose most useful service to us may be as a counter to be traded away in a serious bargaining."

The letter then addressed the ground strategy and its relation to the problem of a bombing halt.

We are pursuing an aggressive ground strategy of attrition in South Vietnam which often involves US troops fighting search-and-destroy battles in totally uninhabited places, in

153

the worst possible terrain for American forces, at the time of the enemy's choosing, and with inconclusive results. This is a strategy devised and executed by the Field Commander with remarkably little detailed guidance from either the JCS or higher civilian authority. Certainly the degree of Washington's critical interest in the way in which the ground war is fought has been in striking contrast to the bombing campaign. This strategy generates an increasing rate of US casualties...

As indicated by discussion of the bombing, there is only a tenuous military link between our bombing in the North and the casualties we suffer in the South. If we should stop bombing North Vietnam, but continue to pursue the present ground strategy, our casualties are not likely to go down and might go up. But it is doubtful whether a rise would be attributable, in military fact, to a bombing halt. Present US casualty levels are a function of the US ground strategy in the South; they are only distantly related to the bombing. Yet as we address the prospect of a bombing cessation, it becomes apparent that, however tenuous the military linkage, a political linkage has been allowed to develop....

In my judgment we thus confront a linkage that is in large part a military fiction, but at the same time a palpable political fact. From this I draw the conclusion that, if the President is to accept the consequences of a bombing halt, he must take a corollary decision to alter the ground strategy in ways that will reduce US casualties; otherwise, the domestic political risks may be too high.

One can... make a strong argument that a different ground strategy, less ambitious in purely military terms and more explicitly devoted to protecting the populated areas of South Vietnam, would improve the likelihood of the kind of untidy, unpleasant compromise which looks like being the best available means of our eventual extraction from the morass. It would give us a better chance to develop a definable geographical area of South Vietnamese political and economic stability; and by reducing the intensity of the war tempo, it could materially improve the prospect of our staying the course for an added number of grinding years without rending our own society. . . .

But the point to be made here is simply that, given the political link between bombing in the North and US casualties in the South, an aggressive ground strategy that generates high casualties may prove to be an insuperable obstacle to a bombing halt, even if such a halt is judged by US officials to be in the national interest.

As you know, the President himself has contributed to this linkage on recent occasions—notably in his State of the Union message and in awarding the Medal of Honor to an Air Force officer on February 2. . . . I do not know what assessment of bombing effectiveness lies behind his words on these occasions, but several key journalists, some of them entirely sympathetic to his dilemmas, believe he is now attributing to the bombing an importance that is seriously at odds with the San Antonio formula. They see a contradiction, but have refrained from pointing it out up to now, out of a concern that this would endanger the San Antonio formula.

. . . I look forward to your coming to the Pentagon, and to working with you on a range of consequential problems in a period of evident storm. You have my abiding respect, and warm wishes for success.

Sincerely,
Townsend Hoopes

THE END OF FEBRUARY

By the end of February the military situation in Vietnam was under better control but, contrary to earlier expectations, the offensive had not been quickly contained and then snuffed out. Despite enormous casualties (estimated in the range of 28–40,000), the enemy had attacked thirty-five major cities and towns and occupied many of them for extended periods; perhaps 25,000 civilians had been killed in the attacks and counterattacks, and physical destruction was very heavy. The U.S.-ARVN forces had weathered the whirlwind and were beginning to recover, but as February ended it was painfully clear that they remained everywhere on the defensive, awaiting fresh attacks, which were now acknowledged to be fully within the enemy's capability. Not only were all of the major cities still threatened by large enemy forces clinging close to their suburbs and outskirts, but nearly half the combat forces at Westmoreland's disposal were concentrated in the northern part of I Corps facing no less than six NVN divisions. Two of these surrounded the beseiged garrison at Khesanh, rained down artillery and mortar barrages upon it, and moved each day apparently closer to a direct assault. Two others threatened U.S. border posts along the DMZ, and two were in the mountains farther to the southeast, threatening the Marine rear and the cities of Quangtrai and Hue.

In addition, the attacks on the cities had pulled 8,000 ARVN troops out of the small villages where they had been protecting the pacification program, and this abandonment of the countryside had opened up very large territories to reoccupation by the Viet Cong. This meant not only physical and psychological destruction of the pacification program, but Viet Cong access to substantial pools of able-bodied men. By persuasion and harsh impressment they could thereby make good a significant percentage of the losses they had suffered in the first offensive.

At home, the situation seemed even more fragile, for the scale, virulence, and tenacity of the Tet offensive had all but severed the remaining strands of the Administration's credibility. The President was speaking out forcefully, but his words and their tone struck listeners as more shrill than reassuring; in them one detected a profound inner discomfort and unease, a thrashing about in uncertainty.

In Dallas on February 27, he said, "There will be blood, sweat, and tears shed. The weak will drop from the lines, their feet sore and their voices loud. . . . Persevere in Vietnam we will and we must. There, too, today we stand at the turning point. The enemy of freedom has chosen to make this year the decisive one. He is striking in a desperate and vicious effort to shape the final outcome of his purposes."

He went on. The enemy has failed "because thousands of our courageous sons and millions of brave South Vietnamese have answered aggression's onslaught with one strong voice. 'No retreat' they have said. 'Free men will never bow to force and abandon their future to tyranny.' That must be our answer, too, here at home. No retreat from responsibility of the hour and the day.... There must be no betrayal of those who fight beside us. There must be no breaking of our trusted commitments.... The peace of Asia and the peace of America will turn on it.... I believe that every American will answer now for the future and for his children's future. I believe he will say, 'I did not retreat when the going got tough. I did not fall back when the enemy advanced, when the terrorists attacked, when the cities were stormed, the villages assaulted and the people massacred ... I stood firm with my government to fight to preserve the way of life we hold dear.' " The more he spoke, the more he descended into bathos. One hard-bitten journalist said to me, "That guy has come unglued again because the real world refuses to shape itself to his personal pre-conceptions."

During the last week of February, the influential television news services took the unusual step of adopting a firm substantive position on the Vietnam issue. Walter Cronkite of CBS, just returned from Vietnam, judged the Tet offensive "a split decision" with heavy losses on both sides. He said the U.S. faced the serious possibility that Khesanh would fall with "a terrible loss of American lives, prestige and morale." He saw a stalemate in the political realm, with the prospect of the GVN hanging on to power but being unable to take the necessary initiatives to gain the confidence of the country or solve its pressing problems. He firmly stated that we were mired in "a military stalemate," but that any attempt to escalate our way out could only lead to "cosmic disaster." He found nothing dishonorable about America going to the

157

conference table "with a full realization that it has met a commitment to defend democracy at a faraway bastion by doing its best." The NBC news staff was even more categorical. It flatly asserted that the war was being lost, if judged against the Administration's expressed reasons for its pursuit. NBC senior commentator, Frank McGee, said the Administration's definition of its goal in Vietnam was to hold off the Communists in order to allow the South Vietnamese to achieve a sense of security and then a stable government. McGee asserted that, with the Communist invasion of the cities and recapture of the countryside, with thousands homeless, and the government weaker than before, the prospect of a free and stable South Vietnam was more distant than ever. All that remains, he said, "is a mutual capacity to lay waste more human beings and more buildings. The initiative has passed to the enemy, and the time has arrived to decide whether it is not a futile policy to destroy Vietnam in an effort to save it."

CHAPTER 8

The Beginnings of Reappraisal

PRELIMINARIES

THE REAPPRAISAL of Vietnam policy began on February 26 with the arrival of a cable from General Wheeler sent from Saigon. He had been dispatched by the President about February 20 "to find out what else Westmoreland might need." For three days he conferred with Westmoreland and inspected the battle areas. Then he sent a cable for McNamara, Rusk, Rostow, and Helms setting forth his assessment of the situation and of the additional "force requirements" that he and Westmoreland considered necessary or at least very desirable. While Wheeler was flying home, McNamara convened the three Service Secretaries and the Chiefs of Staff on the afternoon of February 26 to address the Wheeler cable. My boss, Harold Brown, being out of town, I was present as Acting Secretary of the Air Force.

General "Bus" Wheeler, USA, the Chairman of the Joint Chiefs of Staff, was an intelligent, personable, politically sophisticated staff officer whose talents were admirably suited to the demanding tasks of coordinating the strong (and by no means always common) interests of four powerful military bureaucracies—the Army, Navy, Air Force, and Marine Corps —and of serving as their principal advocate and defender in relations with the Secretary of Defense, the President, and the Congress. Handsome and distinguished in appearance, he was also seasoned, articulate, and courteous, as well as more candid and resilient than most military professionals in his relations with civilian officials and politicians. He understood the importance of intangible factors and readily grasped the limits of what was politically possible. His perception and tact had helped on countless occasions to bridge the sensitive gap between what his colleagues on the JCS insisted was militarily necessary and what the civilian authorities were willing to approve. Though they disagreed often, he and McNamara respected each other greatly.

There was, however, never any doubt of Wheeler's fundamental commitment to a military solution in Vietnam, his determined advocacy of whatever level of effort was required to achieve it, or his unqualified support of Westmoreland. Although more polished and subtle than the Service Chiefs, he was in every respect a convinced and authentic spokesman for the professional military interest.

The Wheeler cable gave authoritative confirmation to many earlier impressions. The fighting was by no means over; indeed large actions appeared in the offing at Khesanh or Hue and all across the central highlands. The enemy had suffered very substantial losses, yet retained sizable reserves and was displaying a greater tenacity than the U.S. Command had seen at any earlier period of the war. He was hanging in close to urban areas in a serious effort to disrupt the inflow of food and other supplies, to paralyze the economy, to intimidate the people by rumor and violence. At least six enemy regiments remained on the edges of Saigon. ARVN had fought well on the whole, but had required reinforcement by U.S. troops in a number of places including Hue. In addition, it had been necessary to position more than half of the 110 U.S. maneuver battalions in northern I Corps to counter the heavy enemy threat there. As a result, there was no remaining theater reserve to meet contingencies. Westmoreland's forces were stretched thin, and required prompt and substantial reinforcement. Wheeler's cable then summarized the "force requirements," which amounted to about 206,000 men divided into three time phases: 107,000 by May 1; another 43,000 by September 1; and the final 56,000 by December. The ground force package (both Army and Marines) totaled about 171,000, the Air Force about 22,000, and the Navy about 13,000.

To say the least, the magnitude of the request was a stunner to those gathered around the table. The Secretary of the Navy, Paul Ignatius, asked why, if U.S. and allied forces had killed more than 30,000 enemy troops since Tet, Westmoreland needed an extra 100,000 men within sixty days. General Harold Johnson, the Army Chief of Staff (and Acting JCS Chairman in Wheeler's absence) replied that, because the Viet Cong were now vigorously recruiting in the countryside, abandoned by ARVN, we had to expect them to recover their losses at least numerically; he thought, however, the quality of VC forces had suffered irretrievably.

I expressed surprise at the size of the request for additional airpower—seventeen tactical fighter squadrons, of which twelve were to be Air Force and five Marine. Two of the twelve had been previously requested, and the Air Force was engaged in preparations to deploy them. I expressed concern that sending more would seriously crowd the airfields in South Vietnam, with resulting higher damage rates from mortar fire and sapper attacks, or, alternatively, would create further adverse political consequences if we introduced another increment of U.S. air forces ino neighboring Thailand. General Johnson replied that the new request simply maintained the existing ratio of air support to ground forces. This was true, but it was a bureaucratic rather than a substantive answer. I did not pursue the point in the meeting, but there was in fact no well-reasoned analysis to support the *existing* air-ground ratio; it had simply evolved out of the early conditions of the war. Moreover, it was a matter of some delicacy in Army-Air Force relations because it touched the boundary line between the assigned roles and missions of

161

the two Services. If the Air Force did not provide close air support in a ratio satisfactory to the Army, that would strengthen the Army's argument for developing its own means of close support. Already, through the development of helicopter gunships of increasing power, speed, and sophistication, the Army had pressed against that boundary. The rote application of that ratio in constructing the new "force requirements" for Vietnam was the first hint that perhaps they had not been entirely made in Saigon, but that Wheeler had carried to his meeting with Westmoreland some rather definite JCS views as to what was needed and could be obtained at this juncture of the war.

The fact remained that we already had thirty land-based tactical squadrons in South Vietnam. Wheeler and Westmoreland were now asking that this be increased to forty-seven. A number of professional airmen considered South Vietnam already saturated with allied airpower, and there was of course the basic question whether large additional forces were available. In response to the *Pueblo* crisis, we had just dispatched 150 aircraft to South Korea. The Air Force was a "can do" outfit; it could generate additional squadrons if the decision were made to do so, but this would take time, cost money, and almost certainly require the further call-up of reserves if we were to avoid a drawdown of the squadrons in Europe or otherwise committed to NATO.

McNamara gave his opinion that to meet the Westmoreland request would create a requirement for about 400,000 more men on active military service (reservists or draftees) and involve an added cost of $10 billion for the first twelve months (at this time he was working on a defense budget for the fiscal year beginning in July 1968 that amounted to about $90 billion, of which roughly $30 billion was attributable to Vietnam). He asked each Service to analyze the Westmoreland request in the light of three possibilities: (1) that we would fully comply, (2) that we would partially comply, and (3) that we would examine alternative political and military strategies in Vietnam. But for purposes of moving ahead, he asked that we concentrate initially on the first alternative.

One of the major ironies of the Wheeler trip was that, had McNamara not been in his final month of office, he, rather than Wheeler, would almost surely have gone to Saigon, and his judgment rather than an undiluted military judgment would have formed the basis of the authoritative request, if any, for more forces. Previously, at every critical turn in the war, McNamara had flown to Vietnam to bargain directly with Westmoreland and the other commanders regarding the manpower and discretionary authority required for the next phase. In every instance, he had reached his own conclusions before departing Washington and had meticulously prepared his position, including a draft of what he would report to the President on his return. In every case he prevailed upon the military commanders to scale down their requests (called "requirements"); in return for their cooperation, he gave his public endorsement to the amended buildup. That pattern had been repeated at approximately six-month intervals since early 1965. It was a technique which exemplified McNamara's mastery of, and strong instinct for, managed decision-making: by holding control within very narrow channels, developing an advance position, and moving fast, he finessed serious debate on basic issues and thus saved the President from the unpleasant task of arbitrating major disputes within his official family. It had worked smoothly, but it had also resulted in a twenty-five-fold increase in the military manpower commitment to Vietnam—from 21,000 to 510,000—over a three-year period.

Even in the advanced state of disenchantment which had overtaken him by late February, McNamara's instinctive reaction on receiving the new military request was to "manage the problem," whittle down the numbers, muffle the differences, and thereby avoid a bruising confrontation within the Administration. The President's initiative of November to move McNamara to the World Bank thus proved a fateful hinge on which swung later events of far-reaching consequence. Phil G. Goulding, the Assistant Secretary of Defense for Public Affairs, thought that if McNamara had remained firmly in the saddle and had made the trip to Saigon, there would have been no request for 206,000 men and probably no immediate and dramatic reappraisal of policy. The matter is of course speculative, but my own view is close to Goulding's.

With McNamara managing the manpower question, it seems likely that agreement inside the circle of advisers would have been rather quickly reached on troop reinforcements of perhaps 50,000, together with a renewed offer to stop the bombing in exchange for reciprocal acts by Hanoi. Such terms would have been set forth in a generally tough, patriotic, hortatory speech by the President. This approach might have bought the Administration another month or two of public toleration. It might have weakened Senator McCarthy's showing in New Hampshire (where public knowledge of the 206,000 figure helped enormously), which in turn might have made Robert Kennedy more hesitant; it might have persuaded President Johnson to stay in the political race. But in the end, I am sure, and well before the summer, an attempt to carry on in Vietnam without significant change, as though the Tet offensive had not really happened, would have generated a wholesale domestic cataclysm, as well as a major explosion in the Democratic party, which neither Lyndon Johnson nor his Vietnam policy could have survived. For the deep-seated, powerful thrust of public opinion in March was that "more of the same" was simply not good enough. The further irony is that an explosive upheaval, produced by yet another effort to finesse the basic issues, might have forced a far more definitive decision on the war sometime in mid-1968, e.g., immediate unilateral reduction of U.S. forces and a phased liquidation of the entire enterprise in twelve to eighteen months. Because circumstances brought about a dramatic reappraisal in March and because the President was thereby persuaded to act as he did—to put a ceiling on the war, to halt

164

the bombing partially, to take himself out of the race—the teeth of the domestic opposition were pulled sufficiently to preserve at least a semblance of Lyndon Johnson's leadership inside the Democratic party and to permit him a tolerably graceful exit at the end of the year with his Vietnam policy still shrouded in ambiguity.

But McNamara did not go to Saigon, and the sending of Wheeler produced an undiluted expression of the true military desideratum—no less than a 40 percent increase in a force level already at 510,000. This was an event that galvanized the Pentagon civilians, who were for the first time able to assert their strong anti-escalation position in a favorable psychological and managerial climate. The Westmoreland request was a catalyst that made serious reappraisal unavoidable, and Clifford's arrival as Secretary of Defense meant that new channels of communication were now available for debate.

FAREWELL TO McNAMARA

On February 28, there was a farewell reception for Mc-Namara at the White House. In the gilded East Room, filled to capacity with his friends, admirers, and official antagonists (ranging from Robert and Ethel Kennedy to L. Mendel Rivers), crowded with television cameras and illuminated to an artificial intensity by klieg lights, McNamara received the Medal of Freedom, and the President spoke with grave eloquence of "this loyal, brilliant and good man" whose prodigious labors and achievements at the Pentagon over seven long years made him "one of America's most valuable public properties." For the first time in his public career, McNamara was overcome by emotion. Two or three times, he breathed deeply and cleared his throat, but the words would not come. Finally he was able to say "Mr. President, I cannot find words to express what lies in my heart today. I think I had better respond on another occasion." It was a moving moment to see this man of cool, controlled power, who had mastered the vast and complicated bureaucracies at the Pentagon for seven years, suddenly overcome by a rush of what must have been intensely conflicting emotions—honest pride in the evident warmth, and truth, of the President's praise for the excellence of his stewardship, misgivings about the morass of a war whose solution had proved beyond his powers, and chagrin that his departure should be under circumstances of ambiguity. To these were added cumulative fatigue from the long bearing of heavy burdens, and the physical and psychic relief at having these burdens suddenly lifted. Everyone departed that brief ceremony uplifted a little in spirit.

The following day there was a final military review at the Pentagon; it seemed predestined to fall apart in a total shambles. The skies were leaden, swollen with the possibility of cold rain, but the military authorities decided at 11:00 to muster the honor guard on the spacious lawn that stands below the River Entrance overlooking a placid lagoon that reaches out to merge with the Potomac. At 11:30 the rains came, but that was by no means all. The President and his entourage, descending from McNamara's office to the street level, overloaded the Pentagon's private elevator and found themselves, with McNamara, stuck fast between floors for twenty minutes, while the civilian and military hierarchy and a crowd of well-wishers shivered outside in the chilling wet. When the principals did appear, they were hatless and coatless. McNamara stood facing the reviewing stand with his back to the honor guard, while Nitze with the President beside him read the citation. McNamara's face was streaming with cold rain; as Nitze began to read, the public address system failed, carrying his eloquent words away on the wind. It was a hapless finale for the exemplar of managerial efficiency. There was a reception afterwards in the Secretary's dining room and, as we warmed ourselves with hot coffee, I had a brief word with Clifford. He thanked me for the February 13 letter and said he wanted to talk about it soon.

Clark Clifford was not, in March 1968, a stranger either to government or the problem of Vietnam. As the youngish, astute Special Counsel in President Truman's White House, he had been a tough-minded and shrewd political adviser, the most eloquent (and some thought by far the most sincere) advocate of the Fair Deal program, and a man who saw the full dimension of the Russian threat from the first skirmishes of the Cold War. Leaving government several months after Truman's spectacular victory over Dewey in 1948, he established a private law practice which made him, some said, the highest paid lawyer in the country. A good friend of Lyndon Johnson, he had been since 1961 a member and since 1964 the chairman of the President's Foreign Intelligence Advisory Board, a position which kept him in the channel of the private and secret information that is the raw material for the conduct of foreign policy and military affairs. Yet there is, as he soon discovered and acknowledged, a vast difference between being an occasional consultant without responsibility and a major cabinet officer with direct and momentous responsibility.

He had come to a general view of the U.S. role in Southeast Asia on a morning in December 1960 at the White House, during the transition period between the Eisenhower and Kennedy Administrations. He was present as Kennedy's coordinator on the transition. At that session in the Cabinet Room, Eisenhower sought to impress upon the President-elect his belief that the United States had a vital interest in assuring that Southeast Asia remained free of "Communist domination." Eisenhower attached special importance to Laos, more so than to Vietnam. According to Clifford, Eisenhower felt a political settlement of the conflict in Laos would be the best solution; if that proved impossible, he favored an "allied military intervention." In the last analysis, however, he felt Laos was important enough to warrant U.S.

military intervention alone. As Kennedy later complained, Eisenhower hardly mentioned Vietnam, and thus failed to provide any special warning of the difficulties to come. It was this appraisal that had formed the basis of Clifford's general support for the Johnson Administration's policy in Southeast Asia.

But there had come a turning point in the summer of 1967 in the course of a trip to Asia with General Maxwell Taylor, at the President's request. The purpose of the mission was to express to those allied governments that had some fighting forces in Vietnam the President's hope that they would increase the level of their combat effort, and to discuss the attendant problems and considerations.

The question of allies remained a sore point. In 1965 the President had made a major effort in both Europe and Asia to get "more flags" into Vietnam as a means of demonstrating the international character of support for the GVN; the President appeared to feel that an appeal to Europeans was also an imperative of U.S. domestic politics. While the latter assumption seemed dubious, his appeal to Europe was a natural, perhaps unavoidable, concomitant of his understanding of the problem. For if Vietnam were indeed the Rhineland in 1936 and Czechoslovakia in 1939, then the European stake in its own security should have been dramatically self-evident. The difficulty was that the Europeans failed to grasp the supposed analogies and made predictably polite, but cool and negative, responses to the President's request for troops. Rusk and the other foreign policy experts were surely aware that the Europeans would not provide troops, and it seemed a measure of either their disingenuousness or their submission to an implacable President that they allowed the cabled instructions to go to U.S. Ambassadors throughout Europe, directing them to undertake a hard sell. The Germans were willing to send a valuable hospital ship and a team of doctors, which operated in the port of Saigon and later at Danang; others contributed bits and pieces of military material or nonmilitary services, but in terms of creating either the fact or appearance of a major allied effort in Vietnam, the European responses were zero. Although the Administration later claimed that thirty-one nations were "aiding" the war effort, Senator Fulbright's Committee showed in 1966 that about half of these had each contributed services or materials amounting to $26,000 or less over a two-year period. When compared to the U.S. field force of 510,000 men and a war expenditure approaching $2.5 billion per month, this did not exactly make the case that the United States was being supported in Vietnam by a panoply of ardent and determined allies.

Australia, New Zealand, Korea, Thailand, and the Philippines did provide forces. By the time of Tet, the Koreans had 48,000 tough combat soldiers in Vietnam, by far the most impressive demonstration of responsive concern by an Asian nation. This stout-hearted effort was of course totally underwritten by the United States—indeed on terms so generous that the Administration found it necessary to cover them with a rather dubious security classification. Except for base pay of the troops, the U.S. provided everything: premium pay for combat in Vietnam, food and shelter, logistics support, and transportation; also an agreement to strengthen the ROK forces remaining in South Korea.

Thailand, located adjacent to North Vietnam and beset by a troublesome incipient insurgency in its northeastern provinces along the Mekong River, was willing to put about 2,200 troops into South Vietnam, asking in return complete U.S. subsidy for these forces, as well as a substantial increase in U.S. military equipment assistance to the Thai forces remaining at home. As a result of Clifford's trip in 1967, the Thai government agreed to add 10,000 men to its Vietnam force, and these were eventually provided in two increments, in the summer of 1968 and the early winter of 1969.

The Philippines provided, after much haggling, a noncombatant engineer battalion numbering about 2,000 men, but here again the price was complete subsidization of the force in Vietnam and a promise to maintain a steady flow of military assistance for the home forces in the Philippines.

Australia provided at its own expense a brigade of 6,000 troops and, after further U.S. pressure, an additional artillery unit and an air squadron, bringing the total to about 8,500. New Zealand contented itself with the astonishingly token contribution of 450 men.

What struck Clifford, as he talked to the Prime Ministers and Defense Ministers of these countries (he did not go to Manila because the Marcos government had made plain that the Philippines did not wish to be asked for a further military contribution), was the casual, business-as-usual attitudes expressed. Especially in Australia and New Zealand he found far less a sense of danger, concern, or even involvement than he had expected; there was a general unwillingness to take the unpopular steps that President Johnson was requesting. To send more than a small number of additional troops would require higher taxes and the enactment of draft laws. The governments in question were unready to risk the attendant political flak. These attitudes impressed Clifford deeply, and he found them in sharpest contrast with the perception of the danger that certain of the same countries had possessed in 1940 and 1941, when an imperialist, militarist Japan was on the march. Australia had raised nearly 682,000 men and had sent them out not only against the Japanese, but halfway across the world to fight for King George and the British Empire. New Zealand had raised 157,000 men in World War II. In 1967, they were unprepared to make anything remotely resembling a comparable effort.

In fairness, it had to be said that these modest contributions were of roughly the same order of magnitude that had obtained in the Korean War (except in the case of South Korea, which mobilized about 300,000 men to defend its own soil). Australia's contribution to Vietnam was three times larger than its effort in Korea, but New Zealand's was only one-third as large. The Thai contribution to Vietnam through 1967 was slightly larger than its earlier effort in Korea; the two Filipino efforts were about the same. But the Vietnam conflict was presumably the acid test of the liberation-war threat, which would define the ability of free nations to contain the militant thrust of Chinese expansion and thus determine the fate of Asia. Apparently, these governments had not been reading Rostow. From this educative encounter, Clifford drew the conclusion that, if the nations who lived in the area and whose security was more directly at stake were not prepared to make a serious and substantial effort, the United States should very definitely reduce its own commitments. General Taylor did not at all share this conclusion. He agreed that the United States was being used, that the Asians were "letting Uncle Sam do it," but this did not alter his view that the U.S. had a special responsibility to counter Chinese Communism and protect freedom, alone if necessary.

Clifford thus entered upon office in March with a sense of uneasiness about the underlying assumptions of U.S. policy in Vietnam, and with his former views in a fluid state. Newspapers in Moscow, Peking, Warsaw, East Berlin, and Hanoi promptly denounced him as "an out-and-out warmonger," "a trusted man of Wall Street financial circles," and "a stubborn opponent of stopping the air raids" against North Vietnam. As it turned out, these cordial Communist greetings were not without their uses, for it helped to have LBJ think that Clifford's later "heretical" views represented a basic reversal of an earlier position. This was not quite the case.

THE AD HOC TASK FORCE ON VIETNAM

Since his Senate confirmation in January, Clifford had of course been preparing himself for his new responsibilities by conferring frequently with McNamara, Nitze, and the Joint Chiefs of Staff. On February 28, two days before the swearing-in ceremony, the President named an *Ad Hoc* Task Force on Vietnam with Clifford as chairman. Its purpose was to examine the Wheeler-Westmoreland request for more forces and to determine the domestic implications. As the principals understood it, the assignment from the President was a fairly narrow one—how to give Westmoreland what he said he needed, with acceptable domestic consequences.

Clifford convened the Task Force that same day in McNamara's Pentagon dining room for an introductory meeting. Beginning on March 1, he held day and evening sessions through March 6. McNamara attended the first session as Secretary of Defense, but did not thereafter participate. The other participants were Clifford, Nitze, Warnke, and Goulding for Defense; Rusk, Katzenbach, William Bundy, and Philip Habib for State; Wheeler for the JCS; Helms for CIA; Rostow for the White House; Fowler for Treasury; and Maxwell Taylor as a special adviser. Initially Clifford adopted a kind of quiet, judicial posture, encouraging others to develop information. He was going through, as he later put it, "the most intensive learning period of my life." Rusk said little at the opening session, it being a familiar trait of his to remain relatively silent at meetings he did not himself conduct, preferring to reserve his position for the President's ear. Thereafter, he did not attend the Task Force discussions.

Clifford moved immediately to broaden the inquiry's frame of reference by stating that, to him, the basic question was whether the U.S. should continue to follow the same course in Vietnam. What was likely to happen if we put in another 200,000 men? Would that bring us any closer to our objectives? Perhaps Westmoreland did need 200,000 additional troops under his present strategic concept, but was that a sensible concept? McNamara said Westmoreland's forces had been asked to carry more of the burden of achieving U.S. political objectives in Vietnam than could be borne by military power; we could not, he said, "by limited military means" force North Vietnam to quit, but neither could they drive us out of South Vietnam; the time had therefore come to recognize the necessity for negotiations and a compromise political settlement. Nitze argued the need to reexamine the involvement in Vietnam in the wider context of U.S. interests and commitments elsewhere in the world; he said that, whatever the result in Vietnam itself, we would have failed in our purposes if the war should spread to the point of direct military confrontation with China or Russia, or to the point where our resources were so heavily committed in Vietnam as to put our other commitments in serious doubt. He thought a less ambitious strategy should be devised, in order to buy time for strengthening ARVN and for getting out. Habib, who was William Bundy's deputy and a specialist on Vietnamese affairs, thought any alternative course would be preferable to sending more U.S. troops, because that would simply take the pressure off the GVN and ARVN to stand on their own feet.

Rostow, Wheeler, and Taylor expounded the hard line, arguing that the Tet offensive was in reality a new and unexpected opportunity. The guerrilla enemy, so long elusive and unwilling to give battle under conditions that favored America's superior firepower, had suddenly exposed himself all over the country. He had come into the open in large numbers, in a desperate attempt to seize cities and promote popular uprisings. This dramatic shift of strategy indicated he could no longer stand the relentless pressure of U.S. military power in a protracted war. Therefore, the prompt and substantial reinforcing of Westmoreland could open the way to victories that would decimate the enemy forces and bring Hanoi, much more quickly than otherwise, to the conference table under conditions favorable to our side. Speaking for the JCS, Wheeler said the full 206,000 men were needed, and that to provide less would be taken by Westmoreland as a vote of no confidence. Taylor doubted whether sending even the full 206,000 would enable Westmoreland "to do what he is trying to do." *

Nitze and Warnke, supported by Katzenbach, sought to counter these arguments. There was, they argued, no very convincing evidence that the enemy's attack was motivated by desperation or that his immediate aims were as ambitious as a popular uprising against the GVN and the wholesale desertion of ARVN. It seemed more likely, they argued, that the enemy had decided the time was ripe for a major effort to achieve several very important, but still limited, purposes: to capture one or more major cities, to cause large-scale panic in the ARVN, to recapture large parts of the countryside in order to destroy the pacification program and gain access to new recruits; above all, to show public opinion in America that, contrary to the optimistic projections of November, the U.S. was not winning the war and in fact could not seriously attempt to win it without undermining its domestic and global interests.

As Warnke saw it, both sides were disappointed by the results. The enemy failed to capture and hold any major city, and he suffered tremendous losses, perhaps 30,000 killed; also, ARVN fought better than expected. But the attacks produced devastating effects on our side as well—many cities were overrun and then gravely damaged or destroyed in the process of recapturing them, with heavy loss of life; the enemy still held the countryside and had demonstrated the inherent fragility of the pacification program; large-scale U.S. forces

* There has been a curious, retrospective effort by the military leaders to argue that an actual request for 206,000 additional troops was never made. That figure, they now claim, merely represented one of several possible force levels in a wide spectrum of "normal contingency plans" that covered plausible future battlefield situations ranging from favorable to ominous. But the Wheeler assessment contained only one set of figures and related them directly to his considered view that Westmoreland needed prompt reinforcements. Certainly the President, in establishing the *Ad Hoc* Task Force on Vietnam, understood that he was organizing to consider a specific manpower request. Finally, Wheeler's own line of argument in the Task Force discussions leaves no doubt that he regarded the figure as a firm military proposal, endorsed by the Joint Chiefs of Staff.

were tied down in remote, uninhabited places like Khesanh and Con Thien, unable to move, pounded by enemy artillery, and with their ability to resist direct assault a matter of growing doubt. Finally, it was clear that public opinion in the United States had been shaken to the roots. In plain truth, Warnke argued, neither side could win militarily. U.S. strategy should henceforth be based on that reality and should aim, not at victory, but at the kind of staying power necessary to the achievement of a compromise political settlement. In military terms, this meant no further troop increases (for the enemy could and would match them), a pullback from isolated posts like Khesanh, and a far less aggressive ground strategy designed to protect the people where they live. A revised directive should be sent to Westmoreland making clear that henceforward his primary mission would be to protect the population of South Vietnam. There should also be a renewed effort to open talks, if necessary by halting the bombing.

With Clifford listening intently and learning fast, but not yet committed to any position, the sheer momentum of the ongoing policy continued to dominate the proceedings. Except for Clifford, who was still neutral, the participating *principals*—Rusk, Rostow, Wheeler, Taylor, and Fowler —were strongly for meeting the request and getting on with the war. They claimed, explicitly or by implication, to know the President's mind, and everyone was aware that he had many times said his commanders in Vietnam would get whatever they needed. In the circumstances, the advocates of change faced a heavy, uphill battle, but they kept doggedly at it. After each Task Force session broke up, Warnke and Goulding stayed behind to express to Clifford their concern over the drift of the discussion, to press a particular point, to counter a particular line of argument. Clifford listened intently, then asked them to go and prepare facts and analysis that he could use at the next session. All during the seven-day period, Warnke and Goulding would thus retire to an office between sessions to develop hasty counter arguments, dictating and correcting drafts at a rapid clip, so that Clifford could have fresh information for the next meeting.

While the Clifford Task Force was meeting, the Army and the Air Force were analyzing possible "alternative strategies" at Clifford's direction. In the Air Force, Harold Brown and I worked steadily through the weekend, receiving drafts from the Air Staff, discussing these with the Vice-Chief, General Bruce Holloway, and a small team of officers, and then sending the drafts back to be amended and refined. The Air Staff brought forward three alternatives: (1) an intensified bombing campaign in the North, including attacks on the dock area of Haiphong, on railroad equipment within the Chinese Buffer Zone, and on the dike system that controlled irrigation for NVN agriculture; (2) a greater effort against the truck routes and supply trails in the southern part of North Vietnam (the narrow area called the panhandle) to be generated by shifting about half the daily sorties away from the Hanoi-Haiphong area; and (3) a campaign designed to substitute tactical airpower for a large portion of the search-and-destroy operations currently conducted by ground forces, thus permitting the ground troops to concentrate on a perimeter defense of the heavily populated areas.

The Air Staff strongly preferred Alternative 1, but Brown and I continued to feel that, while there was little assurance such a campaign could either force NVN to the conference table, or even significantly reduce its war effort, it was a course embodying excessive risks of confrontation with Russia. Alternative 2 was statistically promising (it became the basis for the President's later decision to eliminate all bombing above the 20th parallel), but it too lacked decisiveness. Alternative 3 was pressed on the staff largely at my insistence, and the analysis seemed to show that tactical airpower could provide a potent "left jab" to keep the enemy in the South off balance while the U.S.-ARVN ground forces adopted a modified enclaves strategy, featuring enough aggressive reconnaissance to identify and break up developing

176

attacks, but designed primarily to protect the people of Vietnam and, by population control measures, to force exposure of the VC political cadres. It was a strategy aimed not at winning a military victory, but at providing a strong negotiating posture. Harold Brown forwarded the Air Staff papers together with a memorandum representing his supplementary views and my own. He and I were in full agreement.

THE TASK FORCE RECOMMENDATIONS

These various countermovements notwithstanding, the Task Force ended its seven-day effort by drafting a set of recommendations which in all essential respects confirmed existing policy. In a short, unsigned memorandum for the President, it recommended an immediate deployment of about 20,000 additional troops and the prompt approval of reserve call-ups, larger draft calls, and lengthened duty tours in Vietnam sufficient both to provide the remaining 186,000 men requested by Westmoreland and to restore a strategic reserve force adequate to meet contingencies that might arise elsewhere in the world. There was to be a reiteration of the San Antonio formula, but no new initiative toward negotiations or peace. There was also to be a step-up in the bombing, with Wheeler, Taylor, and Rostow advocating measures beyond those acceptable to the other members of the Task Force, i.e., to expand the targets around Hanoi and Haiphong, and to mine Haiphong harbor. These were the central recommendations. The advocates of change gained only the fringe benefit of delay, i.e., deferment of the actual decision to deploy the remaining 186,000 to Vietnam and agreement to make that decision subject to: (1) evidence of improved political performance by the GVN, (2) studies that might produce new political and strategic guidance for Westmoreland, and (3) week-by-week examination of the developing situation in Vietnam. Beyond these frail and imprecise caveats, the report was entirely silent on the matter of the relevance and adequacy of U.S. political objectives in Vietnam, the validity of the present ground strategy, the usefulness of the bombing, or the effects of Tet. Its spare, terse, emotionless prose typified those papers that go to the President for action on issues of great heat and consequence. They do not reargue the issues, for these are painfully known to all concerned; they state merely the minimal compromise agreement that the contending parties have been able to reach.

Clifford, although he passed along the report, was uneasy about it, for the Task Force deliberations had deepened his doubts as to the wisdom and practicality of existing policy. Moreover, in separate meetings with the Joint Chiefs of Staff, he had probed for their professional assessment of the battle-field effect of adding 206,000 troops, but had received only "vague and unsatisfactory" answers. They could not promise victory; at most, they could say that more troops would add to the cumulative weight of our pressure on the enemy. Nitze, Warnke, Goulding, and I were profoundly discouraged, for we felt that presidential approval of the first increment of troops would implicitly reaffirm both the Bunker-Westmoreland assessment of the Tet offensive and the Westmoreland ground strategy. To me the Task Force report was mindless folly, confirming once more the depressing truth that the inner core of the Administration was frozen solid in misconceptions as to the nature of the war, as to what our military power could accomplish, as to how our real interests in Asia should be served. The advisers seemed incapable of extricating themselves from policies that were manifestly *not* working. The memorandum contained, for example, no mention at all of negotiations, yet it seemed clear we would only begin another dreary cycle of inconclusive bloodshed and widening conflict if, in the wake of Tet, we made the mistake of insisting there could be no talks until we had once again regained the military initiative. As I said in a memorandum to Warnke at this time:

In the see-saw struggle to determine the precisely propitious moment to risk negotiations, we should try to retain a sense of proportion. We are a nation of 200 million—the strongest economic and military power in the world—whereas North Vietnam is an underdeveloped country of 19 million. We should be able to afford a certain magnanimity on this point of the circumstantial "position of strength" prerequisite for entering upon negotiations. In other words, we should not too much insist on our own particular stage setting for talks. If we do, we will probably get no talks at all.

But by far the most serious deficiency of the Task Force report was its failure to gauge the horrendous political implications of its basic recommendation that the military manpower request be met. For this involved a reserve mobilization on the order of 250,000 men as well as increased draft calls. Together, these measures would add 450,000 men to U.S. active duty forces, bringing the total strength to about 3.9 million. With his sensitive journalistic antennae quivering, Goulding hastily dictated an appendix which Clifford circulated within the Task Force, but which did not go forward to the President. Goulding's appendix noted that there had been absolutely no preparation of public opinion for such a large-scale mobilization. The official line had stressed our ability to fight in Vietnam and at the same time to meet commitments elsewhere without undue strain; it had held that we were winning the war and, specifically, that we had emerged victorious from the Tet offensive; it insisted that ARVN was improving every day. Now suddenly 250,000 American reservists were to be separated from their families and careers and another 200,000 men drafted—all in the absence of any new or palpable national crisis.

Goulding argued that the shock wave would run through the entire American body politic. The doves would say the President was destroying the country by pouring its finest men and resources into a bottomless pit. The hawks would cry that the Administration had no moral right to disrupt the lives of all these young men and still insist on waging a war of limited objectives, limited geographical boundaries, and limited weapons. They would demand, Goulding wrote, that the Administration "unleash . . . hit the sanctuaries . . . if necessary invade." The antiwar demonstrations and resistance to the draft would rise to new crescendos, reinforced by civil rights groups who would feel the President had once again revealed his inner conviction that the war in Vietnam was more important than the war on poverty. It would be quite unavailing for the Administration to say that only 20,000 more men were being committed to Vietnam. That might or might not prove to be true; in the larger sense the claim would be irrelevant for, in the context of steady escalation over the past three years, it simply would not be believed. Moreover, the major political damage would be done by the increased mobilization itself, for it was this that would bring on the domestic surprise and disruption, as well as cause the defense budget to rise by $2.5 billion in 1968 and by $10 billion in 1969. The actual deployment of the other 186,000 to Vietnam would be, as the saying went, a "secondary explosion."

Goulding's appendix made clear that the Administration had trapped itself in repeated expressions of overblown optimism and could thus carry into effect the recommendations of the Task Force only if it were ready to accept the gravest domestic political risks. Clifford was deeply impressed by its unanswerable logic; others were equally taken aback. Fowler, who had concluded that a formal war mobilization was the only sure way to obtain the higher taxes and controls that he felt were necessary for a successful defense of the dollar, was apparently chastened by the chilling implications of the Goulding analysis.

The Task Force recommendations were sent to the President on March 7. The following day, Clifford went to the White House to discuss the proposed actions and their implications, and also to lay before the President some of the fundamental questions which had formed in his own thinking about Vietnam. The recommendations, he explained, were responsive to instructions and represented actions that the President could take "if that is the way you wish to go."

He felt obliged to add, however, that, while not yet agreeing or disagreeing with the thrust of the Task Force report, he had developed "doubts" about the efficacy of the ground strategy, the effectiveness of the bombing campaign, and what could really be accomplished by a further large infusion of American troops. He acknowledged that his doubts did not appear to be shared by the other principals on the Task Force, namely, Rusk, Rostow, Wheeler, Taylor, and Fowler.

When the basic differences were out on the table, the President was less than pleased with Clifford's position, notwithstanding its essential tentativeness at that point. Disturbed by what had seemed to him McNamara's progressive emotionalism and apostasy, the President had looked forward to Clifford's coming aboard as a means of reestablishing solid group harmony. Then, as Clifford later said wryly, "this Judas appeared." The warm, longstanding friendship between the two men grew suddenly formal and cool. For with Lyndon Johnson nothing counted for more than personal loyalty, and with respect to Vietnam nothing was so deep-rooted as the President's instinctive bellicosity and will to win. Clifford was affronting both of these feelings, and over the following days he felt the relationship deteriorating. However, it did not during March fall to the point where the President refused to see him alone—that was to be a manifestation of the following summer, during Clifford's struggle to effect a total bombing halt in an effort to get the Paris talks off dead center.

The session on March 8 ended with Clifford emphasizing the tentative nature of his own judgments and expressing the hope that there would be time for further study. Wheeler and the JCS were anxious to move ahead on the Task Force recommendations, but Rusk and Rostow were prepared to have the issues studied further, in part because the domestic implications, political and economic, seemed to grow more ominous with each passing day. Some reasonable delay appeared to meet the President's preferences.

CHAPTER 9

Clifford Resolves His Doubts

DOMESTIC POLITICS

MARCH 12 was the day of the Democratic primary in New Hampshire. While President Johnson won as a write-in candidate with 49.4 percent of the vote, Senator Eugene McCarthy polled 42.2 percent. The shock to Johnson and his supporters was very real, for the voting proved beyond denial that the reports of deep divisiveness in the country were more than newspaper talk. One Democratic politician, reflecting on New Hampshire and watching the storm clouds gather over Wisconsin, where the primary voting would take place on April 2, said "The Democratic Party is on the edge of rebellion."

On Wednesday evening, March 13, Clifford received a call from Senator Edward Kennedy asking for an appointment for his brother Robert. Kennedy said his brother was worried about Vietnam and the crisis in the cities, but mainly about Vietnam. He had been thinking of an approach to the problem. Clifford offered to meet the next morning at the Pentagon.

Robert Kennedy arrived, accompanied by Theodore Sorensen, who had been President Kennedy's Special Counsel in the White House. His conscience urged him, Kennedy said, to try to change the course in Vietnam, and he had been under great pressure to get into the presidential race.

He said that he and Sorensen wanted to present a proposal for the President's consideration, for if there were some way in which he could effect a change in Vietnam policy, he would not feel obliged to run. He then asked Sorensen to explain the plan. The President, said Sorensen, would announce that "under the conditions now prevailing and in light of recent events," he found it necessary to conduct a complete evaluation of Vietnam policies and, for this purpose, had decided to appoint a commission that would conduct an investigation and report its findings to both the President and the American people.

Clifford commented that this would amount to "a confession of error" by LBJ. Kennedy said one could not expect a President publicly to use words like that, but the words would nevertheless have to be strong enough to indicate that he had reached a point of grave doubt as to the wisdom of the present course. Kennedy proposed that the commission be composed of Edwin Reischauer, Kingman Brewster, Roswell Gilpatric, Robert Kennedy, Carl Kaysen, General Lauris Norstad, General Matthew Ridgway, Senator Mansfield; also possibly Senators Cooper and Aiken. Sorensen proposed that Robert Kennedy should be chairman of the commission, but Kennedy said he did not think that was necessary so long as he was a member.

Clifford commented that a Kennedy candidacy would confront the great difficulty of trying to displace an incumbent President who was seeking reelection. Sorensen demurred, saying that 1968 presented "an entirely different situation."

After the meeting, Clifford called the President and made an appointment to see him later that afternoon. In the President's office, he presented the Kennedy plan. LBJ's reaction was "immediate and positive"—the offer was unacceptable for several reasons: (1) no matter how dressed up, it would appear to be a political deal and would tie the Administration's Vietnam policy to the presidential race; (2) the kind of public statements suggested would throw the gravest doubt on present policy; (3) the appointment of an outside group would constitute a usurpation of the functions and powers of the Presidency; (4) such a statement would give the greatest possible lift to Hanoi's morale because it would intimate a new and softer American policy; (5) the people suggested for membership would not need to hold any meetings because the President was entirely familiar with their attitudes; they could not conduct an objective inquiry because their minds were already made up.

Clifford then left the President to telephone Sorensen in Robert Kennedy's office. Sorensen got Kennedy on the phone. Clifford told them the President had found the suggestion unacceptable, and he summarized the President's reasons. He added that the President was willing to talk to individuals or groups, including groups of former government officials, but that the combination of proposed commission and accompanying public statements would constitute a transference of Presidential responsibility. Kennedy asked, "Is that his answer?" Clifford said it was. Sorensen asked, "There is nothing more?" When Clifford said no, Sorensen said thank you and the conversation ended.

On Saturday, March 16, Robert Kennedy announced for the Presidency and embarked immediately on a whirlwind campaign beginning with two speeches that produced the largest political crowds in the history of Kansas—15,000 at Kansas State University, and 17,000 at the University of Kansas. Clifford was uncertain whether Kennedy would have stayed out of the race even if the President had accepted the essential elements of his proposal, but he regarded the President's reasons for refusal as entirely cogent. He also drew the inference from this episode that the President definitely intended to run for reelection.

Certainly Lyndon Johnson was in a combative mood. On March 15, he received an eight-page "eyes only" memorandum from Ambassador Goldberg at the United Nations, arguing for a complete bombing halt in order to get negotiations started. Goldberg had left the Supreme Court in 1965 at the President's urgent request, because the President had persuaded him that he could be of special value in helping to resolve the tortured problem of Vietnam. Now he was frustrated and disillusioned because he felt himself to be without influence on that issue. On Cyprus, the Middle East, and the *Pueblo* crisis, he had a voice. But it wasn't possible, he thought, to get a hearing from the Vietnam "war council," which he defined as the President, Rusk, Rostow, Fortas, and Clifford. He felt the deepest irony and anger at the fact that his former colleague, Justice Fortas, had achieved far greater influence on Vietnam policy, *while remaining on the Court*. He had expressed his desire to resign, but the President had put him off, being concerned about a "bunching" of cabinet resignations in March (McNamara and John W. Gardner were both leaving in that month).

Goldberg favored a complete bombing halt, feeling it was the only way to get substantive talks started and being convinced it would have no serious adverse effect on the war effort; he conceded it might create certain political problems if the President continued to insist on linking bombing in the North with the level of American casualties in the South, particularly at Medal of Honor ceremonies. But the memorandum got a volcanic response at the White House. At a meeting of the inner group on Saturday, March 16—the day Robert Kennedy put himself into the race—the President referred to Goldberg's initiative and then said testily "Let's get one thing clear. I am not going to stop the bombing. I have heard every argument on the subject, and I am not interested in further discussion. I have made up my mind. I'm not going to stop it." A chilled silence settled over the embattled advisers gathered in the Cabinet Room.

MEMORANDUM ON THE INFEASIBILITY
OF MILITARY VICTORY

Deeply discouraged by the apparent results of the reappraisal, which seemed to have produced only a more cautious confirmation of existing policy and strategy, I decided that someone had to make it blindingly clear to Clifford that acceptance of either a little or a lot more of the same involved the purchase of disaster on the installment plan. To hold our own country together and to salvage something from the Vietnam quagmire required, I was convinced, major changes in thought and action. Almost everything tragic and wrong about the present policy flowed from the assumption that we could, within the bounds of recognizably "limited war," win a military victory in Vietnam (or could by military pressure force the NVN-VC to accept our terms, which came of course to the same thing). At an earlier time, victory might not have been beyond reach—if we had knowingly adopted and determinedly sustained a genuine counterinsurgency effort, firmly subordinating military actions to the political aims of rooting out the Viet Cong infrastructure and protecting the people of South Vietnam. But the development of U.S. strategy since 1965—and indeed before that—had taken an entirely different road; by March 1968 it was too late to turn back and start fresh. Hope now lay in the fact that one strong and important cabinet officer, Clifford, was increasingly questioning the assumption that military victory was achievable, and was showing himself receptive to further argument and analysis; moreover, that the President did not appear bent upon an immediate decision on the Task Force recommendations. I therefore undertook to find compelling arguments to support the conclusion that U.S. military victory in Vietnam was infeasible. After a week of hard work, I sent Clifford what I hoped was a definitive memorandum.

Memorandum for the Secretary of Defense
Subject: The Infeasibility of Military Victory in Vietnam

As a contribution to current deliberations and to your own ongoing review of the situation, this memorandum argues the case that the idea of military victory in Vietnam is a dangerous illusion, at any price that would be compatible with US interests, the interests of the people of South Vietnam, or the cause of world peace. Secretary Brown agrees that it should be forwarded for your consideration.

Military victory—that is, the destruction or ejection of NVN forces and the reduction of VC guerrilla forces to impotence or at least to a level that is manageable by ARVN alone—has been the implicit (though not always clearly recognized) goal of US policy at least since the decision to build up American manpower in 1965. It continues to be the unexamined assumption of General Westmoreland's strategy, of his request for additional forces, of the JCS support for his strategy and his requests, and of all other proposals for intensifying or enlarging our war effort in Vietnam.

Moreover, military victory (as defined above) appears to be a necessary precondition for the realization of a US political objective which defines "free choice" for the people of SVN as a process necessarily excluding the NLF/VC from participation in either elections or government. Whether or not this definition reflects the true US intent, it is clearly the position of the GVN and has not been rejected by the USG. As is known, even noncommunist politicians are now being jailed by the GVN out of fear that they will open a dialogue with the NLF. These facts suggest that if military victory is not feasible, the US political objective must be redefined.

One's assumption about the necessity or feasibility of military victory is therefore a critical fork in the road. Reaffirmation will lead in the direction of a larger and wider war effort aimed at destroying the NVN/VC forces. Refutation will lead to adoption of a far less ambitious strategy, aimed at protecting the people of South Vietnam, permitting a stabilization of the US resources commitment at tolerable levels, and followed by a prompt, utterly serious effort to achieve a compromise settlement of the war that reflects the enduring political and military realities in Vietnam. It is imperative, at this watershed in our Vietnam experience, to subject the assumption to the most searching re-examination. Our future ability to formulate rational policies for Vietnam depends on this.

The history of our involvement in Vietnam, particularly since 1965, has been marked by repeated miscalculations as to the force and time required to "defeat the aggression," pacify the countryside, and make the GVN and the ARVN viable without massive US support. Each fresh increment of American power has been justified as the last one needed to do the job. Responsible political and military officials have consistently under-estimated NVN/VC strength and tenacity, have promoted uncritical notions of what US military power can accomplish in the political and geographical environment of SEA, and have indulged in persistently wishful thinking as regards the present capacity and real potential of the GVN and the ARVN. It is important that these misjudgments be kept in mind as we weigh the alternatives that now lie before us.

The following points contain some material that may already have come to your attention. The purpose here is to combine all of the relevant arguments and bring them to focus on the root question of whether military victory is feasible.

The Political Factors

1. The GVN is a narrowly based military clique. While it is systematically corrupt, this fact does not particularly distinguish it from other military governments in Asia.... What does distinguish the GVN are its inefficiency, lack of popular support, and inability to protect or govern large areas of SVN. These deficiencies are interrelated and mutually reinforcing; they are also, of course, gravely aggravated by the powerful challenge of the NVN/VC on both the political and military levels. For better or worse, it is Ho Chi Minh and Hanoi who have harnessed nationalism to their cause and who have demonstrated superior determi-

nation, organization, and fighting qualities. To survive without permanent massive US support, the GVN must win broader allegiance and extend its effective authority. Yet its will and ability to do either of these things have never been in greater doubt.

2. ...At the end of 1967...the GVN actually had dominant influence over only about 30% of the population; pacification was on a tenuous and fragile footing...even though the pacification effort had been greatly expanded during the year.

3. Although our information is still fragmentary, it appears that the recent NVN/VC offensive has achieved the takeover of a large part of the populated countryside. ARVN forces have pulled back to defensive positions around towns and cities, and many of the RD cadres have similarly withdrawn....It is probable that, in those areas where the NVN/VC have regained access to populations formerly under GVN control, they will quickly destroy the GVN structure by eliminating those individuals identified as agents and servants of the GVN.

4. ...ARVN and US forces in the towns and cities are now responding to mortar fire from nearby villages by the liberal use of artillery and air strikes. This response is causing widespread destruction and heavy civilian casualties—among people who were considered only a few weeks ago to be secure elements of the GVN constituency. [This is] another example of our conceptions of military necessity working to undermine our political objective.

5. The present mode and tempo of operations in SVN is already destroying cities, villages and crops, and is creating civilian casualties at an increasing rate. Recent statistics suggest that perhaps 5% of the people of SVN are now homeless refugees. While this is not of course deliberate, US and ARVN forces are contributing heavily to the destruction and dislocation, and the people of SVN are aware of this. We are progressively tearing the country apart in order to win "the hearts and minds" of its people. Unfortunately, the end and the means are mutually exclusive.

The Bombing Campaign

6. The bombing campaign against North Vietnam has now entered its fourth year. Since the beginning of the air strikes in 1965, the flow of men and material from NVN to SVN has definitely increased....

8. NVN has ... made a durable adjustment to the bombing. On balance, NVN is a stronger military power today than before the bombing began....

10. It may be possible to reduce the present infiltration capability by concentrating a greater bombing effort south of the Red River, especially by augmenting the currently productive attacks against trucks in Laos. New technology, new tactics, and particularly such systems as the AC-130 gunship show promise of producing measurable improvement. However, to cut off the required minimal supply flow (50-150 tons per day) to SVN, we would have to improve our present effectiveness by a factor of four or more. Such an improvement is possible *in principle*.

Relative Ground Force Strengths

. . . .

13. If we should decide to meet General Westmoreland's requests for additional manpower, in whole or in part, the probable NVN response would be to offset our advantage by adding *proportionate* forces from NVN. Based on the relative manpower ratios that have existed over the past three years (during which time the fighting has ebbed and flowed, but remained inconclusive), it appears that NVN could neutralize a 206,000 US augmentation by adding less than 50,000 men (a ratio of about 1 to 4).

14. On the basis of [its] untapped manpower resources and in view of the newly gained access to a greater portion of the SVN population, it seems evident that NVN could go on making offsets of this kind for an indefinite period. Nor is there anything to suggest that Hanoi lacks the will. However, even if we assume that additional US measures (e.g., closing Haiphong) were to reduce the infiltration capability, NVN would retain the option of reverting to a lower

scale of warfare, and could take additional casualty-limiting actions to preserve its political and military organization in SVN if that were deemed necessary (there is however nothing in the present situation to indicate that Hanoi is worried about attrition).

15. Assuming we continue to pursue the present strategy of attrition (and give Westmoreland 206,000 men), we would have to expect that US casualties would increase in roughly direct proportion to the higher level of effort. This could mean 1300–1400 KIA per month. Yet it would soon be evident that the increase in casualties had not altered the fundamental condition of stalemate in SVN.

16. There is accordingly no foreseeable military resolution of the conflict at either the present level of US forces (plus ARVN and other friendly forces) or with a full 206,000-man augmentation as requested by General Westmoreland. Nothing that we know of Hanoi's determination, manpower reserves, and available weapons supply, and nothing in the past record, gives us any basis for a confident judgment that we could attrite the enemy, drive him from SVN, or destroy his will to fight as a result of fully meeting General Westmoreland's new requests. What is called into question by these facts is the US strategy of attrition in SVN —the strategy of attempting to wear down the enemy by inflicting more casualties than he can cumulatively bear. . . .

Impact of the Westmoreland Requests

17. The further augmentation of US forces as proposed by General Westmoreland would entail very substantial costs in South Vietnam, in the United States, and elsewhere in the world.

18. In *South Vietnam,* the presence of more than 700,000 US forces would increase the already crushing weight of the American presence on that small country. Worst of all, it would encourage the GVN to believe that the US was prepared to go on fighting its war without making enforceable demands for either administrative efficiency or economic and social reform. . . . It would definitely weaken US leverage on the political situation.

19. A decision to provide 206,000 additional men in the next 12 months would also have a profound impact in the *United States*. It would require mobilizing 250,000 reserves, increasing draft calls, and facing up to substantially increased costs (the annual cost of the VN war would rise from about $25 billion to about $35 billion)....

20. The need for public and Congressional support (both authority and money) of this further force buildup would almost certainly require political rhetoric designed to create an atmosphere of national crisis; yet, barring further dramatic reverses in SVN, the crisis would look synthetic to both war critics and impartial observers (in the sense that the case for larger forces had to be justified by the existence of a situation decisively different from the situation prevailing over the past three years). Extremists in Congress would probably demand, as the price of their support, elimination of all restrictions on bombing of the North, and some might advocate measures designed deliberately to provoke a US confrontation with China or the USSR. There would also be pressures to expand the war into Laos and Cambodia, which, if yielded to, would only serve to spread thinner the US forces in SVN.

21. At the present level, the war is eroding the moral fibre of the nation, demoralizing its politics, and paralyzing its foreign policy. A further manpower commitment to SVN would intensify the domestic disaffection, which would be reflected in increased defiance of the draft and widespread unrest in the cities. Welfare programs on which our domestic tranquility might depend would be eliminated or deeply cut. It is possible that well-placed dissenters in Congress could paralyze the legislative process.

22. The Soviet and Chinese reactions would probably not be extreme, if our additional actions were confined to increasing ground forces and tactical air forces. But they would almost certainly step up their level of materiel support to NVN, as a means of helping Hanoi to offset our manpower increases.... Moreover, if the Soviets believed that our world-wide posture had become seriously unbalanced by the heavy deployment to Vietnam, it is possible

they would test our will in Europe or at other points (e.g., new pressure on Berlin, or stimulation of the Syrians to aggravate the already uneasy Middle Eastern situation).

23. Our progressive diplomatic estrangement would continue. The Scandinavian countries, already visibly wavering, might adopt an open anti-US position. The Labor Government in the UK, which is paying an increasing domestic price for its support of US policy in Vietnam, might be less willing or able to go on paying it.

The Alternative of Intensified Bombing

24. As an independent alternative to ground force augmentation, we could greatly increase the bombing of North Vietnam. There is no doubt that an area bombing campaign, with emphasis on closing the ports of Haiphong, Hon Gai, and Cam Pha, and on attacking over-the-beach deliveries, dispersed storage facilities, and the northeast and northwest rail lines leading into China could impose further serious strains on the already overstressed NVN social and economic structure. The hopeful assumption is that North Vietnam would then be forced to decide on a priority of imports (war-making goods vs. life-supporting goods) and would choose the latter. . . .

26. Should we undertake an expanded bombing effort, the Soviets, Chinese, and North Vietnamese could be expected to devote more effort to the movement of supplies by truck from China along the northeast and northwest routes, and to over-the-beach operations. In the face of such efforts and in the light of our Korean war experience, we could probably cut the NVN import capability in half—to 4,000 tons a day; and it is remotely possible that it would fall to 2,000 tons. But NVN could still import the required munitions and other war-supporting materiel, most of the needed POL, and anywhere from very little (at 2,000 tons) to most (at 4,000 tons) of the needed manufactured goods and food. Living standards in NVN would fall, but this would not necessarily interfere with the capability to support actions in SVN. Household handicraft and family food plots would probably sustain them.

27. Only by a bombing campaign aimed at crop destruction does it appear that food import requirements could be increased to near the import capacity (if they increased from 10% to 50% of total rice needs, the requirement would rise from 1,000 to 5,000 tons per day). Only this kind of increased food requirement could seriously impact on the current level of military imports.

28. In military terms, an intensified area bombing campaign could limit NVN actions in SVN at or near the pre-Tet level, and below the level of February 1968. But such a campaign ... would be unlikely to reduce NVN capability in SVN substantially below the 1967 level. It is possible that a more drastic reduction could be effected, but given the long season of poor bombing weather (between November and May, the weather permits an average of 5 days per month of visual bombing), the NVN transportation system would begin to be reconstituted.

29. Notwithstanding its probable inconclusiveness, an intensified area bombing campaign would have far-reaching military and diplomatic repercussions. A major effort to close Haiphong would have to accept serious risks of hitting Soviet shipping; and if Soviet ships were struck, the USSR could not fail to react. Reaction could cover a wide range of possibilities from introducing minesweepers and naval escort vessels carrying anti-aircraft guns, to providing bomber aircraft and pilots to NVN, to creating a diversionary crisis in Europe or the Middle East. We could be sure only that it would be an utterly determined reaction. ...

The Alternative of Unlimited Manpower

32. It is conceivable (but no more than that) that we could drive out or totally defeat the North Vietnamese in SVN, destroy the Viet Cong and its infrastructure, and thus provide the remaining South Vietnamese with a "free choice" ... if we were to *treble* the number of US forces in SVN. As earlier noted, the present tempo of operations in SVN is already destroying cities, villages and crops, and is creating civilian casualties at an increasing rate. While this is not deliberate, our forces are contributing heavily to the de-

struction. The commitment of 1.5 million men (or any number approaching that magnitude) would inevitably produce a policy of scorched earth. Even assuming the battle could be contained without the intervention of Chinese ground forces or Soviet air forces, and without a serious Russian diversionary action in another part of the world, we could hardly avoid totally crushing the country and its people, leaving a wasteland. As was said of the Romans at Carthage, "You made a desert and called it peace."

33. A *trebling* of effort would probably raise the US cost of the Vietnam War to about $85–90 billion per year. It is difficult to believe the American people would accept such a burden or such a risk. Disaffection would be rampant.... Large segments of our society would be totally alienated...

34. If there were a serious prospect (as there would be) that the NVN/VC effort would be totally defeated, China might well enter the war with large-scale combat forces. The Soviets would almost surely increase the quantity and the level of sophistication of their material support; they might introduce Russian pilots and bomber aircraft; and they would more than likely create a serious diversion in another part of the world. World opinion would totally condemn the US for a Carthaginian policy.

Conclusion

35. Anything resembling a clear-cut military victory in Vietnam appears possible only at the price of literally destroying SVN, tearing apart the social and political fabric of our own country, alienating our European friends, and gravely weakening the whole free world structure of relations and alliances. Russian or Chinese military intervention on the side of NVN, or at another geographical point in the world, would be a serious risk if we greatly increased our own effort. They clearly have the capacity, and give every evidence of having the will, to prevent the outright defeat of NVN.

36. Judged against any rational scale of values, a military victory in Vietnam is therefore infeasible at any price consistent with US interests.

37. What follows inexorably from the foregoing conclusion is the need for a redefinition of our political objective in Vietnam, and a basic shift in military strategy. The objective should be an honorable political settlement of the war followed by the organization of an international agreement to guarantee the military neutralization of Vietnam, Laos, and Cambodia. Our military strategy should accordingly be adjusted to give maximum support to a negotiating posture.

38. A well-coordinated program of action will of course require the detailed attention of the USG. In particular, the State Department must seriously tackle the unpleasant realities of a genuine compromise settlement to be hammered out in negotiations with a weakened, but not a beaten foe. To date the matter has been carefully avoided, avoidance being sustained by the tacit assumption that negotiations would involve little more than ratification of the other side's surrender, or that there would be no negotiations at all, but only a "fading away" of the Viet Cong. Negotiations will be painful and might be protracted, and they will inevitably involve severely disappointing the present GVN.

39. If, however, these unpleasant realities are faced, the actions required are apparent. They are a cessation of the bombing to get talks started, as soon as we have regained our military poise; a shift of our forces to the primary task of protecting the population centers; willingness to talk to the NLF and to accept a coalition government; organization of the international community, including especially the Soviet Union, to guarantee the military neutralization of Vietnam, Laos, and Cambodia; and ultimately the phased withdrawal of US forces.

Townsend Hoopes

The memorandum was at once a compendium of my own convictions and a distillation of other men's diligence and wisdom. Some of the arguments had come to Clifford's attention between February 28 and March 7, but mainly in fragments, as the discussion ebbed and flowed in meetings of the Vietnam Task Force. Moreover, arguments of the complexity and consequence of these require reiteration. If my effort had merit, this lay in its having brought most of the relevant and telling points to bear upon the root question for a man whose judgment and intellectual grasp were of the highest order, but who was in major respects a newcomer to the problems. I gave it to Clifford on March 14; there was soon evidence that its reasoning and its conclusion had helped to crystallize the views that were already forming in his mind.

THE FULBRIGHT HEARING

On March 12, the Senate Foreign Relations Committee opened its annual hearings on the Foreign Aid Bill (of which the Military Assistance Bill was a part). The first witness was Rusk and, as had been unanimously anticipated, the discussion quickly turned from economic and military aid to an extended, painful, and frustrating renewal of the public debate on the Vietnam War. For two full days the sorely tried Secretary of State bore the skeptical, troubled, hostile questions from the Senators with admirable dignity and an invincible politeness, but without satisfying any of their doubts. Forced to defend the past and unable to speculate on possible new departures that might emerge from the still ongoing reappraisal, Rusk was in a deeply unenviable position. The resulting dialogue was stale and unedifying fare for both official Washington and the presumed millions of television viewers.

Senator Case of New Jersey, a liberal Republican and a rather quiet man, asked Rusk whether the U.S. commitment really called upon us to persevere to the point of destroying South Vietnam in order to save it. Rusk replied that he doubted the premise of the senator's question, since most of the battles were being fought in essentially uninhabited areas. He went on to imply that all would be well in the end, if only the faint-hearted would refrain from irrelevant criticism of the war and would demonstrate steadfastness. The gentle Case was provoked. "Mr. Secretary, you don't have to persuade this committee, or even me, that it is necessary to be steadfast and patriotic, that it is good to meet commitments, that a nation like the U.S. has responsibilities in the world. You really do not. But there is a line to be drawn between the honorable meeting of commitments and pigheaded pushing in the direction of a course which has become more and more sterile. We are trying to find out which is which. . . . For myself, it seems that a course which more and more is producing agony and destruction for the people we are trying to help, and degradation at home, requires more justification than has been made and presented for it."

Fulbright had also requested Clifford to testify immediately following Rusk, this being the normal sequence for foreign aid hearings, but Clifford, still uncertain as to the depth of his own disaffection from the Administration's Vietnam policy, had declined with the ploy that he was too new to the office and too preoccupied with Vietnam (*sic*) to have developed mature judgments on the Military Assistance Program. The President was also negative about a Clifford appearance before the Fulbright Committee, having concluded that the circumstances of Rusk's testimony—before hostile questioners seeking to exploit the medium of nationwide television—had resulted in a net detriment to the Administration's position. After discussing the problem together, Clifford and the President agreed that Nitze, as Deputy Secretary of Defense, should testify if this was agreeable to the senators. Fulbright promptly concurred, but Nitze then advised Clifford that he was not in a position to defend the Administration's Vietnam policy. Since it was clear, in light of Rusk's experience, that the senators would quickly finesse the subject of foreign aid and direct their questions to Vietnam, Nitze reasoned that he could not avoid the issue and that accordingly he should not testify. He had drafted a letter to the President which he then showed to Clifford. It stated briefly and politely his central position, going on to say that he placed hope in the range of alternative options that were, as he understood it, still under consideration in connection with the reappraisal. The letter concluded with a short paragraph recognizing the possibility that, in view of Nitze's stated position, the President might prefer that he "not continue."

Paul Nitze possessed wide and relevant experience in foreign-military affairs, a sophisticated intellect, and a considerable charm edged with a somewhat Prussian quality. The son of a college professor, he had made his money as a young man in Wall Street before World War II, married well, and thereafter addressed himself primarily to a public career with emphasis on the study and management of strategic problems. After service on the Strategic Bombing Survey in 1946–47, he became Acheson's distinguished Director of Policy Planning at State. Exiled from direct government service during the Eisenhower period by reason of Republican antipathy to the Truman-Acheson foreign policy with which he had been closely associated, Nitze became a noted thinker on strategic problems and foreign policy, operating from the convenient base of the presidency of the Foreign Service Educational Foundation, a part of Johns Hopkins University; eventually he also became an influential consultant to the Eisenhower White House. In 1961, President Kennedy appointed him Assistant Secretary of Defense for International Security Affairs (ISA), and in the ensuing years President Johnson, at McNamara's urging, promoted him to Secretary of the Navy and then to Deputy Secretary of Defense. Basically a hardliner in his attitudes toward Russia, China, and Communism, he was however noted for his sense of proportion, knowledge, and sound judgment on matters of both policy and technique. He was that rare combination of intellectual and manager, as well as a man of unquestioned loyalty and integrity. To those seriously concerned with the effective management of defense affairs, he was a pearl of great price.

Clifford, who was impressed by the depth of Nitze's conviction and who badly needed Nitze's professional expertise to handle major strategic, technical, and administrative problems which time had not yet permitted him to come to grips with, was concerned that the President, acutely sensitive on the matter of loyalty, might in his current frame of mind resent the tone of Nitze's letter and ask for his resignation. Clifford agreed to convey the letter to the President, but urged Nitze first to delete any reference to resigning, and also to soften certain passages, assuring him it was very important, both politically and substantively, that he stay on. Nitze was willing to amend the letter, but even in its revised form it got a sour reception from Lyndon Johnson. Clifford and the President next agreed that Warnke should be the Defense witness, on the logical grounds that his office was directly responsible for planning and managing the Military Assistance Program. Warnke was agreeable, notwithstanding his profound misgivings about Vietnam policy, for, not having been in government at the time of the 1965 decisions, he felt he could roll with the punches. Fulbright however demurred, insisting that the Committee could accept only Clifford or his deputy. So the ball was hit back into Clifford's court. Either he would have to testify personally or the Defense Department would have to bear the onus of refusing to comply with a request from the Senate Foreign Relations Committee.

There is reason to believe that this was the moment—about March 16—when all of Clifford's unresolved uneasiness and doubt crystallized into a firm conviction that the Administration's policy in Vietnam was indefensible. Moved by Warnke's persuasive skepticism, chilled by Goulding's appendix, in receipt of my long memorandum, impressed by Nitze's readiness to resign, his own thoughts coalesced into solid form. Certainly, the idea of having to defend a highly dubious enterprise before informed and vehement congressional critics, and under klieg lights for the benefit of a national television audience, was a prospect calculated to concentrate the mind wonderfully. Clifford decided he would not do it. Instead, he paid a private call on Fulbright and, in the course of a talk that was frank on both sides, spoke of the ongoing reappraisal within the Administration and of his own deepening doubts with respect to the current policy. He urged Fulbright to understand that the prospects for change might be damaged if he were to testify while the major issues were still being debated at the White House, but he thought a more propitious time for testimony would develop. Fulbright, who was heartened by what he heard, dropped all Committee pressure for Clifford's appearance and wrote a letter which in effect invited the Secretary of Defense to name his own time and convenience.

CHAPTER 10

The President at Bay

FURTHER STORM WARNINGS

BY MID-MARCH, storm warnings were coming in from all points of the political-economic compass. Newspaper dispatches of March 10 had disclosed the magnitude of the military manpower request, and this was producing a sharp aggravation of the chronic balance-of-payments problem, with attendant and serious strains on the international monetary system. In the Congress, there was rising criticism of Westmoreland, alarm at the threat to the dollar, opposition to a large-scale call-up of reserves, and uneasiness at the apparent drift and indecision that seemed to have descended upon the Administration. The Gallup Poll reported that 49 percent of the American people now believed the United States was wrong to have become involved in Vietnam with its own military forces.

There was heavy fire from intellectuals of consequence. Max Lerner noted that Washington's response to the acute post-Tet crisis seemed to involve the same deficient mix: "The rituals of reappraisal, the dispatch of a high official to Vietnam, and the decision to hold tight, interpret the new situation as a substantive gain, and probably call for more American soldiers." He noted that this process was producing only frustration, resentment, and bitterness among

Democrats and Republicans alike because it was "obviously wrong." Commenting on the stubbornness of the Westmoreland doctrine of attrition, he said, "To fight a war of corpse statistics on Asian terrain, with China's endless millions in the background, is to move ever farther away from the world of reality." George Kennan called the war a "massive miscalculation and error of policy, an error for which it is hard to find any parallels in our history." He found the Administration's policy "grievously unsound, devoid throughout of a plausible, coherent and realistic object," and he thought the President and his inner circle were "like men in a dream, seemingly insensitive to outside opinion, seemingly unable to arrive at any realistic assessment of the effects of their own acts."

The *New York Times* called the situation a "man-made disaster." On March 15, *Time* magazine commented that the debate was being conducted in a vacuum, that the President had retreated into an ever-narrowing circle of advisers with no one outside the coterie knowing what was on his mind, what questions he was asking or what alternatives he foresaw. The Senate and the country were troubled by the prospect that the Administration would announce new military measures without so much as a by-your-leave to Congress; indeed Fulbright thought the President's authority further to expand the war without consent of the Congress was the principal issue. Senator Church saw the Administration "poised to plunge still deeper into Asia where huge populations await to engulf us, and legions of young Americans are being beckoned to their graves." Robert Kennedy said "There is a question of our moral responsibility. Are we like God of the Old Testament that we can decide in Washington, D.C. what cities, what towns in Vietnam are going to be destroyed? I know that some have said we should intensify the bombing of the North. They should be heard. I do not happen to believe this is the answer to the problem, but I do know that what we have been doing is not the answer . . . that it is immoral and intolerable to continue it."

Clifford, having now reached the firm conclusion that the war was not winnable in military terms under any conditions compatible with American interests, began to state his case for a fundamental change of policy—aimed squarely at disengagement. He was still groping for the precise formula, but the ingredients were apparent: a bombing halt to get talks started, a shift to a less costly ground strategy, measures to strengthen ARVN, a clear warning to the GVN that U.S. military power would not remain indefinitely in Vietnam, and that therefore the GVN must posture itself for a serious political settlement involving compromise with the NLF.

ACHESON'S ROLE

Despite strident declarations which reflected the visceral Johnson, the President was privately troubled and uneasy during February and early March. Whatever his strong instinctive preferences, he could not responsibly ignore the hard realities of the human and financial cost of the war, the fading support for it in the country, the malaise in the foreign-military bureaucracy, and the galloping deterioration of the Democratic party. However unpalatable, these were facts that could not be wished away.

In late February he had consulted Dean Acheson whom he held in the highest regard as a brilliant mind, a courageous and distinguished former Secretary of State, and the toughest of Cold Warriors. When the President asked him his opinion of the current situation in Vietnam, Acheson replied he wasn't sure he had a useful view because he was finding it impossible, on the basis of occasional official briefings given him, to discover what was really happening. He had lost faith in the objectivity of the briefers: "With all due respect, Mr. President, the Joint Chiefs of Staff don't know what they're talking about." The President said that was a shocking statement. Acheson replied that, if such it was, then perhaps the President ought to be shocked. The President said he wanted Acheson's considered judgment; Acheson replied he could give this only if he were free to make his own inquiry into the facts so that he would not be dependent on "canned briefings" from the JCS, Rostow, and the CIA. The President agreed he should have the necessary resources for an independent study.

Acheson thereupon assembled a small group of knowledgeable people at the second and third levels and worked with them over a two-week period, holding meetings at his home where he cross-examined them at length. The group included Philip Habib of State, George Carver of CIA, and Major General William DuPuy of the Joint Chiefs of Staff organization. On March 15, Acheson gave the President his findings, at a luncheon where the two men were completely alone. Acheson told the President he was being led down a garden path by the JCS, that what Westmoreland was attempting in Vietnam was simply not possible—without the application of totally unlimited resources "and maybe five years." He told the President that his recent speeches were quite unrealistic and believed by no one, either at home or abroad. He added the judgment that the country was no longer supporting the war. This was tough, unvarnished advice in the Acheson manner, though served with the customary polish and elegance. The President obviously did not like it, but he greatly respected the purveyor.

The luncheon with Acheson took place just three days after the New Hampshire primary, on the same day that Ambassador Goldberg's bombing memorandum arrived from New York, and one day before Robert Kennedy entered the presidential race. In the face of these unpalatable new pressures and of unwanted but unignorable advice, Lyndon Johnson began to feel "crowded"; his immediate reaction was to lash out in a kind of emotional tantrum. On March 17, he flew to the Middle West to deliver two thoroughly truculent speeches—to the National Alliance of Businessmen and the

National Farmers Union—in the drafting of which Rostow and Fortas had a major hand. Pounding on the lectern, jabbing his finger at the audience, resorting frequently to extemporaneous additions to his prepared text, he said: "Your President has come here to ask you people, and all the other people of this nation, to join us in a total national effort to win the war, to win the peace, and to complete the job that must be done here at home. . . . Make no mistake about it—I don't want a man in here to go back thinking otherwise—we are going to win." Attacking the advocates of a different ground strategy, he charged that "Those of you who think that you can save lives by moving the battlefield in from the mountains to the cities where the people live have another think coming."

Back in Washington on March 19 to address the National Foreign Policy Conference at the State Department, he introduced a definite note of chauvinism: ". . . danger and sacrifice built this land, and today we are the Number One Nation. And we are going to stay the Number One Nation." He then misquoted Lincoln: "With firmness in the right as God gives us the right [sic], let us strive on to finish the work we are in."

I was, along with others, profoundly discouraged by these outbursts, for they suggested that all our efforts, including especially Clifford's courageous stand, were coming to nothing, that the President at bay was stubbornly determined to steer the ship his own way, giving his critics—who by this time probably numbered a large majority of the American people—the back of his hand, conspicuously failing to face the truth about the inadequacy of his preconceptions and his policy. He had also taken to invoking the spirit of the Alamo which, as someone noted, seemed an unfortunate Freudian slip, since everyone there had died. I telephoned Warnke, who was briefly in Florida, and told him I thought we had lost and that the time had come to resign. I was writing a letter of resignation. He was equally discouraged, but closer than I to the day-to-day developments, and he said, "Clark hasn't given up yet. I don't think we should until he does." Clifford was still counting on the innate mysteries of presidential decision-making, and perhaps on the ultimate inscrutability of Lyndon Johnson.

But there was no immediate break in the political weather. In the almost daily meetings on Vietnam at the White House, Clifford found himself outnumbered "7 or 8 to 1" and "not getting very far with the President." After the bellicose speeches of March 18 and 19, he feared "the game was lost." Yet with characteristic persistence, he searched for allies, talking to Dean Acheson, McGeorge Bundy, and Douglas Dillon, all of whom were members of the informal "Senior Advisory Group on Vietnam," a body of distinguished former diplomats, soldiers, and public servants who had rendered great service to the country in foreign policy or in military posts of high responsibility. The group had counseled with the President one or twice a year since 1965. At the last meeting in November 1967, all members, except George Ball, had expressed support for the Administration's policy as well as general satisfaction with the progress of the war (as presented to them by the official briefings). But now Acheson had given the President a far different view, and Clifford also perceived significant shifts in the positions of Bundy and Dillon. From these straws in the wind, he developed the suggestion that the President ought to have the benefit of the group's post-Tet assessment and advice before he decided the consequential issues now before him. The President agreed that a new meeting should be held, and the dates of March 25–26 were scheduled.

By March 20, the President appeared to have passed through his first explosive reaction to the mounting pressures and to have recovered a measure of calm. On that day he had Goldberg come down from New York to discuss his bombing halt memorandum of March 15. The two men met alone, Goldberg unaware of the President's earlier outburst. The

President put forth a number of interested questions, and it was in general a harmonious session. Before they parted, he asked Goldberg to join the meeting of the Senior Advisory Group on March 25, and expressed the hope that the Ambassador would reiterate his views on that occasion. Two days later, on March 22, he announced that Westmoreland would be relieved of his command and come home to be Army Chief of Staff.* No successor was immediately named and no date fixed for the return. In light of his major decisions several days later, it seemed that by these acts President Johnson was tentatively clearing away the accumulated underbrush and preparing the site for the construction of a possibly different policy. Neither act was conclusive, or committed him to substantive change. Those who knew him very well thought in retrospect that the process was largely subconscious, but it did seem that, in a mysterious way peculiar to the U.S. Presidency, something was stirring and changing. Clifford continued to see hope in the mere fact that the debate went on, that the President remained willing to hear him out, rather than turning him off "which he was perfectly capable of doing."

THE MEETING OF MARCH 22

On March 22, the inner circle of advisers, plus George Christian, the press secretary, and Harry McPherson met with the President to discuss a speech on Vietnam that the President had now decided to make. He had instructed McPherson in early February, just a few days after the onset

* By interesting coincidence, a letter by Arthur Schlesinger appeared in the *Washington Post* the same day. Scornful of the caliber of military generalship that had led to the ordeal of the surrounded garrison at Khesanh, Schlesinger wrote: "President Johnson likes to compare himself with Lincoln— 'sad but steady'—but he lacks one prime Lincolnian quality: that is, the courage to fire generals when they have shown they do not know how to win wars. Lincoln ran through a long string of generals before he got to Grant. It is not likely that he would have suffered Westmoreland three months... Let us not sacrifice our brave men to the folly of generals and the obstinacy of Presidents."

of the Tet offensive, to prepare something appropriate; by the first of March, McPherson had proceeded through five drafts, progressively revising and refining his text on the basis of comments from responsible officials in the interested departments. But there seemed in February no sense of urgency about a speech, and the comments were desultory. There was a simple explanation for this: throughout February and into early March, Washington was still trying to find out what was happening in Vietnam, and the prevailing uncertainty made a policy speech premature. By late March, the Administration thought it had a better grip on the situation; moreover, time was running out. Increasing pressures beat upon the White House demanding that the President explain the situation and define anew the nation's course, that he "get on television and level with the people."

The speech draft that the group addressed on March 22 was essentially a tough and uncompromising reiteration of Administration policy (McPherson later called it the "We Shall Overcome draft"). While it left open the question of troop reinforcements, it proposed a call-up of 50,000 reserves, refused any consideration of a bombing halt without clear reciprocity, and urged the surtax as recommended by Fowler. It was patriotically hortatory, calling upon the nation to persevere in a difficult undertaking.

The draft was dismaying to Clifford, who later described it as "everything I hoped it would not be," and he immediately urged that it be amended to include some serious gesture toward peace. He argued for at least a partial bombing halt, as a means of starting a process of tacit, mutual deescalation. This would not, he argued, violate the President's injunction against a total halt and would not jeopardize American troops in northern I Corps. At the very least, it would improve the Administration's public posture and thus extend the lease on public support for the war. The trouble with a partial halt, as everyone recognized, was that it almost certainly wouldn't meet Hanoi's minimal condition for talks.

Vice-President Humphrey, having in mind the impending Wisconsin primary on April 2, felt that the bombing had to be fully stopped, if any political benefit were to be derived. Katzenbach and Harriman also supported a total bombing halt, but somewhat later—around the end of April—because they wanted to allow further time for the U.S. to regain its poise in Vietnam after the Tet onslaught. The meeting, which lasted nearly seven hours, ended with a brisk summary by Rusk. He said the consensus seemed to be that some U.S. move toward negotiations was desirable, but that this was necessarily qualified by the recognition that a mere curtailment or partial cessation of the bombing would not, in all probability, bring Hanoi to the conference table. It was a familiar argument. A year before, in the spring of 1967, McNamara and McNaughton had proposed a similar plan to pull the bombing down to the 20th parallel, with the intention of concentrating the attacks in the narrow "panhandle" through which the infiltration of men and supplies had to pass. In the summer of 1967, Rusk had also proposed a heavily qualified, partial halt to McNamara and Nitze. In both cases, the hope was that, if Washington made the first de-escalatory move, Hanoi might match it, thus setting in motion a cautious step-by-step reduction in the level of violence. But the President had refused to accept these proposals in 1967, in part because the JCS and the Senate hawks were adamantly opposed.

On the night of March 22, as he lay between waking and sleeping, McPherson, the able young speech writer, was visited by an idea. It involved the establishment of some middle ground between the broad desire to make a gesture toward peace and the fear of its rejection by Hanoi. The next morning, McPherson spelled it out in a short memorandum for the President. What he proposed was that the President should unconditionally stop the bombing north of the 20th parallel and, simultaneously, offer to stop it entirely in exchange for assurances that Hanoi would show restraint at the DMZ and would not attack Saigon and other major cities. To McPherson's surprise, the President acted very swiftly, sending the memorandum to Rusk the same day, and thence to Saigon for consideration by Ambassador Bunker with Rusk's implicit endorsement. Bunker responded without great enthusiasm, but to the effect that he could live with it.

LIFTING THE SIEGE OF KHESANH

By early March the siege of Khesanh had so tightened that the Marine garrison could be supplied only by air. Enemy bombardment was heavy and unremitting, and it provided partial cover for the extensive tunneling operations which reached out like sinister fingers from the enemy trenches toward Khesanh's barbed wire perimeter. On March 1, 500 NVN troops frontally assaulted the base, but were driven off by the defenders, materially assisted by B-52 strikes, which laid tons of explosives only 750 yards from the base's outer ring, caving in the tunnels and disrupting the attack force. Between March 5 and March 11, not only Khesanh but several other American strongholds along the southern rim of the DMZ were subjected to intense daily shelling. On March 8, an enemy group of 100 men suddenly emerged from a tunnel at the edge of the airstrip. They were fiercely attacked and driven back by the defenders.

March 12 was awaited with a special anxiety; it was the fourteenth anniversary of the fall of Dien Bien Phu, and it seemed logical to believe that General Giap fully understood the psychological advantage of creating a historical parallel. Fortunately, the U.S. command had at last arranged itself to provide the best chance of preventing a tragic and humiliating defeat. Several weeks before, Westmoreland had turned to Momyer, his air deputy who commanded the 7th Air Force in Saigon, and told him he was placing primary responsibility for the defense of Khesanh on airpower. Momyer had accepted the assignment on the condition that he be given "single management" of airpower in the area of Khesanh, which meant operational control of all USAF, Navy, and Marine tactical strikes, and also primary call on B-52 strikes. The condition was granted. The first thing Momyer did was to photograph the entire five-mile circle around Khesanh with high resolution cameras, using color film. This enabled the U.S. Command, for the first time, to locate all of the NVN troop formations, trench systems, and supply points in the area, and that information in turn formed the basis of the relentless, systematic bombing program that subsequently shredded the NVN forces. The resulting victory was in large measure a triumph of good military intelligence and its orderly application. On March 11 and 12, U.S. aircraft carried out their heaviest attacks up to that time; fighter-bombers flew 250 sorties and successive flights of giant B-52s dropped their unanswerable devastations on the carefully plotted enemy positions. March 12 passed without an attempted ground assault and, as the worst of the monsoon weather began to lift, offering the welcome prospect of clearer skies, one began to sense that the tide might be turning, that the Khesanh affair, so ill-conceived, so tragically and unnecessarily made the symbol of American military honor, might not end quite so badly.

The issue however was still in doubt. On March 17, 120 rounds of enemy artillery fell on the base, blew up a major ammunition dump, and seriously damaged the telephone antennae. There followed, between March 18 and March 25, an extremely violent and intense exchange of NVN artillery fire and American air strikes. The airstrip at Khesanh was now under almost constant interdiction, making it much too hot for a steady stream of cargo aircraft. Major supply became dependent on medium-level parachute drops and an ingenious technique called LAPES (meaning low-altitude parachute extraction system) in which sliding pallets are pulled out of the rear cargo door by a small drag-chute while the aircraft is flying at an altitude of 3–6 feet. But medical evacuation and the bringing in of replacement personnel and certain delicate cargo still required some aircraft to land at Khesanh. Remarkably, although more than a dozen aircraft were destroyed on the ground, only two were hit while in the landing pattern. In one accident, the crew made their way without injury to the comparative safety of sand-bagged bunkers beside the airstrip; in the other, forty-four Marine replacements and the crew of five were all killed.

By the end of March, it was evident that Momyer's "single management" application of airpower had crippled the besiegers beyond their capacity to recover and fight. In about six weeks, U.S. aircraft had dropped 100,000 tons of bombs and fired 700,000 rounds of machine gun fire into a circular area roughly five miles in diameter. B-52s operating from Guam and Thailand had pulverized the thick jungle canopy and the surrounding hills with 2,500 sorties; USAF fighter-bombers had flown 9,700 sorties, the Marines 7,000, and the Navy 5,000. An Air Force colonel, who commanded an F-100 wing, said "The tonnage of ordnance placed in that circle is unbelievable. In mid-February, the area looked like the rest of Vietnam, mountainous and heavily jungled with very little visibility through the jungle canopy. Five weeks later, the jungle had become literally a desert—vast stretches of scarred, bare earth with hardly a tree standing, a landscape of splinters and bomb craters."

On April 1, photoreconnaissance indicated that perhaps 20,000 of the 35,000-man enemy force had withdrawn from the area, the 325th C Division into Laos, the 2nd Division back to the North. On April 5, a 30,000-man U.S.-ARVN column (Operation Pegasus) began a ground drive along Route 9 to relieve Khesanh. Encountering little ground resistance, but coming under sporadic artillery fire, the relieving force reached the base on April 6 and 7. In the smashed land beyond the base perimeter, it found evidence of a rout—1,200 enemy dead strewn about the battlefield, caches totaling 20,000 rounds of small arms ammunition,

5,000 mortar shells, 600 rockets, 5,000 grenades. During the seventy-day ordeal, Marine casualties within the base had been remarkably low—199 dead and about 1,600 wounded. The enemy dead were estimated at more than 10,000.

A senior Army general called Khesanh "probably the first major ground action won entirely or almost entirely by airpower," and it was without question a signal triumph for the high competence and courage of professional airmen from all branches of U.S. military aviation—indeed the one decisive victory for airpower in the Vietnam War. But by no means did it redeem the Westmoreland strategy. What it did was to retrieve a serious blunder by the skillfully improvised and determined application of airpower under the urgent stress of imminent defeat. And it involved, of course, its own distortions. For the relief of tiny Khesanh had required a greater bomb tonnage than had been dropped on any other single target in the history of warfare, including the atomic drop on Hiroshima. David Douglas Duncan called it "defense through deluge" and complained that only America could afford such a "bankruptcy of tactics."

THE MEETING OF THE SENIOR ADVISERS ON VIETNAM

The Senior Advisory Group on Vietnam met in the White House on March 25 and 26. Those present were: Dean Acheson, Secretary of State under President Truman; George Ball, Under Secretary of State in the Kennedy-Johnson period; McGeorge Bundy, Special Assistant to Presidents Kennedy and Johnson; Douglas Dillon, Ambassador to France under President Eisenhower and Secretary of the Treasury under President Kennedy; Cyrus Vance, Deputy Secretary of Defense under McNamara and a diplomatic troubleshooter for President Johnson; Arthur Dean, chief Korean War negotiator; John J. McCloy, High Commissioner to West Germany under President Truman and Assistant Secretary of War during World War II; General Omar Bradley, World War II Commander and the first JCS Chairman; General

Matthew Ridgway, Korean War Commander and later NATO Commander; General Maxwell Taylor, JCS Chairman under President Kennedy and later Ambassador to Saigon; Robert Murphy, a senior career Ambassador of the Truman-Eisenhower period; Henry Cabot Lodge, former U.S. Senator and twice Ambassador to Saigon; Abe Fortas, a sitting Associate Justice of the Supreme Court and a personal adviser to President Johnson; and Arthur Goldberg, Ambassador to the United Nations and a former Secretary of Labor and Supreme Court Justice.

They assembled in the afternoon to read a number of background papers, and then went on to dinner with the principal cabinet officers plus Rostow, Harriman, and William Bundy whom they questioned at length. After dinner, the entire group heard briefings from Habib of the State Department, Carver of the CIA, and Major General DuPuy. The discussion continued late into the evening and resumed at a session the next morning preparatory to luncheon with the President. It was apparent at an early stage that the unanimity of October had evaporated and that a majority was now deeply troubled. Some were seeking a means of cutting back the war enough to make it politically and economically endurable for an indefinite period; others felt that disengagement was now the only answer. There was, as one member recalls it, a pervasive awareness that the enterprise in Vietnam stood at a historic turning point, that this was a period of the most earnest soul-searching. A small minority —Taylor, Fortas, and Murphy—stayed hard-nosed, defending the strategy of attrition as viable, proposing heavier bombing, advocating no shift in the tactics of search-and-destroy. But Acheson, McGeorge Bundy, Dillon, Vance, Goldberg, Ball, and General Ridgway were strong for change. McCloy, Lodge, Dean, and General Bradley were somewhere in the middle, troubled and in doubt, but less ready to declare for a dramatic shift in policy. As Vance later told a reporter, "We were weighing not only what was happening in Vietnam, but the social and political effects in the United States, the impact on the U.S. economy, the attitude of other nations. The divisiveness in the country was growing with such acuteness that it was threatening to tear the United States apart."

At luncheon with the President, McGeorge Bundy performed the role of *rapporteur,* summarizing with appropriate shadings what he felt to be the general view in the wake of the previous evening's briefings and discussion, and of the further debate just before lunch. The consensus, as Bundy described it, was that present policy had reached an impasse, could not achieve its objective without the application of virtually unlimited resources, was no longer being supported by a majority of the American people, and therefore required significant change. Bradley, Murphy, and Fortas objected that Bundy's summary did not accurately reflect the views of the full group. Acheson, who was seated beside the President, interjected to say that Bundy's summary clearly reflected *his* view and that he thought it also represented the great majority of those present. He repeated his conviction that military victory in Vietnam was impossible under conditions consistent with U.S. interests, and that the fundamental U.S. purpose should be to get out rather than further in. He said that insistence on a military solution had dragged the President and the country into a morass which could only get worse unless the goals and the strategy of the war were both changed.

General Wheeler, who had not attended the previous evening's briefings, stated that, if the group's views were derived from those briefings, then he would have to say that the briefers must have been men who didn't know the true situation. Moreover, he insisted that Acheson was incorrect in describing U.S. policy as bent upon a military solution. Westmoreland and the JCS, he said, clearly understood that "a classic military victory" was not possible in the special circumstances presented by Vietnam. Acheson replied that it was disingenuous to argue about semantics; if the employment of a half million men to eradicate every Viet Cong and drive the North Vietnamese Army out of the South was not an effort aimed at a military solution, then words had lost their meaning. Murphy backed the superiority of military advice in wartime and objected to the interposition of civilian judgments. Fortas continued to play the curious role he had assumed on other occasions in the running debate on Vietnam—as spokesman for those private thoughts of Lyndon Johnson that the President did not wish to express directly.

At the end of a rough, gloves-off session during which the President queried each man as to his personal view, Lyndon Johnson was left in no doubt that a large majority felt the present policy was at a dead end, and that the U.S. strategic interest required basic change. The group did not attempt to spell out the specific elements of a new policy, but the unmistakable thrust of their thinking was toward de-escalation, negotiations, and disengagement.

The President was visibly shocked by the magnitude of the defection, and perhaps even more by the fact that some, like McGeorge Bundy and Vance, were now associating themselves with it. Bundy had been a major architect of intervention in 1965; Vance had been McNamara's able right-hand at the Pentagon and more recently a distinguished diplomatic troubleshooter in Greece, Turkey, Korea, and Detroit. Acheson, whose high ability and measured toughness he probably admired most, had previously expressed the same view in the strongest terms. Nevertheless, the President was stung by what seemed to him an unexplainable shift of sentiment, if judged in terms of the information that formed the basis of his own assessment. The next day he demanded to see the men who had briefed the Senior Advisory Group. Carver and DuPuy dutifully presented themselves, but Habib was out of town making a speech. The two men repeated for the President the essentials of their earlier briefing. He asked, "What did you tell them that you didn't tell me?" They replied there were no discrepancies. The President was insistent: "You must have given them a different briefing; you aren't telling me what you told them because what you're telling me couldn't account for the inferences they drew." It was a tense moment, but there was no immediate explanation.

In retrospect, it was my impression that the President's sense of incongruity reflected the extent to which he had become the victim of (1) Rostow's "selective briefings"—the time-honored technique of underlining, within a mass of material, those particular elements that one wishes to draw to the special attention of a busy chief—and (2) the climate of cozy, implicit agreement on fundamentals which had so long characterized discussions within the inner circle on Vietnam, where never was heard a disparaging word. In addition, it was evident that the members of the Senior Advisory Group brought to the meeting a wider, better balanced view of America's world role, a more direct exposure to the swift-running currents of public opinion after Tet, and of course a less fixed commitment to one policy. It was also true that Habib, the briefer who was unavailable for the President's interrogation, had probably provided a more candid, pessimistic assessment of the post-Tet situation in Vietnam than the other two men. Yet it was my impression that this latter distinction was not decisive. What counted was the breadth and depth of relevant experience that the Senior Advisers brought with them. Hearing the bleak facts from the briefers, whether tinged with optimism or pessimism, they reached their own conclusions.

THE FINAL BATTLE

Two days later, on March 28, Clifford met in Rusk's office together with Rostow, William Bundy, and McPherson. He was unaccompanied by anyone from the Pentagon. The announced purpose of the meeting was to "polish the draft" of the speech the President was now scheduled to make just three days later. Prepared by McPherson, the draft presumably reflected the long discussion of March 22. Because of the uncertainty of the President's position, however, it did not take account of the proposed two-step bombing halt put forward by McPherson on March 23 and implicitly accepted by Rusk and Bunker. For similar reasons, and also owing to the pressures of time, it did not reflect the majority view of the Senior Advisory Group. It was still essentially a defiant, bellicose speech written to be delivered between clenched teeth. It made a *pro forma* plea for negotiations, but said nothing whatever about a bombing halt, which was of course the prerequisite for talks. Significantly, it proposed a troop increase of only 15,000 men, which was of course a far cry from the original request; this appeared to reflect a second meeting between Wheeler and Westmoreland in the Philippines on March 24. Presumably, Wheeler had on that occasion conveyed to the Field Commander a far different assessment of the operative realities in Washington than he had provided on his trip to Saigon in February.

After reading the draft, Clifford said, "The President cannot give that speech! It would be a disaster! What seems not to be understood is that major elements of the national constituency—the business community, the press, the churches, professional groups, college presidents, students, and most of the intellectual community—have turned against this war. What the President needs is not a war speech, but a peace speech." This opening comment seemed to place his main argument on the grounds of domestic considerations, but in the course of a comprehensive presentation he dealt fully with the military situation in Vietnam and elsewhere in the world. For the first hour or so, Clifford still appeared to be alone, meeting only silent patience from Rusk and Rostow, and with Bundy and McPherson "not taking substantive positions, but simply sitting in as aides." But significantly Rusk did not attempt to cut him off, as he might have, with the comment, "I know your views, but let's get on with the reading." As he talked on, Clifford began to feel he was making progress with Rusk who was "troubled and sincerely anxious to find some way to the negotiating table." The Clifford manner is deliberate, sonorous, eloquent, and quite uninterruptable. It gathers momentum as it proceeds, and soon achieves a certain mesmerizing effect; the perfection of the grammar is uncanny. During the course of several hours, speaking slowly, his fingertips pressed together, and glancing occasionally at an envelope on which he had scribbled a series of points, Clifford mustered every available argument in the powerful arsenal of reasons why it was not in the United States' interest to go on pouring military resources into South Vietnam; he drew heavily on the earlier analyses provided by Nitze, Warnke, Goulding, and myself. When the meeting finally broke up at 5 P.M., the group had inadvertently reviewed not only the speech draft, but the whole of Vietnam policy. Moreover, Rusk had agreed that McPherson should prepare an alternative draft, in order that the President might have two speeches to consider and thus the benefit of a clear-cut choice. Rusk did not object to giving the President a choice. Clifford thought Rostow refrained from making a fuss because he considered the President had already made up his mind not to stop the bombing—which was now the central point at issue.

The occasion had a major impact on McPherson, who was deeply impressed by Clifford's "brilliant and utterly courageous performance" and who from that point forward became not merely a semicovert dove, but an aroused and powerful ally. Working all through that night, McPherson wrote the first draft of the "peace speech," containing an unconditional bombing cut-off at the 20th parallel and a promise of total cessation if Hanoi provided assurances that it would respect the DMZ and refrain from attacking the cities. He sent this draft to the President early on Friday, March 29, with a note saying that it seemed to reflect the views of "your leading advisers." Later in the day, the President telephoned to ask about a passage "on page 3." McPherson had to compare the two texts in his own office before he discovered to his relief that the President was now working from the alternative draft, the peace speech. From then until the late afternoon of Sunday, March 31, the President worked with McPherson, Clifford, and a number of others to polish the new speech.

THE PRESIDENT DECIDES

At 9 o'clock on Sunday evening, speaking from his office in the White House, the President said "Good evening, my fellow Americans. Tonight I want to talk to you of peace in Vietnam and Southeast Asia." He reviewed his Administration's efforts "to find a basis for peace talks," especially the San Antonio formula of the preceding September, and asserted that there was "no need to delay the talks that could bring an end to this long and this bloody war." He then moved to the principal conclusion of the reappraisal and the pivotal element of the new approach to Hanoi. He said "So, tonight...I am taking the first step to de-escalate the conflict. We are reducing—substantially reducing—the present level of hostilities...unilaterally and at once. Tonight, I have ordered our aircraft and our naval vessels to make no attacks on North Vietnam, except in the area north of the Demilitarized Zone where the continuing enemy buildup directly threatens allied forward positions..." This meant stopping the bombing, he said, in areas inhabited by "almost 90 percent" of North Vietnam's population. "I call upon President Ho Chi Minh to respond positively, and favorably, to this new step toward peace."

He referred to the emergency deployment in mid-February of 10,500 Marine and airborne troops, and argued that to enable these forces to reach maximum combat effectiveness "we should prepare to send—during the next five months—support troops totaling approximately 13,500 men." He announced that President Thieu had, in the previous week, ordered the mobilization of 135,000 additional South Vietnamese, which would bring the total strength of ARVN to more than 800,000, and he pledged an effort to "accelerate the re-equipment of South Vietnam's armed forces" which "will enable them progressively to undertake a larger share of combat operations against the Communist invaders." The tentative estimate of these additional U.S. and ARVN costs was, he said, $2.5 billion in 1968 and $2.6 billion the following year. He then made a strong pitch for a ten percent surtax, saying "The passage of a tax bill now, together with expenditure control that the Congress may desire and dictate, is absolutely necessary to protect this nation's security, to continue our prosperity, and to meet the needs of our people."

Turning to "an estimate of the chances for peace," the President said, "As Hanoi considers its course, it should be in no doubt of our intentions. . . . We have no intention of widening this war. But the United States will never accept a fake solution to this long and arduous struggle and call it peace. . . . Peace will come because Asians were willing to work for it—and to sacrifice for it—and to die by the thousands for it. But let it never be forgotten: Peace will come also because America lent her sons to help secure it."

Finally, and somewhat surreptitiously, he came to his surprise withdrawal from the presidential race. Asserting that the country's "ultimate strength" lies in "the unity of our people," he acknowledged that "There is division in the American house now. There is divisiveness among us all tonight. And holding the trust that is mine, as President of all the people, I cannot disregard the peril to the progress of the American people and the hope and prospect of peace for all people. . . . With America's sons in the fields faraway, with America's future under challenge right here at home . . . I do not believe that I should devote an hour or a day of my time to any personal partisan causes. . . . Accordingly, I shall not seek, and I will not accept, the nomination of my party for another term as your President."

Clifford and his wife, Marney, had been invited to the

family quarters on the second floor of the White House for a drink, half an hour before the President's address. Without a word, the President motioned him into a bedroom and handed him the last two paragraphs. A few minutes later, as Clifford disclosed the President's secret to his own wife and to Rostow's wife, Elspeth, a photographer snapped a picture. "The ladies look," Clifford said later, "as though they had just been hit by a wet towel." At home in McLean, Virginia, I was unaware as to how the battle of the "war" and "peace" drafts had finally been decided, but expecting the worst, I worked at polishing a letter of resignation for submission the following morning. Immediately after the President's address, the electricity failed throughout the house. I found a cold bottle of champagne in the cellar and for the next hour sat on the bedroom floor with my wife, sipping thoughtfully by the light of a single candle.

In retrospect, the most important effect of the March 31 decisions was to put a ceiling on the resources the United States was henceforward willing to allocate to Vietnam. They applied the brakes to the war, finally bringing to a halt the open-ended escalation which had been rising with gathering momentum and heedlessness since 1965. They met the primary need expressed by the Fourteen Asian Scholars—i.e., to show "a capacity for innovation of a de-escalatory nature, indicating there is no inevitable progression upwards in the scope of the conflict." In addition, the decisions began, at least in principle, the shift of ultimate responsibility to the GVN and ARVN; they implied a repudiation of military victory as a valid goal and of search-and-destroy as a valid strategy. When public opinion quickly endorsed both the decisions and their implications, there was born a new policy of finite means which became in fundamental respects irreversible.

How did the President come to these decisions? No one can be sure. He seemed finally to have grasped the seismic shift in public opinion and the absolute political imperative of yielding to it, at least temporarily. This shift was borne in upon him by the New Hampshire primary, Robert Kennedy's entrance into the presidential race, the solid congressional opposition to mobilizing larger reserves, and the almost unanimous hostility of the press. The intractable nature of the new environment was made personal by the sharply changed outlook of Acheson, McGeorge Bundy, Vance, and Dillon. Without question, Clifford played a pre-eminent—and I believe the decisive—role. He was the single most powerful and effective catalyst of change, bringing each day to the stale air of the inner circle a fresh perception of the national interest, unfettered by connection with the fateful decisions of 1965. He rallied and gave authoritative voice to the informed and restless opposition within the government, pressing the case for change with intellectual daring, high moral courage, inspired ingenuity, and sheer stubborn persistence. It was one of the great individual performances in recent American history, and achieved in the remarkably taut time span of thirty days. Moreover, it retained its luster and its central effectiveness amid all the backsliding and ambiguity of the Administration's final ten months in office. If, as later events showed, these prodigious efforts did not really change President Johnson's mind about the Vietnam war, at least they compelled him to decide—in favor of reason, restraint, and a new approach. And such decisions by the incumbent of perhaps the most powerful office on earth created a new situation that virtually precluded a return to the old.

Clifford's own view of the March 31 decisions was both modest and mystical: "Presidents have difficult decisions to make and go about making them in mysterious ways. I know only that this decision, when finally made, was the right one."

Epilogue

WHAT HAPPENED with respect to Vietnam policy during the final ten months of the Johnson Administration—from April 1, 1968 to January 20, 1969—deserves, of course, and will no doubt get, a full telling. But that story is not the subject of this book, and others are better placed to tell it. Suffice it to say that the policy struggle between rival coalitions within the U.S. government continued almost unabated, even though the decisions of March 31, had they been applied by a President who meant what he said, ought to have resolved it in favor of the moderates; as it was, the fact that the American people promptly endorsed the decisions did put new limits on the debate.

To Washington's surprise, North Vietnam responded quickly and affirmatively to President Johnson's new call for negotiations, accepting the half-loaf of a partial bombing halt as an adequate basis for preliminary talks, while adding the significant caveat that initial meetings could have only one purpose—to determine how and when the bombing of North Vietnam was to be totally stopped. Because Hanoi's acceptance included the essential element of face-to-face contacts, the Administration was hardly in a position to refuse, and so had to take the caveat as well. But there was immediate evidence of confusion and thinly veiled discord inside the Administration. Rusk and Rostow tried to slow down and, if possible, avoid altogether the kind of initial talks proposed by North Vietnam. Rusk, who was in New Zealand attending a closed meeting of SEATO Foreign Ministers at the time of the President's speech, reportedly told his colleagues that neither the neutralization of Vietnam nor a coalition government was a workable solution. Returning promptly to Washington, he lost no time in making evident his general distaste for the enterprise, emphasizing the limited purpose of the talks and denigrating the possibility of a total bombing halt.

On April 3, the U.S. proposed Geneva as the site for initial talks. North Vietnam, in its response, proposed the Cambodian capital of Phnom Penh. Although the President had repeatedly said he would "meet anywhere, at any time" —most recently in his speech of March 31—the Administration quickly refused Hanoi's proposal. On April 9, the U.S. proposed Vientiane, Rangoon, Djakarta, and New Delhi. On April 11, Hanoi proposed Warsaw, which had been the site of desultory but undisturbed U.S.-Chinese diplomatic exchanges for a number of years. This too the Administration refused. When Hanoi reiterated its preference for Warsaw and lobbied in the world press, Washington thereupon trotted out a further counterproposal consisting of an additional ten cities: Colombo, Tokyo, Kabul, Katmandu, Rawalpindi, Kuala Lumpur, Rome, Brussels, Helsinki, and Vienna. On May 3, North Vietnam proposed Paris. By this time the matter had become a travesty, with the American and foreign press charging the U.S. government with "bad faith" and "quibbling." The unedifying spectacle of the American President chivying Hanoi on a location for the talks, after having told the world several dozen times that he set no conditions on the time and place of negotiations, was painful in Clifford's memory. He had opposed Phnom Penh on the grounds that it afforded inadequate communications facilities, but he saw no objection to Warsaw and told the President so. When Paris was finally agreed upon, the President took credit for it and lectured Clifford as follows: "You've got to stand up to the Communists and not give in even on minor points; that's how we got Paris. You wanted to give them Warsaw, etc."

Clifford got that LBJ speech at least ten times, but declined to respond because the issue seemed to him *de minimis*.

This fight over where to talk was merely the opening skirmish in the renewed conflict between the opposed coalitions within the Administration. The President's speech had brought momentary harmony based, it was apparent in retrospect, on the assumption of the hard-liners that Hanoi would give a negative response thus creating a situation in which all issues dealt with in the reappraisal could be reopened. Emerging from a Senate Committee hearing in mid-April, Rusk said he had seen "no evidence of restraint" by the other side, and emphasized that infiltration was continuing "perhaps at an increasing rate." Maxwell Taylor was soon sending "innumerable memoranda" to the President telling him how serious were the military consequences of the partial bombing halt; Rostow and the Joint Chiefs of Staff were taking a similar line. In early June, when enemy rockets were falling again on Saigon, Ambassador Bunker urged retaliatory bombing attacks on Hanoi. On the other side, Clifford in Washington and Harriman and Vance in Paris pressed hard for a total bombing halt and thus a beginning of substantive talks.

The hard-liners were soon arguing that Hanoi's affirmative response showed that North Vietnam was all but beaten, that its coming to Paris reflected the crushing military defeats administered by American firepower in the post-Tet period. With a little more delay and stone-walling, so the argument ran, and with steady military pressure, the U.S. could soon have Hanoi over a barrel and could thus negotiate on far more favorable terms. "Militarily," said Westmoreland in late April, "we have never been in a better relative position in South Vietnam . . . the spirit of the offensive is now prevalent. . . ." That the renewal of these discredited arguments had any force at all was attributable to the fact that the President himself remained instinctively disposed toward military victory and opposed to compromise. In March, he had been reluctantly persuaded of the need to take dramatic steps toward de-escalation and disengagement by the arguments of Clifford, Acheson, and others, and by the irresistible pressure of events. In April and May, it was clear that his conversion had been, at most, intellectual but never visceral; his continued susceptibility to hard-line arguments during the spring, summer, and fall amounted to serious backsliding from the major implications of the March 31 decisions, and produced an official U.S. posture of acute ambivalence. He understood that domestic political realities would not sustain a policy of renewed escalation of the bombing or any significant reinforcement of U.S. ground troops, but he remained receptive to the idea that the enemy could be worn down by sustained military pressure even within the newly established limits on resources.

The Johnson Administration thus never acquired the necessary unity to redefine the U.S. political objective in Vietnam in the context of the post-Tet realities. Military victory had been foreclosed both by events and the decisions of March 31, yet half the government, tacitly encouraged by the President, continued its ardent pursuit. And because military victory was not firmly put aside as an unreality, the idea of an "independent South Vietnam free of communist influence" continued to circulate in influential places as a valid, viable objective of U.S. policy. Until October, when Clifford, Harriman, and Vance succeeded in bringing off a total bombing halt, the bombing effort was not really curtailed, but only geographically rearranged; statistically, there was an intensification. On the ground, General Abrams made a number of sensible adjustments, including a greater emphasis on protecting the populated areas and undertaking fewer cavalier sallies to the uninhabited borderlands, but these changes hardly constituted a dramatic new strategy born of the knowledge that search-and-destroy had failed. They reflected primarily the fact that additional forces could no longer be obtained merely by telephoning the White House. There were 550,000 American troops in Vietnam, casualties were running between 200 and 400 KIA a week, and the war was still costing $30 billion a year. The policy and the strategy had failed, but there was an inability, arising out of disunity within the Administration and the President's own ambivalence, to acknowledge the failure and thus the painful necessity for definitive new thinking.

The President told Clifford in the autumn that his primary purpose was now to leave his successor with "the best possible military posture in Vietnam." Clifford argued that, for the sake of the President's ultimate standing before the bar of history, he ought to want something much broader and more positive, namely, to leave his successor "an ongoing, substantive negotiation, firmly committed to ending the war and reducing the American involvement in Vietnam." The President was finally willing to accept a total bombing halt in late October, but in November and December he was still listening to the siren song of those who clung tenaciously to the prospect of resolving the conflict by military pressure. He was listening despite evidence that the enemy's determination to fight seemed unimpaired and that his capacity to regenerate his forces remained significant. As the Administration left office, therefore, ambivalence remained at the very heart of its Vietnam policy. Were we in Paris to negotiate a political compromise on the clearly accepted premise that military victory was infeasible? Or were we there to stone-wall Hanoi in the belief that, given enough time, we could grind out something resembling a military victory in South Vietnam and thus avoid the dangers, and the further affronts to our prestige, that would attend a compromise political settlement? There were no clear answers to these questions.

THE PROSPECT NOW BEFORE US

At this writing (early August 1969), the answers to these questions are only a little clearer. President Nixon is on record as believing there can be no military solution, but large murky patches remain on the fabric of American policy in Vietnam. Perhaps understandably, Nixon has insisted on going through the whole painful learning process at first hand; in any event, he has thus far declined to come down firmly on a clear-cut course of action and has maneuvered skillfully, yet with increasing evidences of improvisation, to avoid fateful choice. The choice, basically, is between trying yet again to strengthen and salvage the Thieu regime for the sake of a gradual, far from complete, but hopefully honorable American disengagement from a war that might, in such circumstances, continue for years to come; and casting that government aside for the sake of a fairly quick, probably unpalatable political settlement which would however permit—indeed require—the prompt and complete withdrawal of American forces. The Nixon Administration has not yet bitten the bullet; in fact it seems to be pursuing a deliberately hedged policy of carrot and stick.

The carrot elements are embodied in the formal U.S. proposal of May 14 that the "major portion" of all foreign forces in South Vietnam be withdrawn within twelve months; the remaining "non-South Vietnamese forces" would thereafter retire to base areas, thereby creating a *de facto* cease-fire and setting the stage for internationally supervised elections. The stick elements are embodied in a supposedly tough alternative aimed at threatening the enemy with the grim prospect of interminable war, through a combination of strengthening ARVN and withdrawing enough U.S. forces to assure that American public opinion will support the continued participation of the remainder for an indefinite period. This alternative is known as "Vietnamization." The Nixon Administration appears to be experimenting with various combinations of carrot and stick—tabling presumably generous offers in Paris, while exerting "maximum military pressure" in South Vietnam in an effort to enlarge the area of GVN control before the onset of significant U.S. force withdrawals. The result thus far is continued stalemate in Vietnam and deepening deadlock in Paris. Such a result should not be surprising, for, unfortunately, this approach confronts the fundamental weakness of the U.S. bargaining position at this stage of the war.

The Nixon offer of mutual withdrawal plus elections may indeed be generous by past U.S.-GVN standards, but it depends for success on reciprocal action by Hanoi. But Hanoi gives no indication that it feels the need to make significant concessions (like promising to withdraw its forces) in order to achieve large-scale U.S. troop withdrawals or avoid resumption of the bombing against North Vietnam. This position is no doubt based on Hanoi's quite accurate assessment that, nearly eighteen months after Lyndon Johnson's proclaimed de-escalation, American public opinion more than ever favors and expects a liquidation of the U.S. war effort (I would go so far as to say that the American people have just about written off this war). The evidence strongly suggests that Hanoi is not going to reciprocate, but intends simply to wait us out.

The alternative of "Vietnamization" suffers from similar frailties, for in truth its viability as a threat to the enemy depends far less on augmented material support for ARVN, than on the long-term retention of significant U.S. combat power (air and ground). Effective "Vietnamization" would probably pose a genuinely bleak prospect for the enemy, notwithstanding his determination to return, if necessary, to a strategy of low-level protracted guerrilla war. Here again, however, the political situation in the United States palpably deprives this Nixon alternative of any real credibility. Those who still cling to the hope of vindicating the strategy of victory-through-attrition have of course warmed to the concept of "Vietnamization," but they have assumed it would involve a very gradual and carefully calibrated U.S. withdrawal—say, 50,000 men per year. Such an assumption seems however to stand on a gross misreading of domestic political feasibilities, as President Nixon himself has now substantially conceded. In his press conference of June 19, when asked what he thought of Clark Clifford's proposal to bring home 100,000 troops in 1969 and all of the remaining combat ground forces by the end of 1970, he expressed the "hope" that his Administration could beat the Clifford schedule. The reply, whether deliberate or accidental, sowed consternation in Saigon and among the supporters of "Vietnamization" at home, for it seemed to make the real situation crystal clear to Hanoi. It has produced stiffened NVN intransigence in Paris and a protracted lull on the battlefield—a lull rather openly designed to induce larger and faster U.S. troop withdrawals and thus to deprive Nixon's "tough" alternative of its credibility.

At this writing, then, the United States remains in a tenuous position; its strategy has not succeeded, but the national leadership has thus far refused to accept either the consequence of failure (which is defeat in some degree) or the need to devise a new strategy for carrying on the war. It is very late in the day—much too late—to try a new and different military strategy. But even if it were not, "Vietnamization" would seem an unpromising horse to bet on. For, so far as one can tell, such a strategy would involve essentially more of the same—further enlargement of the already too large and cumbersome ARVN, organized in conventional formations, heavily armed with artillery, equipped with helicopters, supported by large-scale U.S. tactical air power, and sent out to vindicate the Westmoreland doctrine. The painful trials and frustrations of Vietnam have, momentarily at least, exhausted the intellectual capital of our military leaders and brought American military doctrine to a conceptual impasse. So we limp along, Micawber-like, hoping for something to turn up in Paris or Saigon.

THE DANGEROUS POLICY OF PARTIAL WITHDRAWAL

Beyond the immediate tactical weaknesses of the Nixon Administration's apparent policy, there are, I believe, inherent dangers in a policy of substantial, but less than total, withdrawal from Vietnam. Such a policy was perhaps seriously proposed for the first time by McGeorge Bundy in October 1968. More recently, Clark Clifford argued for it in the July 1969 issue of *Foreign Affairs*. Speaking at DePauw University on the occasion of a symposium in memory of John T. McNaughton, a graduate of that institution, Bundy said: "Until the present burden of Vietnam is at least partly lifted from our society, it will not be easy—it may not even be possible—to move forward effectively with other great national tasks. This has not always been my view, but I think it was John McNaughton's before he died, and it seems to me wholly clear now that at its current level of effort and cost the war cannot be allowed to continue for long."

He went on to argue that "decisive change" could come about in only three ways—by imposing a military solution, by negotiating a real settlement with the enemy, or by a unilateral decision to change our own level of effort. On the possibility of a military solution, he was unequivocal: "There is no prospect of military victory against North Vietnam by any level of U.S. force which is acceptable or desirable either in our own interest or in the interest of world peace. The last three years have demonstrated plainly that American forces can prevent defeat.... But they have also shown us that they cannot produce victory." He favored a negotiated settlement, but felt it was improbable that Hanoi would agree to any arrangement acceptable to the American people. Having thus set out three possible solutions and demolished two, he arrived by a process of elimination at the third—the unilateral, but partial, withdrawal of U.S. forces: We must "steadily, systematically and substantially reduce the number of American casualties, the number of Americans in Vietnam, and the dollar cost of the war" through a phased, unilateral withdrawal of American forces down to a level of approximately 100,000 men.

Bundy argued at DePauw that a withdrawal down to about 100,000 men was now possible without the need to lose "what has been gained in the strategic sense." Clifford argued in *Foreign Affairs* that withdrawal of all U.S. combat ground forces by the end of 1970 would "be consistent with continued overall military strength"; indeed, he thought it might confront Hanoi with the painful possibility that ARVN could "with continued but reduced American support, prove able to stand off the Communist forces." Yet the idea that the U.S. can resolve its difficulties in Vietnam through the progressive, but still partial, unilateral withdrawal of its forces rests on two crucial assumptions: (1) either ARVN can really supply substitute power equal to that of the departing U.S. forces, or (2) the present and future situations in South Vietnam can be managed at a lower level of aggregate allied power than has been required in the past. Clifford has no trouble with the second assumption, arguing cogently that present allied power is excessive, if the aim of military victory is excluded: "There is, in fact, no magic and no specific military rationale for the number of American troops presently in South Vietnam. The current figure represents only the level at which the escalator stopped." Nevertheless the two assumptions are in a real sense interdependent, and both are inherently fragile; the first requires a dramatic improvement of ARVN that we have not in fact seen over the past seven years; the second requires a belief not only that the NVN-VC are much weaker than they have been, but also that their weakness is now a permanent condition.

Should the U.S. government pursue a course of partial withdrawal in Vietnam, while leading the American public to believe all will end well, I am afraid a number of unpleasant shocks, surprises, and politically dangerous consequences would arise to confront us. For at best, such a course is a prescription for an interminable war; partially disguised by the declining level of U.S. participation, it would in fact require our country to sustain a continuing burden of war casualties and heavy dollar costs that would become explicitly open-ended as we leveled off our forces at 100,000 men or thereabouts. Sooner or later, and probably sooner, the American people would reawaken to the fact that they were still committed to the endless support of a group of men in Saigon who represented nobody but themselves, preferred war to the risks of a political settlement, and could not remain in power for more than a few months without our large-scale presence. These things are predictable because the Thieu regime is both self-serving and wholly unrepresentative—its strong anti-Communist stance (which our support has both nurtured and hardened) bears little or no relation to the vaporous, myth-filled, un-ideological, village-oriented political sentiments of the vast majority of people who inhabit the non-country of South Vietnam. That government, as one perceptive journalist has remarked, is a creation as artificial and improbable as an air-conditioned motel in the middle of a trackless jungle. If therefore we offer continued, even though reduced, combat support for an indefinite period, we may be sure that the Thieu group will accept it and that the war will go on—with a continuing heavy drain on American lives, money, national purpose, and moral reputation. In my judgment, such an unfolding would be plainly alien to our national interest; moreover, it would seriously risk a snapping of the national patience under circumstances that would endanger fundamental U.S. foreign policy interests in Asia, and that might well threaten the political life expectancy of the incumbent Administration in Washington.

At worst, the course of partial withdrawal would produce a progressive erosion of the military situation in Vietnam, leading downward to a time when we faced the prospect of outright defeat. With U.S. strength reduced to 100,000 men, with no corresponding enemy reduction, and with no dramatic improvement of the GVN and ARVN, developments could seriously threaten the safety of our smaller forces and thus pose the same hard question we faced in 1965—to escalate or liquidate. Were the United States to face, several months or years from now, the serious prospect of military defeat in Vietnam, I believe that fact would strain our capacity for wise choice beyond the breaking point, and that any decision in such circumstances could only further divide our people and imperil our political process.

There is, unfortunately, an unbreakable interconnection between victory and the avoidance of defeat in the Vietnam situation. You really must have the first in order to ensure the second; or, as others have said, if guerrilla insurgents are not totally defeated, then they win. If victory is not possible, defeat in some degree (and by whatever name you arrange to call it) is not avoidable. A concept of partial unilateral withdrawal that tries to have it both ways—to forswear victory yet avoid defeat—is an inherent contradiction. It won't work.

THE POLICY OF COMPLETE WITHDRAWAL

Deliberate, orderly, but complete withdrawal has become, in my judgment, the only practical course open to the United States, if we are to restore our foreign policy to coherence, regain our psychological balance, alleviate the deep-seated strife in our society, and re-order our national priorities in ways that will win the support of a large majority of our own people. Vietnam is not of course the only source of division in America today, but it is the most pervasive issue of our discord, the catalytic agent that stimulates and magnifies all other divisive issues. In particular, there can be no real truce between the generations—no end to the bitterness and alienation of even the large majority of our youth that is neither revolutionary nor irresponsible—until Vietnam is terminated.

A major premise of the Johnson Administration's war effort was that a vital U.S. interest was at stake in Vietnam, requiring a total and tireless commitment to cleansing that area of Communist influence. That presumption has now fallen of its own weight—even if one broadens the context to include the argument that an unlimited commitment in Vietnam, though not vital per se, was necessary to safeguard other vital U.S. interests in Asia.

If we can forthrightly acknowledge the basic, unpalatable

236

truth—that our intervention in 1965 was misconceived, that viewed through cold, clear eyes it could not be justified on the grounds that a vital national interest was at stake—then we can bite the bullet in Vietnam. We can acknowledge past failure and the inevitability of some degree of defeat. We can move to a phased, unilateral, and total withdrawal of forces, not as a means of pretending we have discovered a painless way to achieve partial victory or even a settlement consistent with our original objectives, but as a means of liquidating an enterprise that is beyond retrieval and a condition that is poisoning the bloodstream of our society; as a means of putting the Thieu government on notice that, after a reasonable period of months, our military forces will no longer be there; as a means of demonstrating beyond words that the GVN must either move decisively to a settlement during the limited time our remaining military presence can provide supplementary leverage, or else decide to fight on alone without U.S. troops beside them. The deed once done would, in my judgment, be accepted by American and European opinion and would be adjusted to by Asia without serious repercussions in areas of principal strategic concern to us. I do not say we should abruptly abandon the GVN; I do say we should give them a definitive indication of our intention to be totally gone by a given date—a date that affords a reasonable time for leaders throughout South Vietnamese society to chart their own course.

Such a United States policy would be extremely painful for several strata of South Vietnamese, bringing to the surface the root question of whether they could accommodate to the new political uncertainties or would have to leave the country. But only such a policy could push the Thieu group to a serious contemplation of settlement. In any event, the consequences in South Vietnam of an American military withdrawal must be weighed against the consequences in the United States of keeping open the running sore of heavy U.S. military involvement. Measured by that test, I believe that U.S. interests in the broadest sense require an orderly and phased, but resolute and total, military withdrawal from Vietnam. If our course is resolute, the chances are fairly good that the various factions in South Vietnam will come to an accommodation or a balance which will be able to avoid domination of a new government by the National Liberation Front. Almost certainly, there will be major changes in the social order, producing a different distribution of political, economic, and social power. But Vietnamese society, twisted and torn by the colonial era, the French-Indochina war, the Diem period, and the Great American Infusion, clearly needs reorientation and self-rediscovery. For despite our massive economic assistance and its accompanying rhetoric of revolutionary development and social change, our presence and our actions there have in fact tended to confirm and even to strengthen the old order. But that order cannot be upheld, except by external military support.

THE PROBLEM OF PRESTIGE

A severe loss of U.S. prestige in Asia and throughout the world is frequently cited as the compelling reason why we cannot withdraw unilaterally from Vietnam. It is accordingly of central importance to see this problem in perspective, admitting that Americans face a special difficulty here. Russia, Germany, Japan, France, and Great Britain have all suffered terrible military failures throughout long and checkered histories; some have barely managed to survive the attendant domestic convulsions. But the United States, alone among the powers of consequence now on the world scene, has never known a major defeat. We should be able to understand that, in the nature of things, we could not expect our record to remain permanently unblemished, especially not when our involvement has pervaded the globe in an era of seething change, instability, and violence. Yet the apparent perfection of the past record is admittedly an obstacle to our taking setbacks in stride. Before World War II, a large body of domestic opinion believed implicitly that America was somehow morally superior, and by this fact protected against the terrible disasters that regularly befell less splendid and upright nations. We are, I think, clearer today that such attitudes reflected the immaturity and naïveté of a people not yet fully involved in the complexities of the world; we now understand that the life history of any great nation must show over time its fair share of victories and defeats.

Such understanding can provide perspective as we address the situation now before us, for many other nations have bounded back from far graver reverses than the loss of prestige that would attend a gradual and orderly withdrawal from Vietnam. Moreover, it is an advantageous truth that mere loss of prestige for a Great Power is always transient and usually brief. Many times in the past two decades, the Soviet Union has suffered painful rebuffs—in the Greek Civil War in 1947, at the Turkish straits the same year, in the Berlin Blockade of 1948, in the determined U.S.-UN response to the attack on South Korea of 1950, which so badly disrupted Stalin's calculations, and most emphatically in the Cuban Missile Crisis of 1962. Yet no one would deny that the Soviets quickly recovered from each of these setbacks; no one doubts that they have subsequently projected their foreign policies with undiminished vigor and determination, backed by undiminished, indeed growing, resources. The point is that Great Powers quickly recover from blows to their prestige alone, precisely because of their power. When the world wakes up the next morning, the Great Power has not quit the scene. It is there, as solid as yesterday, and the world must make new arrangements to cope with it.

As with the Soviet Union, so essentially with the United States. We too have had our share—although a far smaller share—of deflations affecting our prestige since the end of World War II, and they have not affected our fundamental strengths in any way. There was the shooting down of the U-2 over Russia, the besieging of President Eisenhower by Tokyo rioters, and the travesty at the Bay of Pigs. At the time of the latter fiasco, President Kennedy gave evidence that he understood the limited requirements of U.S. national prestige, and he refused to inflate these by injecting considerations of presidential face. By quickly admitting his own error and by nobly taking on the full burden of responsibility, he enabled the country to see the incident in true proportion and to be steadied by his candor.

I have no trouble in believing that, had he lived, he would have similarly cut off the U.S. involvement in Vietnam—possibly at the time of General Khanh's coup in January 1964, but in any event well below the astronomical level it finally reached. It was the country's tragedy that Lyndon Johnson tended instinctively to equate the nation's prestige with his own, and that his personal needs were greater than the objective requirements of the nation. Johnson was at bottom a combination of sentimental patriot and gambler which led him to compound original misjudgments many times over, rather than risk the loss of prestige associated with an American "defeat" in Vietnam. Kennedy was too skeptical, too attuned to cold reality (as one admirer said, "too smart an Irish Mick") not to have foreseen the developing morass. He would, I believe, have overridden the quite predictable military arguments and acted to cut the nation's losses, accepting and absorbing whatever deflation was required in terms of national and presidential prestige, and taking such measures as lie within the national power and interest to cushion the consequences in places like Thailand, Korea, and Japan. This is still the road to the recovery of our lost sense of proportion, to the healing of our deep domestic divisions, to the reestablishment of a wise and respected foreign policy.

Supplement, 1969-73

IN THE longer perspective, perhaps the most remarkable fact of the first Nixon term will be that he was able to maintain an American combat military presence in Indochina throughout the whole four-year period. Given the state of American opinion in 1969, such a feat had seemed unlikely. But by gradually reducing American ground forces, the number of Americans killed, and the size of draft calls, Mr. Nixon was able to tranquilize the most sensitive domestic political nerves and thus position himself to yield with glacial slowness to the powerful public yearning for an end to the American involvement in Vietnam. Where sedatives proved ineffective, he applied raw presidential power, inherent in the fluid conditions of war, to create situations on the battlefield that were beyond the power of his critics to prevent or undo. In all this he showed himself to be not a consensus president, but a determined commander-in-chief, with a strong personal view that the national interest required a clear-cut anti-Communist solution in South Vietnam, and with a readiness to accept searing domestic division and demoralization in order to continue trying to get it.

THE NIXON EFFECT

By the end of March 1973, the United States finally withdrew the last of its combat forces (ground and air) from South Vietnam and in return received all American soldiers and airmen held prisoner by Hanoi or the Viet Cong. This narrow but important exchange was the centerpiece, indeed the only effective element, of a cease-fire and truce agreement signed two months before, on January 23. All the other elements of that agreement, without exception, quickly broke down. At mid-May, wholesale violations of the truce by both parties and steady deterioration of the fragile supervisory machinery indicate that the protracted struggle is not even at a temporary stopping point, but at the threshold of a new phase that will probably, at some future time, resume the form of open warfare on a large scale. Nor has the United States accomplished a genuine extrication. Although American ground and air forces are out of South Vietnam, at least 10,000 American "civilians" and other "contract personnel" remain to advise, support, and help operate the Saigon armed forces, while the American air effort continues from bases just outside Vietnam. American B-52s based in Thailand, and tactical aircraft operating both from Thailand and from aircraft carriers positioned in the Tonkin Gulf, are pounding targets in Cambodia every day on a large scale. On May 10, for the first time in the war, the House of Representatives voted to cut off all funds for U.S. military operations in or over Cambodia, and the Senate has followed suit. But President Nixon has insisted that he will continue the bombing, even if it proves necessary to defy the explicit will of Congress. A major constitutional crisis thus impends, at a time when Mr. Nixon's moral authority is gravely weakened by the Watergate scandals.*

During the first few months after he assumed office in 1969, the new President could have taken definitive steps toward liquidating the American role in the war without serious political risk to himself, indeed with political benefit for both his party and the cause of national unity. In fact, his opportunity was broader. It was no less than the chance to lead the nation firmly away from two decades of self-deception in Indochina, to admit a national mistake and by that cleansing act begin to uncoil the contradictions and restore the national balance. He could have set himself the task of educating the public with respect to two central realities: (1) that the tangled political issues which divide and torture

* Further congressional action in July finally forced Mr. Nixon to stop bombing on August 15.

Vietnam can be settled only among the Vietnamese; and (2) that, contrary to the erroneous assumptions on which American military intervention was based, the particular constitutional form and the particular ideological orientation of Vietnamese politics do *not* affect the vital interests of the United States. Adoption of such a posture could have led to a prompt and total American withdrawal from Indochina, on condition that our prisoners be returned, leaving all political questions to be settled by the Vietnamese. Such a settlement, indeed involving not only withdrawal in exchange for prisoners but also Hanoi's implicit willingness to defer the issue of Vietnamese unification for a reasonable period of years, appeared to be readily available at the end of 1968, as a result of the Harriman-Vance negotiations with Xuan Thuy in Paris.

It is now clear, however, that President Nixon did not want, or felt he could not politically afford, that kind of settlement; so deep were his convictions on the matter that he was willing to squander the honeymoon period and allow the war to become unmistakably a Republican rather than a Democratic responsibility—indeed to become increasingly his own personal undertaking. While his reasons were subject to conflicting speculation at the time, it now seems clear that he acted as he did out of two related considerations: (1) he could not fully rid himself (even after his 1972 rapprochement with China and his efforts to regularize summit meetings with Russia) of the Cold War notion that the war in Vietnam is, and always was, a moral struggle between anti-Communist good and Communist evil; and (2) he continued to believe (like his predecessors) that domestic political defeat awaited the president who acknowledged that American intervention in Vietnam had been based on a misperception, or who left behind a Saigon regime so fragile that it would quickly collapse after the American withdrawal. He was accordingly unready to contemplate any genuine American letting-go in Vietnam. In order to stay, however, he had to make both rhetorical and physical adjustments.

President Nixon asserted several times during 1969 that it was his intention to end the war. On November 3 he explained he was proceeding on two fronts: "A peace settlement through negotiations or, if that fails, ending the war through Vietnamization." His early efforts at negotiations predictably failed—chiefly because his aim of securing the mutual withdrawal of American and North Vietnamese forces from the South exceeded Washington's bargaining power. What had not been possible to coerce with 549,000 men under General Westmoreland was hardly possible to gain by negotiation while Mr. Nixon was withdrawing 110,000 troops and promising the return home of an additional 150,000 by the end of 1970. Within the narrow logic of his own formulation, then, if the negotiating position proved unproductive, he was thrown back on the alternative of strengthening the Saigon armed forces. On June 3, 1970, he pledged "to end this war" and insisted that "Vietnamization would lead to a 'just peace.' " "Vietnamization" seemed to mean the progressive transfer of the military burden to South Vietnamese forces; as such, it could serve as a useful vehicle for the extrication of American troops, but it was not in fact a process capable of ending the war. For by strengthening the Saigon army (ARVN), it would reinforce the natural resistance of the Thieu regime to any compromise settlement. At the same time, it could not hope to change the military balance sufficiently to defeat Hanoi's forces, nor to coerce Hanoi to negotiate on Saigon's terms. "Vietnamization" was thus a formula for endless war, even though it would presumably permit the total removal of American forces.

At least through 1970, however, it was not clear that Nixon intended a full withdrawal of American forces. As he manipulated the variable factors, his definition of "Vietnamization" seemed to include the indefinite retention of a significant U.S. military component—at a level just low enough to render American political anxieties manageable. The Nixon approach to Vietnam in 1970 appeared to involve three basic aims: (1) endeavoring to hold U.S. forces in Vietnam at a level of substantial power, but at a level that would also be politically acceptable to American public opinion; (2) striving to strengthen ARVN to the point where, in collaboration with remaining U.S. forces, it would confront Hanoi with a superior and unassailable military posture; and (3) forcing Hanoi to recognize the enduring nature of that dual posture, thereby inducing Hanoi to negotiate a settlement in Paris satisfactory to both Washington and Saigon. The Nixon formula for a "just peace" thus depended on Hanoi's recognition and rational acceptance of a position of permanent military inferiority in South Vietnam.

The difficulty with this vision of the future as a basis for policy was that it bore little relation to reality in either America or Vietnam. On the evidence, the American people were not prepared to sustain a military commitment in Vietnam for an indefinite period: there was a widening awareness that no vital U.S. interest was at stake and that the regime we were sustaining was narrow, corrupt, and self-serving. Moreover, absolutely nothing in the history of the war, nor in the existing or prospective power balance in Vietnam, indicated that Hanoi could be forced to come to terms with the Thieu regime. The Nixon plan for achieving an end to the war and a "just peace" thus appeared to many as a remarkable extension of the illusion that had led his predecessors into the quagmire. To be sure, it differed in one important respect: it assumed a larger dependence on the Saigon armed forces, particularly the ground forces, and a correspondingly smaller role for the American Army; on the other hand, as gradually became apparent, Mr. Nixon's "just peace" assumed the indefinite availability and employment of American air power in Indochina.

That his plan involved the use of American power for an indefinite period seemed clear in his vehement rejection of a proposal that was gaining wide public support by mid-1970: announcing a fixed timetable for total American withdrawal.

His objections were twofold: (1) it would rob our side of all bargaining power, and (2) it would permit Hanoi simply to wait until we had departed, when it could then resume the offensive. But the dust already gathered at the Paris peace talks showed how little bargaining power the United States possessed. And even in the absence of a fixed, public time-table, it was manifestly Hanoi's strategic aim to await the American departure. The only counterpoise to such a waiting strategy was for America to remain in force on a permanent basis, yet that was by now accepted as a political impossibility. But if Mr. Nixon's objections were thus unpersuasive, they revealed that he was still working strenuously to have it both ways—to maintain control of events in Southeast Asia even as he withdrew American forces in response to domestic political imperatives. A secure anti-Communist regime in Saigon remained the first priority.

SPREADING THE WAR TO CAMBODIA

In part, his determination to secure the Thieu regime in South Vietnam was derived from his Cold War perception that it was not possible to divorce the Indochina struggle from a larger test of wills with Peking and Moscow, a truth confirmed by the "incursion" of American forces into Cambodia on April 30, 1970. The head of that state, Prince Sihanouk, had been deposed by coup d'etat on March 18, while he was out of the country, and his successor, an incompetent named Lon Nol, had given the North Vietnamese forces in the "sanctuaries" along the Cambodia-South Vietnam border an ultimatum to depart Cambodia within seventy-two hours. In a fateful act, President Nixon ordered American forces to move across the border to "clean out the sanctuaries" because, as he put it, recent Communist activities in those areas "posed an unacceptable threat to our remaining forces in South Vietnam." This patently unpersuasive rationale was contradicted a day or two later by Secretary of Defense Melvin Laird, who told newspapermen that the attacks were intended to exploit "an opportunity," as the North Vietnamese in Cambodia, unsettled by the Lon

Nol coup, were at that time facing westward toward Pnompenh. Beneath the smokescreen of these statements, President Nixon seemed, above all, determined to prevent Cambodia from preserving its neutral status. As he told Stewart Alsop of *Newsweek*, he was apprehensive that, if neither side moved following the Lon Nol coup, an "ambiguous situation" might arise, making it difficult for the United States thereafter to attack the border sanctuaries without being charged by international opinion with attacking a neutral country. To avoid such embarrassment, one side or the other had to make a belligerent move. Mr. Nixon made it.*

The move proved catastrophic for Cambodia, and involved a serious Nixonian miscalculation of American public reaction. A roar of protest and dismay rose up even from those who supported the war. The action seemed precipitate, unnecessary, widening out the political complications, the cost, the casualties and the human tragedy, while making settlement far more difficult. A large, affluent crowd marched in bitter protest along the streets of Washington, including at least a platoon of impeccable Wall Street lawyers, one of whom declaimed in a high-ceilinged Senate hearing room that "wars are too important to be left to Presidents."

The resulting political pressure from the Congress forced the Administration to promise that American ground forces would leave Cambodia and would not re-enter, but the damage had been done. The invasion of Cambodia set in motion imponderable new political forces (in Pnompenh, Vientiane, Bangkok, Saigon, Hanoi, Peking, Moscow, and Washington), promising that the newly kindled war in that country would spread, would be protracted, would reopen old tribal hatreds, and would continue to involve the United States in situations that the American presence could aggravate but could do nothing to resolve. Whether Mr. Nixon foresaw the consequences of his rash and unwise act is doubt-

* In early August 1973, it was revealed that, months before the ground incursion, Mr. Nixon had secretly directed at least 3500 bombing raids against Cambodia.

ful. He made a very personal, arbitrary decision, one that found a close linkage between his assessment of the local situation in Vietnam and his sense of contending with the global implications of "International Communism." Amid stories circulated by his press aides that it was important for a free world leader to demonstrate "unpredictable" tendencies to Communist adversaries, Mr. Nixon posed in his later television address (June 5, 1970) a question which made clear that he perceived the playing field as much wider and the stakes much higher than Cambodia or even Indochina: "If an American President had failed to meet this threat to 400,000 American men in Vietnam," he asked, "would those nations and people who rely on America's power and treaty commitments for their security—in Latin America, Europe, the Middle East, or other parts of Asia— retain any confidence in the United States?" If the speech was less than persuasive, it was because it posed a false question; few officials in Saigon or Washington perceived any real threat to American forces arising out of the Lon Nol coup. The incident thus served mainly to illuminate the disturbingly solitary method of Mr. Nixon's decision making and his apparently deliberate isolation from varied sources of advice.

In the same speech, delivered as American forces were pulling out of the Cambodian sanctuaries, he described the military action in Cambodia as "the most successful operation of this long and very difficult war." Ten months later, (mid-February 1971), close to half of Cambodia had passed out of the Cambodian government's control; the country's productive capacity—embracing rubber plants, cement plants, fertilizer plants, paper mills, and rice mills—had been severely damaged by heavy American air strikes and other war operations; roads, railroads, bridges, and other communications had been extensively cut. Although the Cambodian armed forces had grown from 35,000 to 165,000 men, most of the major cities were in rebel hands and the capital was under virtual siege by a combination of indigenous rebel forces and North Vietnamese. All of this had produced a Cambodian budget deficit of $40 million in 1970 and an estimated shortfall of $400 million in 1971. The United States continued to disclaim any commitment to uphold the Lon Nol government, but actions steadily belied words. Initially, a few thousand captured Russian rifles and American carbines were quietly provided to the Cambodian Army; later, $100 million in emergency military and economic aid was transferred from other programs. Then Congress was pressed to vote $250 million in exchange for the Administration's promise that no American ground forces would re-enter Cambodia. By the end of 1972, with American aid continuing at the rate of $5 million per week, the growing Cambodian Army was mired in sloth and corruption, with officers enriching themselves by grossly padding the payrolls. Meanwhile, the strength of the Cambodian dissidents had grown to 45,000 men organized into regular battalions and equipped by North Vietnam with modern weapons including mortars and recoilless rifles. They controlled perhaps 80 percent of the country and had virtually cut off all access to Pnompenh.

THE ISSUE OF PRISONERS

On September 17, 1970, the Viet Cong representative in Paris offered to negotiate the release of American prisoners immediately following a *public announcement* of a definite United States timetable for total withdrawal. The proposal proved embarrassing to the Nixon Administration precisely because it offered a practical exit at a time when American public opinion had conclusively lost its capacity to believe that Washington's tenacious war aims were any longer attainable, important, or moral. It was an undisguisable truth that the American Army in South Vietnam was beset by a galloping deterioration of discipline and morale—soldiers refused orders to go on patrol and frequently resorted to "fragging" their officers with hand grenades. And the mass killing of unarmed men, women, and children by American troops at the village of My Lai was a sickening, sobering revelation for a nation that needed to feel it was fighting an honorable war. The Viet Cong proposal further embarrassed Washington by underlining the truth that "Vietnamization," whatever its merits, could not bring American prisoners home; it could promise no better than an indefinite extension of the war. Apparently feeling suddenly vulnerable on the politically sensitive issue of prisoners, the President ordered a bizarre helicopter raid on an empty prisoner compound at the village of Sontay in North Vietnam. It seemed an effort to demonstrate that the Administration was not "standing idly by" while Americans languished in North Vietnamese prisons, yet it was in fact designed to bring back few if any prisoners (the determining factors in selecting the Sontay site were its accessibility to helicopter assault and the ease with which the attackers could get in and out of the compound). It was a strained exercise in public relations.

In a related effort to defend "Vietnamization" against the widening realization that it could not end the war or secure the return of American prisoners, Mr. Nixon asserted (February 17, 1971) that so long as North Vietnam held American POWs, American military forces would remain in Vietnam: moreover, that they would remain in sufficient numbers to give the other side "an incentive to release the prisoners." The statement implied the curious proposition that American tenacity would at some point break the will of the North Vietnamese and cause them to negotiate on American terms. Taken at face value, it was another manifestation of the strange delusion that Washington somehow had more at stake in Vietnam than did Hanoi. On the record, it seemed more accurate to reverse the President's proposition and to say that, so long as American forces remained in Vietnam, North Vietnam would continue to hold American prisoners. The truth of this counter-proposition was indeed so evident that it was difficult to believe the President had somehow failed to understand it. To many it seemed he was manipulating the prisoner issue as another means of prolonging American involvement in the war, in order to gain more time for strengthening Saigon through "Vietnamization."

Domestic pressures for faster withdrawal and total extrication nevertheless continued to mount, accompanied by a widening inability to understand or share Mr. Nixon's purposes. The Saigon regime now boasted 1.2 million well-armed and well-trained men in the regular forces, backed by additional thousands of territorial guards—the total number of South Vietnamese under arms being at least three times greater than the combined strength of the Viet Cong and the North Vietnamese. U.S. military aid was extensive and sophisticated, and had been going on for seventeen years. American forces had been fighting on a large scale to defend South Vietnamese territory for six years. How could it still be argued that the American commitment had not been fully discharged? Yet, at the end of 1970, 414,900 American military men were still in South Vietnam. And an adamant President, refusing to consult with Congress or to engage in genuine public debate, sternly refused to accept the kind of settlement—American prisoners in exchange for American withdrawal—that seemed to meet the essential requirements of national security and national dignity.

THE TEST IN LAOS

Feeling the pressure, Mr. Nixon in early February 1971 accepted the judgment of the American military command that "Vietnamization" was now ready for a major test. The test chosen was to send a force of several ARVN divisions into Laos to disrupt the network of trails running down from North Vietnam, draw the enemy into major engagements, and hold the territory for a period of several months. While no American ground troops or ground advisers would participate, still the whole panoply of U.S. artillery, air support, and helicopter lift would support the operation. Begun with a flourish of trumpets on February 10, the operation was abruptly terminated with heavy ARVN casualties and disorderly retreat before the end of March, despite the use of 2,000 American combat aircraft that flew 5,000 helicopter missions, 7,000 tactical air strikes and 420 B-52 bombing raids in the first two weeks alone. News photographs of besieged, panic-ridden ARVN troops scrambling for places on the landing skids of evacuation helicopters did not convey a reassuring impression of that army's fighting qualities. Stewart Alsop wrote in *Newsweek* that "the Laotian operation was a military failure in Laos and a political disaster in the United States." Yet President Nixon (on April 21, 1971) could nevertheless declare that "tonight I can report that Vietnamization has succeeded." And despite a now unbreachable credibility gap, the American people as a whole reacted with more apathy than anger, revealing a mood of moral exhaustion, a war weariness mixing incredulity with resignation, a profound sense of the futility of trying to influence the Indochina policy of its own government.

On April 22, five Democratic senators, Edmund Muskie, Hubert Humphrey, George McGovern, Harold Hughes, and Birch Bayh—all presidential aspirants—urged total withdrawal from Vietnam by the end of 1971. The Nixon response was to announce the withdrawal of another 100,000 American troops by December, but to reject any public announcement of a "date certain" for total extrication. That, he said, would "throw away a principal bargaining counter to win the release of American prisoners of war"; moreover, it would give "enemy commanders the exact information they need to marshal their attacks against our remaining forces at their most vulnerable time." Both the Nixon arguments were spurious. Hanoi was clearly willing to pay the price of prisoners to get the American colossus out of Vietnam. (Ho Chi Minh had once been quoted as saying that his side would strew the Americans' departing path with roses.)

DELUSIONS OF FINAL SUCCESS

After the Laotian fiasco, military activity in Indochina fell to a lower level, the pace of American troop withdrawal was dramatically quickened, and secret negotiations (not disclosed until April 1972) were opened between Henry Kissinger and Le Duc Tho. Through this combination of events and a deepening public apathy, Mr. Nixon entered 1972 with enough confidence to express in his State of the World message that "Vietnam no longer distracts our attention from the fundamental issues of global diplomacy or diverts our energies from priorities at home." In domestic political terms, one vital part of the statistical record now supported his statement: in the three years and four months since he had assumed office (January 1969–April 1972), American forces had been reduced from 549,000 to 69,000; casualties from 300 to 20 per week; draft calls from 30,000 to 5,000 per month. What further induced Americans to hope for an end in Vietnam was the President's trip to Peking (February 1972) and his announced visit to Moscow in May, for these summit meetings promised to alter the strategic context in which the Vietnam War was being faught. A rapprochement with China and a strengthening of American political and economic ties to the USSR would tend to isolate North Vietnam, to deny it the assurance of unqualified material and political support from the major Communist countries. On his return from Peking, the President sought to convey the impression that Hanoi was now checkmated and the Vietnam War was practically over.

Hanoi indeed saw the writing on the wall and, with characteristic toughness and a misplaced confidence in its ability to influence American opinion in a presidential election year, launched a large-scale invasion of South Vietnam on March 30. On that day, three North Vietnamese divisions attacked through the Demilitarized Zone and immediately seized most of Quangtri Province in the northeast sector. Once more, the poor showing of ARVN cast doubts on the effectiveness of "Vietnamization" and indeed brought Washington face to face with the prospect of sudden defeat. On April 15, Mr. Nixon, charging North Vietnam with "flagrant violations" of the 1968 bomb-halt understandings, ordered B-52 strikes against Hanoi and Haiphong, and also intensified American close air support for the hard-pressed ARVN forces. American opinion reacted with further shock and dismay, having tended to accept the earlier assurances that the war was all but over. The *Washington Post* found a "grim logic" in the Nixon reaction: "Vietnamization" had not in fact worked well enough to assure Mr. Nixon the kind of outcome he could be personally comfortable with—in Vietnam itself, at the forthcoming Moscow summit in May, and in the presidential campaign; therefore he had moved instinctively to apply the one instrument of force that remained available to him.

In a major television report to the nation (April 26), the President sought to meet the renewed charge that his policy involved endless American participation in an endless war. He insisted that "we aren't trying to conquer North Vietnam or any other country. We want no territory. We seek no bases. We have offered the most generous peace terms. . . . But we will not be defeated; and we will never surrender our friends to Communist aggression. . . . As we come to the end of this long and difficult struggle, we must be steadfast. We must not falter. For all that we have risked and all that we have gained over the years now hangs in the balance during the coming weeks and months. If we now let down our friends, we shall surely be letting down ourselves and our future as well. If we now persist, history will thank America for her courage and her vision at this testing time." In this same television report, he disclosed that secret negotiations with Hanoi had been going on since the previous October, and that the American proposals had included an immediate cease-fire, a complete prisoner-of-war exchange, and a withdrawal of all forces within six months to be followed by internationally supervised elections in South Vietnam. All political elements, including the Viet Cong, would be permitted to participate; moreover, one month before such elections, President Thieu and Premier Huong would resign. These were generous terms, he said, but Hanoi had broken off the talks and had now launched a new invasion of South Vietnam.

Neither the renewed American bombing of North Vietnam nor the intensified American air support for ARVN troops had any immediate effect on the course of the new battle in eastern and central South Vietnam. ARVN yielded ground and was reluctant to counterattack. In a situation of deepening anxiety in Washington, President Nixon decided on a further gamble. On May 8 he chose to do what Presidents Johnson and Kennedy had steadfastly sought to avoid for over a decade—to bring the war in Indochina to the point of explicit confrontation with the Soviet Union. On that day, again without consulting Congress, Mr. Nixon announced his decision to widen air attacks against population centers near Hanoi, and to sow aerial mines in Haiphong harbor, thereby creating a blockade supported by a massive American naval armada off the North Vietnamese coast. The evident purpose of the unprecedented latter move was to stop the flow of Russian shipping to North Vietnam, accepting the possibility of a Russian military reaction. The risks involved in thus confronting the Soviet Union seemed highly disproportionate to the advantages that might be gained in Vietnam, for the President was placing in jeopardy the broad issues of strategic arms talks (SALT), European détente, increased trade with Russia, indeed the whole favorable development of Soviet-American relations. The decision seemed designed to protect and salvage, not the central American interest in Vietnam, but the personal honor and credibility of a President facing re-election. With tough defiance, Mr. Nixon asserted that the United States now faced "a clear, hard choice among three courses" and seemed to make plain by his announcement of the bombing and mining measures that he favored "decisive military action to end the war" over either "immediate withdrawal of all American forces" or "continued attempts at negotiation."

The new military measures were, however, accompanied

by a dramatic shift in the American negotiating position. The United States, the President said, would now withdraw all American forces and installations and cease all military operations *within four months*, in return for a cease-fire and the release of American prisoners. Official American requirements for a military truce were thus rapidly narrowed. The advocates of total withdrawal seemed to have won their point. Political columnist Joseph Kraft said of the new terms: "that, in effect, is the whole ball game. The other side is being asked to afford Mr. Nixon a respite, to pull out our troops and get back the prisoners. Then the Communists would be free to go to work on the Saigon regime with the virtual certainty of taking over South Vietnam." It seemed evident that the new Nixon offer did not proceed from any deliberate policy or "game plan"; certainly it had not been in his mind when he invaded Cambodia in 1970 or Laos in 1971, or when he issued his optimistic State of the World message in early 1972. It was a sudden shift in reflecting Washington's anxiety at the new evidence that 1.5 million South Vietnamese soldiers could not assure the protection of 60,000 Americans against 100,000 North Vietnamese. It was motivated by the desire to minimize the risk of undisguisable failure in a presidential election year. The cost of such a face-saving gesture proved to be very high in American airmen and aircraft lost and in thousands of Vietnamese civilians killed and hundreds of structures destroyed.

To the world's deep relief, Moscow decided that its commitments to Hanoi were not worth a dangerous military confrontation with the United States, indeed that its own hopes for strategic arms reduction and increased trade required the maintenance of correct, even forthcoming American-Soviet relations. On that basic point, President Nixon had won his gamble. Nevertheless, to allay the strains on both U.S.-Soviet and Soviet-North Vietnamese relations caused by the new American military measures, he agreed to resume secret negotiations in Paris between Henry Kissinger and Le Duc Tho. Hanoi was deeply angered by Moscow's mild reaction to the bombing and aerial mining, and roundly denounced those who had succumbed to "the Machiavellian policy of American imperialism." In Paris, talks proceeded sporadically through the summer; meanwhile, the North Vietnamese ground offensive failed to achieve a dramatic breakthrough and the war gradually returned to stalemate.

The diplomatic pace quickened in September; and then, on October 8, Le Duc Tho formally unveiled what he called "a new, extremely important initiative." As Dr. Kissinger later described it, the latest Hanoi offer involved an abandonment of the link between military and political issues on which all earlier negotiations had foundered. Kissinger said, "They dropped their demand for a coalition government which would absorb all existing authorities." The coalition idea, however, seemed not to have been wholly dropped, for the North Vietnamese proposal included a "Council of National Reconciliation and Concord," comprising three equal elements (Saigon, Viet Cong, and the neutrals in South Vietnam) to "promote the implementation" of agreements reached between the Viet Cong and the Thieu regime, and also "to organize general elections." Hanoi further announced that agreement had been reached whereunder (1) the United States would stop all bombing on October 18, (2) the two parties would initial the text of the accord in Hanoi on October 19, and (3) the Foreign Ministers would formally sign it in Paris on October 26.

Washington was somewhat unsettled by the detailed nature of Hanoi's closure, as there had been as yet no opportunity to present the agreement to the Saigon government. Nevertheless, on October 26, Dr. Kissinger acknowledged the essential correctness of Hanoi's announcement, saying, "We believe that peace is at hand. . . . Peace is within reach in a matter of weeks or less." That was the posture in which the Nixon Administration went into the November 7 election and won a landslide victory. Meanwhile, however, the timetable for initialing and signing was allowed to slip. A part of the reason was almost surely the Nixon Administration's private determination to avoid a consummation before election day, owing to the uncertain impact of a cease-fire on the American voters. A larger obstacle was President Thieu in Saigon who soon launched a public and private attack on any settlement that would install "a disguised coalition" in Saigon, permit North Vietnamese forces to remain in the South, and fail to recognize the existence of South Vietnam as "an independent state."

Nixon could have disregarded Thieu's angry objections to these key elements of the tenuous accord, but in the crunch he would not "impose" a settlement on Saigon. At the same time, he would not accept all Thieu's objections— he refused, for example, to press for the withdrawal of North Vietnamese troops from the South. Nevertheless, he declined to force the Saigon regime to accept anything resembling a coalition, and indeed instructed Dr. Kissinger to return to Paris on November 20 to argue Thieu's case for a separate South Vietnamese entity—an *independent South Vietnam.* Kissinger did so, and his effort had the effect of tearing the fragile fabric of the tentative agreement and of provoking Hanoi to reinstate earlier demands of its own—a refusal to release American military prisoners unless Saigon also freed the political prisoners in the South. The upshot was a decisive break in the talks. On December 18, again without consulting Congress or even trying to explain his action to the American people, Mr. Nixon suddenly ordered unrestrained bombing attacks on Hanoi and Haiphong, using B-52s. The devastating raids continued throughout the Christmas holiday, dropping millions of tons of explosives on the North, destroying hospitals, foreign embassies, and residential areas and killing hundreds. The sheer intensity of the attacks gave rise to the widespread charge, both at home and abroad, that President Nixon was resorting to deliberate terror bombing—to punish Hanoi for having had the temerity to resist his attempts to alter, in Saigon's favor, the accord previously reached between Dr. Kissinger and Le Duc Tho. Finally, the raids were halted on December 30, and talks were resumed in Paris on January 2. The accords were then worked out and initialed on January 23, 1973.

In essence, they provided for the complete withdrawal of all American troops and military advisers and the dismantling of all American military bases in South Vietnam within sixty days, in exchange for the return of all captured American servicemen and civilians throughout Indochina, and the release of captured North Vietnamese and Viet Cong troops within the same time period. There was to be a ban on the introduction of new troops and munitions into South Vietnam. There was a pledge to maintain the Demilitarized Zone at the 17th parallel, with the question of eventual reunification to be settled "through peaceful means." An international Control Commission (Canada, Hungary, Indonesia, and Poland) was created to supervise the cease-fire and help enforce other provisions. An international conference was to convene within thirty days to supervise the Control Commission and the broad implementation of the agreement. All foreign troops were to be withdrawn from Laos and Cambodia (although no deadline was set for this), and the use of these territories as base areas was prohibited.

At the present time, the steady deterioration of the supervisory machinery and the increasing return to open warfare suggest that the Vietnam war is far from finished for the accords reflected neither a military victory nor a political compromise. A war not concluded decisively on the battlefield cannot be easily settled at the conference table, since there is no victor to impose conditions on the vanquished. What is required in such circumstances, even for a stable truce, is compromise. But compromise is built on confidence, and that ingredient is wholly lacking in relations between North and South Vietnam. After the first four Nixon years, the United States finally succeeded in recovering its prisoners and extricating its forces—and also in preserving the Thieu regime. Mr. Nixon's ambitious hopes for "ending the war" with a "just peace" have proved illusory, however, as many predicted they would, in 1969 and earlier. The January 1973 accords achieved only what could have been achieved in 1968 or 1969: the withdrawal of American forces and the return of American prisoners. The cost of deferring this necessary but unspectacular achievement until 1973 was about $50 billion in additional direct war costs, at least 20,000 additional American combat deaths, hundreds of thousands of Vietnamese, Laotian, and Cambodian casualties, and a new and widening war in Cambodia.

In the early months of 1973, a question crucial for the future in Indochina seemed to be, What does Mr. Nixon want? Would he rest content with a "decent interval" of non-Communist control in Saigon, or would he insist on the enduring survival of the Thieu regime (that is, at least throughout his own second term)? Moreover, how would he express his support of that regime? With money and supplies? With equipment and advice? With massive bombing? In May 1973, uncertainties surrounded all these questions, but the crucial factor now seems to be not what Mr. Nixon wants, but rather what residual power to govern, if any, in either domestic or foreign affairs, he will still possess after the Watergate scandals have run their course. The evidence of the Congressional inquiry headed by Senator Ervin of North Carolina already suggests that the White House apparatus is guilty of something much wider and deeper than a resort to political dirty tricks for the sake of influencing the 1972 election. It reveals attitudes at the highest political levels so inimical to the moral and political traditions of America that they have produced a corruption of the entire governing system. Mr. Nixon continues his efforts to treat the Watergate scandal as "an unfortunate incident," but it reaches to the very door of the oval office and threatens to cripple his capacity to work his will in the governing process even if he escapes formal impeachment. The prudent conclusion is still that the United States has not yet rid itself of the Indochina problem, but if Mr. Nixon should lose his authority to govern, this could change.

Notes

1. Philip L. Geyelin, *Lyndon B. Johnson and the World* (New York: Frederick A. Praeger, 1966).

2. Zbigniew Brzezinski, *Alternative to Partition* (New York: McGraw-Hill Book Company, 1965).

3. Geyelin, *Lyndon B. Johnson and the World.*

4. Alastair Buchan, quoted from *Encounter Magazine* (September 1967).

5. Major Nguyen Be, Army of the Republic of South Vietnam, quoted by Peter Arnett, *Santa Barbara News Press* (November 23, 1967).

6. David Halberstam, "Return to Vietnam," *Harper's Magazine* (December 1967).

7. Robert F. Kennedy, *To Seek a Newer World* (New York: Doubleday & Company, 1967) pp. 190–91.

8. Harry S. Ashmore and William C. Baggs, *Mission to Hanoi* (New York: G. P. Putnam's Sons, 1968).

9. McGeorge Bundy, Letter to the *Washington Post* (September 11, 1967).

10. Participants in the drafting of the "Bermuda Statement" of December 12, 1967:

Harding F. Bancroft	Franklin A. Lindsay
Lincoln Bloomfield	Richard Neustadt
Charles G. Bolte	Matthew B. Ridgway
John Cowles	Marshall D. Shulman
Daniel Ellsberg	Donald B. Straus
Miss Frances FitzGerald	Kenneth W. Thompson
Ernest A. Gross	James C. Thomson
Roger Hilsman	Stephen J. Wright
Joseph E. Johnson	Adam Yarmolinsky
Milton Katz	Charles Yost
George Kistiakowsky	

11. List of the Fourteen Asian Scholars who issued the statement on Asia of December 23, 1967:

Edwin O. Reischauer	Richard L. Park
Leo Cherne	Lucian Pye
Guy J. Pauker	I. Milton Sacks
Chancellor Harry D. Gideonese	Robert A. Scalapino
A. Doak Barnett	Paul Seabury
Oscar Handlin	Fred Von Der Mehden
William W. Lockwood	Robert W. Ward

12. Ashmore and Baggs, *Mission to Hanoi.*

Index of Names